Early praise for *Rails 5 Test Prescriptions: Build a Healthy Codebase*

This is my favorite Rails testing book! I love the prescriptions. It's like collecting big thoughts and organizing little ideas within them.

➤ **Maricris S. Nonato**
Senior Ruby on Rails Developer, Premiere Speakers Bureau

I found Noel Rappin's *Rails 4 Test Prescriptions* so helpful, and I was pleased to see Noel's humor and thorough explanations continue in this edition. Every time I thought, "What about such-and-such?" it was covered within a paragraph or two. Best of all, this edition does more than update the previous edition—there is a substantial amount of new material. I'm planning to read it again and reference it often!

➤ **Tara Scherner de la Fuente**
Software Developer, Allovue

If you're new to Rails, or new to the idea of testing within Rails, this thorough book will definitely set you on the right path.

➤ **Sean Miller**
Solution Developer and Consultant

Sometimes testing sucks. This book magically makes testing not suck; it makes it easy and rewarding with well-written explanations. It is the essential resource for any developer testing Rails applications. It's more than just a testing primer; developers will learn how to create optimal and efficient test suites for Rails. A must-read for beginners and seasoned programmers alike.

➤ **Liz Abinante**
Senior Software Engineer, GitHub

Noel is an exceptional teacher and it shows! This book is a balanced and pragmatic introduction to testing your Rails applications. It effectively communicates the benefits of various approaches while providing sufficient context on situations where the approach might be less applicable.

➤ **Ashish Dixit**
Software Engineer

Rails 5 Test Prescriptions

Build a Healthy Codebase

Noel Rappin

The Pragmatic Bookshelf

Raleigh, North Carolina

Our Pragmatic books, screencasts, and audio books can help you and your team create better software and have more fun. Visit us at *https://pragprog.com*.

The team that produced this book includes:

Publisher: Andy Hunt
VP of Operations: Janet Furlow
Managing Editor: Brian MacDonald
Supervising Editor: Jacquelyn Carter
Development Editor: Katharine Dvorak
Indexing: Potomac Indexing, LLC
Copy Editor: Candace Cunningham
Layout: Gilson Graphics

For sales, volume licensing, and support, please contact *support@pragprog.com*.

For international rights, please contact *rights@pragprog.com*.

ISBN-13: 978-1-68050-250-3
Printed on acid-free paper.
Book version: P1.0—February 2018

Contents

Acknowledgments

It's been nine years since I first started working on a book called *Rails Test Prescriptions*. In that time, many people have helped me make this book better than I could have made it on my own. This includes but is by no means limited to the following people.

Without the encouragement of Brian Hogan and Gregg Pollack, this might still be a self-published book.

Katharine Dvorak has been my editor on this version of the project and has shaped the material this time around. I've worked with Susannah Pfalzer on all my Pragmatic projects, and she's always been helpful and great to work with.

Many technical people reviewed this version of the book and had their comments incorporated. They include Sean Boyle, Mike Coutermarsh, Ashish Dixit, M. Scott Ford, Derek Graham, Luis Cabezas Granado, Josh Justice, Kaan Karaca, Nigel Lowry, Sean Miller, Maricris Nonato, Tara Scherner de la Fuente, and Charley Stran.

I've been very fortunate to be working at Table XI while writing this book. Not only have they been very supportive of the project, but I've also had the chance to get insights and corrections from my very skilled coworkers.

This book is a commercial product built on the time and generosity of developers who create amazing tools and release them to the world for free. Thanks to all of you. In particular, the maintainers of several of the tools discussed were generous in answering my questions, particularly Eileen Uchitelle from the Rails core team, and Sam Phippen from the RSpec core team.

My family has always been encouraging. Thanks to my children, Emma and Elliot, who are more amazing and awesome than I ever could have hoped. And thanks to my wife Erin, the best part of my life and my favorite person. I love you very much.

Preface

Throughout the course of this book, you'll learn how to apply a test-driven development (TDD) process to the creation of applications that use Ruby and Rails. I'll talk about how to apply TDD to your daily coding and about the tools and libraries that make testing in Rails easier.

The goal is to show you how to apply a test-driven process and automated testing as you build a Rails application. Being test-driven allows you to use testing to explore your code's design. You'll see what tools are available and learn when those tools are best used. Tools come and tools go, so I'm really hoping you come away from this book committed to the idea of writing better code through the small steps of a test-driven development process.

Who You Are

I'm assuming some things about you.

I'm assuming you're already comfortable with Ruby and Rails and that you don't need this book to explain how to get started creating a Rails application in and of itself. I'm *not* assuming you have any particular familiarity with testing frameworks or testing tools used within Rails.

Over the course of this book, I'll go through the tools that are available for writing tests, and I'll talk about them with an eye toward making them useful in building your application. This is Rails, so naturally I have my own opinions, but the goal with all the tools and all the advice is the same: to help you write great applications that do cool things and still catch the train home.

What's in This Book

We'll start with an introduction to test-driven development in general: what it is, why it works, and when to use it. In the next two chapters we'll walk through a tutorial using RSpec to create tests for a new Rails application. You'll start testing without using Rails-specific features, and then you'll start to test Rails functionality. We'll also talk a bit about what makes testing and tests most valuable.

After that we'll spend a few chapters going through basic unit tests, talking about models, multiple ways of generating data for tests, and using test doubles to simulate objects and specify hard-to-reach states.

Then we'll zoom out a little bit and talk about end-to-end tests. We'll also start talking about JavaScript, first as an extension to end-to-end tests for code that has JavaScript, and then about unit-testing JavaScript by itself. Then we'll tour the remaining parts of Rails that we haven't covered and show the tool support for those systems.

Once we've gone though all that, we'll walk through most of it again using Minitest instead of RSpec.

Once we're done talking about tools, we'll cover specific scenarios for testing, including testing for security and testing third-party services. We'll talk about troubleshooting failing tests and how to improve your test environment and run your tests quickly. And we'll end with the very common case where you need to add tests to untested legacy code.

What You'll Need

The sample code and mini application you build in this book use Ruby 2.5.0 and Rails 5.2.0,[1] [2] which are the current versions of these tools as I write. (Older versions will run most of the book's examples.) Installation of these tools is beyond the scope of the book, but you can find instructions at their footnoted websites.

The application also uses the SQLite database. I chose SQLite for ease of installation. You may already have it installed on your system; if not, you can find installation instructions on the SQLite website.[3]

A Word About Tools, Best Practices, and Teaching TDD

Two test libraries are in general use in the Rails community—Minitest and RSpec—which means I had a choice of which tool to use as the primary library in this book. This book is about how to test Rails in general; therefore, the details of the testing library in use are secondary to most of it. Still, the examples have to be presented using one tool or the other.

---

1. https://www.ruby-lang.org
2. http://www.rubyonrails.com
3. https://sqlite.org

Minitest is part of the Ruby Standard Library and is available everywhere you might use Ruby (1.9 and up). It has a straightforward syntax that is the Ruby translation of the original SUnit and JUnit libraries (for Smalltalk and Java, respectively), and it is the default alternative for a new Rails project. Minitest is used by the Rails core team to test Rails and has Rails-specific extensions.

RSpec is a separate testing tool designed to support an emphasis on specifying behavior rather than implementation, sometimes called behavior-driven development (BDD). Rather than using terms like "test" and "assert," RSpec uses "expect" and "describe." BDD emphasizes setting expectations about the code not yet written rather than assertions about code in the past.

RSpec has a quirky syntax that sometimes depends on metaprogramming and that people often have strong feelings about, both positive and negative. It's more flexible, which means it's more expressive but also more complicated, and it has a larger ecosystem of related tools. I believe that more Rails applications use RSpec than Minitest, though this is also disputed.

The primary testing tool used in this book is RSpec, because after going back and forth quite a bit, I decided that its expressiveness makes it easier to work with over the course of the entire book, even if it has a slightly steeper learning curve. It's also the tool that I use in my own day-to-day work, which counts for something. That said, there's a whole chapter on Minitest, and I'll discuss most of the extra tools in a way that references both RSpec and Minitest. Most RSpec examples in the downloadable code have a corresponding Minitest version.

That leads to a more general point: sometimes the best practice for learning isn't the best practice for experts. In some cases in this book, I'll use relatively verbose or explicit versions of tools or tests to make it clear what the testing is trying to do and how.

Changes in This Edition

A lot has changed in the Rails testing world over the past seven years, even if the general principles have stayed more or less the same. The entire community, including me, has had more years of experience with these tools, building bigger and better applications, learning what tools work, what tools scale, and what tools don't.

Rails 5 Test Prescriptions has several updates from the Rails 4 version:

- All tools have been upgraded to their latest versions, including Ruby 2.5.0, Rails 5.2.0, Minitest 5.11.3, and RSpec 3.7.1. New features of these and any other tools are described throughout the book when appropriate.

- Controller testing has been deprecated in Rails 5, and is largely gone from this book. In its place, we're using the new Rails 5 system tests and other integration-test tools in accordance with my best understanding of desired practice from the Rails testing and RSpec-Rails maintainers.

- The JavaScript material is completely new and split into two chapters, one that discusses integration-testing JavaScript and one that discusses unit-testing it. The unit testing chapter uses ES6 syntax and Rails Webpacker to develop the JavaScript code.

- Capybara integration now uses headless Chrome as the JavaScript driver, and the Capybara section has been updated to reflect this.

- The code samples have been rewritten to allow for minor changes in best practice over the last few years, and to bring them more in line with my day-to-day practice. In particular, once factory_bot is introduced as a data-creation method, we use it in later tests.

Online Resources

The source code for the application you'll build throughout the course of the book is available as a zip file on the book's web page at The Pragmatic Bookshelf.[4] The readme.md file included in the source code has other information you'll need to run the application. The source code from the zip file may also include any errata discovered after the book's publication. Each directory in the zip file is a complete version of the Rails application in progress. Throughout the book, the code samples specify which directory, and therefore which version of the app, they are from.

You'll also find an interactive forum on the book's web page, where you can post questions for me or for other readers. You can contact me directly via my own website.[5]

Now, let's get started!

---

4. http://pragprog.com/book/nrtest3
5. http://www.noelrappin.com

CHAPTER 1

A Test-Driven Fable

Imagine two programmers working on the same task. Both are equally skilled, charming, and delightful people, motivated to do a high-quality job as quickly as possible. The task is not trivial, but not wildly complex either. For the sake of discussion, let's say it's a new user logging in to a website and entering some detailed pertinent information.

The first developer, who we'll call Sam, says, "This is pretty easy, and I've done it before. I don't need to write tests." And in five minutes Sam has a working method ready to verify.

Our second developer is named Jamie. Jamie says, "I need to write some tests." Jamie starts writing a test describing the desired behavior. The test is executable and passes if the corresponding code matches the test. Writing the test takes about five minutes. Five additional minutes later, Jamie also has a working method, which passes the test and is ready to verify. Because this is a fable, we're going to assume that Sam is allergic to automated testing, while Jamie is similarly averse to manually verifying against the app in the browser.

At this point you might expect me to say that even though it has taken Jamie more time to write the method, Jamie has written code that is more likely to be correct, robust, and easy to maintain. That's true. I'm going to say that. But I'm also going to say that there's a good chance Jamie will be done before Sam even though Jamie is taking on the additional overhead of writing tests.

Let's watch our programmers as they keep working. Sam has a five-minute lead, but both of them need to verify their work. Sam needs to test in a browser; I said the task requires a user to log in. Let's say it takes Sam one minute to log in and perform the task to verify the code in a development environment. Jamie verifies by running the test, which takes about 10 seconds. (At this point Jamie has to run only one test, not the entire suite.)

Perhaps it takes each developer three tries to get it right. Since running the test is faster than verifying in the browser, Jamie gains a little bit each try. After verifying the code three times, Jamie is only two and a half minutes behind Sam. (In a slight nod to reality, let's assume that both of them need to verify one last time in the browser once they think they are done. Because they both need to do this, it's not an advantage for either one.)

At this point, with the task complete, both break for lunch (a burrito for Jamie, an egg-salad sandwich for Sam—thanks for asking). After lunch they start on the next task, which is a special case of the first task. Jamie has most of the test setup in place, so writing the test takes only two minutes. Still, it's not looking good for Jamie, even after another three rounds trying to get the code right. Jamie remains a solid two minutes behind Sam.

Let's get to the punch line. Sam and Jamie are both conscientious programmers, and they want to clean up their code with a little *refactoring*, meaning that they are improving the code's structure without changing its behavior. Now Sam is in trouble. Each time Sam tries the refactoring, it takes two minutes to verify both tasks, but Jamie's test suite still takes only about 10 seconds. After three more tries to get the refactoring right, Jamie finishes the whole thing and checks it in three and a half minutes ahead of Sam. (Jamie then catches a train home and has a pleasant evening. Sam just misses the train and gets caught in a sudden rainstorm. If only Sam had run tests.)

My story is simplified, but look at all the things I didn't assume. I didn't assume that Jamie spent less actual time on tasks, and I didn't assume that the tests would help Jamie find errors more easily—although I think Jamie would, in fact, find errors more easily. (Of course, I also didn't assume that Jamie would have to track down a broken test in some other part of the application.)

It is frequently faster to run multiple verifications of your code as an automated test than to always check manually. And that advantage only increases as the code gets more complex. Additionally, the automated check will do a better job of ensuring that steps aren't forgotten.

There are many beneficial side effects of having accurate tests. You'll have better-designed code in which you'll have more confidence. But the most important benefit is that if you do testing well, your work will go faster. You may not see it at first, but at some point in a well-run, test-driven project, you'll notice that you have fewer bugs and that the bugs that do exist are easier to find. It will be easier to add new features and modify existing ones. You'll be doing better on the only code-quality metric that has any validity:

how easy it is to find incorrect behavior and add new behavior. One reason why it is sometimes hard to pin down the benefit of testing is that good testing often just feels like you're doing a really good job programming.

Of course, it doesn't always work out that way. The tests might have bugs. They might be slow. Environmental issues may mean things that work in a test environment won't work in a development environment. Code changes will break tests. Adding tests to existing code is a pain. As with any other programming tool, there are a lot of ways to cause yourself pain with testing.

Testing First Drives Design

Test-driven development, or TDD, is the counterintuitive idea that developers will improve both the design and the accuracy of their code by writing the tests before they write the code. When adding new logic to a program, the TDD process starts by writing an automated test that describes the behavior of code that does not yet exist. In a strict TDD process, new logic is added to the program only in response to a failing test.

Writing tests before code, rather than after, allows your tests to help guide the design of your code in small, incremental steps. Over time this creates a well-factored codebase that is easy to change.

Success with test-driven development starts with trusting the process. The classic process goes like this:

1. Create a test. The test should be short and test for one thing in your code. The test should run automatically.

2. Make sure the test fails. Verifying the test failure before you write code helps ensure that the test really does what you expect.

3. Write the simplest code that could possibly make the test pass. Don't worry about good code yet. Don't look ahead. Sometimes, write just enough code to clear the current error.

4. After the test passes, refactor to improve the code. Clean up duplication. Optimize. Create new abstractions. Refactoring is a key part of design, so don't skip this. Remember to run the tests again to make sure you haven't changed any behavior.

Repeat until done. This will, in theory, ensure that your code is always as simple as possible and is always completely covered by tests. I'll spend most of this book talking about how to best manage this process using the tools of the Rails ecosystem and solving the kinds of problems that you get in a modern web application. And I'll talk about the difference between "in theory" and "in practice."

If you use this process, you'll find that it changes the design of your code.

Software design is a tricky thing to pin down. We use the term all the time without really defining it. For our purposes in this book, *design* is anything in the code structure that goes beyond the logical correctness of the code. You can design software for many different reasons—optimization for speed, clarity of naming, robustness against errors, resistance to change, ease of maintenance, and so on.

Test-driven development enables you to design your software continuously and in small steps, allowing the design to emerge as the code changes.

Specifically, design happens at three different points in the test-driven process:

- When you decide which test to write next, you're making a claim about what functionality your code should have. This frequently involves thinking about how to add that functionality to the existing code, which is a design question.

- As you write a test, you're designing the interaction between the test and the code, which is also the interaction between the part of the code under test and the rest of the application. This part of the process is used to create the API you want the code to have.

- After the test passes, you refactor, identifying duplication, missing abstractions, and other ways the code's design can be improved.

> **Prescription 1** Use the TDD process to create and adjust your code's design in small, incremental steps.

Continually aligning your code to the tests tends to result in code that is made up of small methods, each of which does one thing. These methods tend to be loosely coupled and have minimal side effects. As it happens, the hallmarks of easy-to-change code include small methods that do one thing, are loosely coupled, and have minimal side effects.

I used to think it was a coincidence that tested code and easy-to-change code have similar structures, but I've realized the commonality is a direct side effect of building the code in tandem with the tests. In essence, the tests act as a universal client for the entire codebase, guiding all the code to have clean interactions between parts because the tests, acting as a third-party interloper, have to get in between all the parts of the code to work. Metaphorically, compared to code written without tests, your code has more surface area and less work happening behind the scenes where it's hard to observe.

This theory explains why testing works better when the tests come first. Even waiting a little bit to write tests is significantly more painful. When the tests are written first, in very close intertwined proximity to the code, they encourage a good structure with low coupling (meaning different parts of the code have minimal dependencies on each other) and high cohesion (meaning code that is in the same unit is all related).

When the tests come later, they have to conform to the existing code, and it's amazing how quickly code written without tests will move toward low-cohesion and high-coupling forms that are much harder to cover with tests. If your only experience is with writing automated tests long after the initial code was written, the experience was likely quite painful. Don't let that turn you away from a TDD approach; the tests and code you'll write with TDD are much different.

When you're writing truly test-driven code, the tests are the final source of truth in your application. This means that when there is a discrepancy between the code and the tests, your first assumption is that the test is correct and the code is wrong. If you're writing tests after the code, then your assumption must be that the code is the source of truth. As you write your code using test-driven development, keep in mind the idea that the tests are the source of truth and are guiding the code's structure.

> **Prescription 2**
> In a test-driven process, if it's difficult to write tests for a feature, strongly consider the possibility that the design of the underlying code needs to be changed.

What Is TDD Good For?

The primary purpose of test-driven development is to go beyond mere verification and use the tests to improve the code's structure. That is, TDD is a software-development technique masquerading as a code-verification tool.

Automated tests are a wonderful way of showing that the program does what the developer thinks it does, but they are a lousy way of showing that what the developer thinks is what the program actually should do. "But the tests pass!" is not likely to be comforting to a customer when the developer's assumptions are just flat-out wrong. I speak from painful experience.

The kinds of tests written in a TDD process are not a substitute for acceptance testing, where users or customers verify that the code does what the user or customer expects. TDD also does not replace some kind of quality-assurance phase where users or testers pound away at the actual program trying to break something. Quality-assurance testing can expose flaws in the developer's understanding of the task that are unlikely to be exposed by the developer's own tests.

Further, TDD does not replace the role of a traditional software tester. TDD is simply a development process that produces better and more accurate code. A separate verification phase run by people who are not the original developers is still a good idea. For a thorough overview of more traditional exploratory testing, read *Explore It! Reduce Risk and Increase Confidence with Exploratory Testing [Hen13]*.

Verification is valuable, but the idea of verification can be taken too far. You sometimes see an argument against test-driven development that says, "The purpose of testing is to verify that my program is correct. I can never prove correctness with 100 percent certainty. Therefore, testing has no value." (RSpec, which is designed for a process its creators called behavior-driven development, was created to combat this attitude.) Ultimately, though, testing has a lot of benefits to offer for coding, even beyond verification.

Preventing regression is often presented as one of the paramount benefits of a test-driven development process. And if you're expecting me to disagree out of spite, you're out of luck. Being able to squash regressions before anybody else sees them is one of the key ways in which strict testing will speed up your development over time.

You may have heard that automated tests provide an alternative method of documenting your program—that the tests provide a detailed functional specification of the program's behavior. That's the theory. My experience with tests acting as documentation is mixed, to say the least. Still, it's useful to keep this in mind as a goal. Tests can be valuable in documenting the expected behavior of the system when things go wrong, and most of the things that make tests work better as documentation will also make the tests work better, period.

To make your tests effective as documentation, focus on giving them names that describe the reason for their existence, and keeping tests short and simple. When a test has a lot of complex setup and assertions, it can be hard for a reader to focus on the important features. As you'll see, a test that requires a bunch of tricky setup often indicates a problem in the underlying code.

In a testing environment, blank-page problems are almost completely nonexistent. I can always think of something that the program needs to do, so I write a test for that. When you're working test-first, the order in which pieces are written is not so important. Once a test is written, the path to the next one is usually more clear: find some way to specify something the code doesn't do yet.

When TDD Needs Some Help

Test-driven development is helpful, but it won't solve all of your development problems by itself. There are areas where developer testing doesn't apply or doesn't work very well.

I mentioned one case already: developer tests are not very good at determining whether the application is behaving correctly according to requirements. Strict TDD is not great at acceptance testing. There are, however, automated tools that do try to tackle acceptance testing. Within the Rails community, the most prominent of these are Capybara and Cucumber; see Chapter 8, *Integration Testing with Capybara and Cucumber*, on page 151. Acceptance testing can be integrated with TDD—you'll sometimes see this called *outside-in testing*. That's a perfectly valid and useful test paradigm, but it's an extension of the classic TDD process.

Testing your application assumes that you know the right answer to specify. And although you sometimes have clear requirements or a definitive source of correct output, other times you don't know what exactly the program needs to do. In this exploratory mode, TDD is less beneficial, because it's hard to write tests if you don't know what assertions to make about the program. Often this lack of direction happens during initial development or during a proof of concept. I also find myself in this position a lot when view-testing—I don't know what to test for until I get some of the view up and visible.

The TDD process has a name for the kind of exploratory code you write while trying to figure out the needed functionality: *spike*, as in, "I don't know if we can do what we need with the Twitter API; let's spend a day working on a spike for it." When working in spike mode, TDD is generally not used, but code written during the spike is not expected to be used in production; it's just a proof of concept to be thrown away and replaced with a version written using TDD.

When view-testing, or in other nonspike situations where I'm not quite sure what output to test for, I often go into a "test-next" mode, where I write the code first but in a TDD-sized small chunk, and then immediately write the test. This works as long as I make the switch between test and code frequently enough to get the benefit of having the code and the test inform each other's design.

TDD is not a complete solution for verifying your application. I've already talked about acceptance tests; it's also true that TDD tends to be thin in terms of the quantity of unit tests written. For one thing, in a strict TDD process you would never write a test that you expect to pass before writing more code. In practice, though, you may do this all the time. Sometimes I see and create an abstraction in the code, but there are still valid test cases to write. In particular, I'll often write code for potential error conditions even if I think they are already covered in the code. It's a balance because you lose some of the benefit of TDD by creating too many test cases that don't drive code changes. One way to keep the balance is to make a list of the test cases before you start writing the tests—that way you'll remember to cover all the interesting cases.

And some things are just hard. In particular, some parts of your application will be dependent on an external piece of code in a way that makes it difficult to isolate them for unit testing. *Test doubles*, which are special kinds of objects that can stand in for objects that are part of your application, are one way to work around this issue; see Chapter 7, *Using Test Doubles as Mocks and Stubs*, on page 129. But there are definitely cases (though they're not common) in which the cost of testing a complex feature is higher than the value of the tests.

Recent discussions in the Rails community have debated whether TDD's design benefits are even valuable. You may have heard the phrase "test-driven design damage." I strongly believe that TDD, and the relatively smaller and more numerous classes that a TDD process often brings, do result in more clear and more valuable code. But the TDD process is not a replacement for good design instincts; it's still possible to create bad code when testing, or even to create bad code in the name of testing.

Words to Live By

- Any change to the program logic should be driven by a failed test.

- If it's not tested, treat it like it's broken.

- Testing is supposed to help for the long term. The long term starts tomorrow, or maybe after lunch.

- It's not done until it works.

- Tests are code that doesn't have tests; keep them simple.

- Start a bug fix by writing a test.

- Tests monitor the quality of your codebase. If it becomes difficult to write tests, that often means your codebase is too interdependent.

What You've Done

In this introductory chapter, you learned what automated testing and test-driven development are, and how they can help you write better code. You also looked at the basic TDD process, where that process is most useful, and where it needs a little help.

Now it's time to start writing code using test-driven development. Let's start your application with a small example.

CHAPTER 2

Test-Driven Development Basics

You have a problem.

You're the team leader for a development team that is distributed across multiple locations. You'd like to be able to maintain a common list of tasks for the team. For each task, you'd like to maintain data such as the status of the task, which pair of developers the task is assigned to, and so on. You'd also like to be able to use the past rate of task completion to estimate the project's completion date. For some reason, none of the existing tools that do this are suitable (work with me here, folks) and so you've decided to roll your own. You're calling it Gatherer.

As you sit down to start working on Gatherer, your impulse is going to be to start writing code immediately. That's a great impulse, and I'm just going to turn it about 10 degrees east. Instead of starting off by writing code, you're going to start off by writing tests.

In the introductory chapter, I talked about why you might work test-first. In this chapter you'll look at the basic mechanics of a TDD cycle. Your starting point will be to create some business logic with our models, because model logic is the easiest part of a Rails application to test—in fact, most of this chapter won't touch Rails at all. In the next chapter, you'll start testing the display parts of the Rails framework.

Infrastructure

First off, you'll need a Rails application. You'll be using Rails 5.2.0 and Ruby 2.5.0. Let's start by generating the Rails application from the command line:

```
% gem install rails
% mkdir gatherer
% cd gatherer
% rails new .
```

This will create the initial directory structure and code for a Rails application. It will also run bundle install to load initial gems. You're going to mostly stick with the initial gem set for the moment. I assume that you're already familiar with Rails core concepts; I won't spend a lot of time reexplaining them. If you're not familiar with Rails, *Agile Web Development with Rails [Rub13]* is still the gold standard for getting started.

You need to create your databases. For ease of setup and distribution, stick to the Rails default—SQLite.[1] Run the following in your terminal to create the database:

```
% rake db:create:all
% rake db:migrate
```

You need the db:migrate call even though you haven't actually created a database migration, because it sets up the schema.rb file that Rails uses to rebuild the test database. The test database is automatically maintained when the schema.rb file changes.

The Requirements

The most complex business logic you need to build concerns forecasting a project's progress. You want to be able to predict the end date of a project and determine whether that project is on schedule.

In other words, given a project and a set of tasks, some of which are done and some of which are not, use the rate at which tasks are being completed to estimate the project's end date. Also, compare that projected date to a deadline to determine if the project is on time.

This is a good example problem for TDD because, while it's not hard to have a sense of what the answer is, the best way to structure the code is not clear. TDD will help, guiding you toward reasonable code design.

Installing RSpec

Before you start testing, you'll need to load RSpec, your testing library.

To add RSpec to a Rails project, add the rspec-rails gem to your Gemfile:

```
group :development, :test do
  gem "rspec-rails", "~> 3.7.0"
end
```

---

1. http://www.sqlite.org

The rspec-rails gem depends on the rspec gem proper. The rspec gem is mostly a list of other dependencies where the real work gets done, including rspec-core, rspec-expectations, and rspec-mocks. Sometimes rspec and rspec-rails are updated separately; you might choose to explicitly specify both versions in the Gemfile. Here we're putting rspec in the development group as well as in the test group so that you can call rspec from the command line, where development mode is the default. (RSpec switches to the test environment as it initializes.)

Install with bundle install. Then you need to generate some installation files using the rspec:install generator:

```
$ bundle install
$ rails generate rspec:install
      create  .rspec
      create  spec
      create  spec/spec_helper.rb
      create  spec/rails_helper.rb
```

What's a Spec?

What do you call the things you write in an RSpec file? If you're used to TDD and Minitest, the temptation to call them tests can be overwhelming. However, as I've discussed, the BDD planning behind RSpec suggests it's better not to think of your RSpec code as tests, which are things that happen after the fact. So, what are they?

The RSpec docs and code refer to the elements of RSpec as "examples." The term I hear most often is simply "spec," short for "specification," as in "I need to write some specs for that feature." I've tried to use "spec" and "example" rather than "test" in this book, but I suspect I'll slip up somewhere.

This generator creates the following:

- The .rspec file, where RSpec run options go. In RSpec 3.6 the default currently sets --require spec_helper, which ensures that the spec_helper file is always required.

- The spec directory, which is where your specs go. RSpec does not automatically create subdirectories like controller and model on installation. You can create the subdirectories manually or Rails generators will create them as needed.

- The spec_helper.rb and rails_helper.rb files, which contain setup information. The spec_helper.rb file contains general RSpec settings while the rails_helper.rb file, which requires spec_helper, loads the Rails environment and contains settings that depend on Rails. The idea behind having two files is to make it easier to write specs that do not load Rails. You're not going to touch the configuration at the moment.

The rspec-rails gem does a couple of other things behind the scenes when loaded in a Rails project:

- Adds a Rake file that changes the default Rake test to run RSpec instead of Minitest and defines a number of other Rake tasks, such as spec:models, that filter an RSpec run to a subset of the overall RSpec suite. I don't recommend using those, as the RSpec command line is more fully featured.

- Sets itself up as the test framework of choice for the purposes of future Rails generators. Later, when you set up, say, a generated model or resource, RSpec's generators are automatically invoked to create appropriate spec files.

Where to Start?

"Where do I begin testing?" is one of the most common questions people have when they start with TDD. Traditionally, my answer is a somewhat glib "start anywhere." While true, this is less than helpful.

A good option for starting a TDD cycle is to specify the initialization state of the objects or methods under test. Another is the "happy path"—a single representative example of the error-free version of the algorithm. Which starting point you choose depends on how complicated the feature is. In this case it's sufficiently complex that I'll start with the initial state and move to the happy path. As a rule of thumb, if it takes more than a couple of steps to define an instance of the application, I'll start with initialization only.

> **Prescription 3** Initializing objects is a good starting place for a TDD process. Another good approach is to use the test to design what you want a successful interaction of the feature to look like.

This application is made up of projects and tasks. A newly created project would have no tasks. What can you say about that brand-new project?

If there are no outstanding tasks, then there's nothing left to do. A project with nothing left to do is done. The initial state, then, is a project with no tasks, and by that logic, the project is done. That's not an inevitable decision; you could specify that a project with no tasks is in some kind of empty state.

You don't have any infrastructure in place yet, so you need to create the test file yourself—we're deliberately not using Rails generators right now. We're using RSpec, so the spec goes in the spec directory using a file name that is parallel to the application code in the app directory. We think this is a test of a project model, which would be in app/models/project.rb, so put the spec in spec/models/project_spec.rb. We're making very small design decisions here, and so far these decisions are consistent with Rails conventions.

Here's your spec of a project's initial state:

```
basics/01/spec/models/project_spec.rb
Line 1  require "rails_helper"
2
3  RSpec.describe Project do
4    it "considers a project with no tasks to be done" do
5      project = Project.new
6      expect(project.done?).to be_truthy
7    end
8
9  end
```

Let's talk about this spec at two levels: the logistics of the code in RSpec and what this test is doing for you in your TDD process.

Compared to other testing libraries, RSpec shifts the tone from an "assertion," potentially implying already-implemented behavior, to an "expectation," implying future behavior. The RSpec version, arguably, is easier to read than the Minitest version (though some strenuously dispute this). Later in this chapter I'll cover some other tricks RSpec uses to make expectations read like natural language.

The project_spec.rb file uses four basic RSpec and Rails features:

- It requires rails_helper.
- It defines a test suite with RSpec.describe.
- It creates an RSpec example with it.
- It specifies a particular state with expect.

On the first line, the file rails_helper, which contains Rails-related setup common to all tests, is required. (You'll peek into that file in the next chapter, when I talk about more Rails-specific test features.) The rails_helper file, in turn, requires a file named spec_helper, which contains non-Rails RSpec setup.

The RSpec.describe method is used on line 3. In RSpec, the describe method defines a suite of specs that can share a common setup. The first argument to describe is either a class name or a string. The first argument documents what the test suite is supposed to cover. You can then pass an optional number of metadata arguments, of which there are none at the moment. The metadata is used to specify additional behavior for the spec. Finally, describe expects a block, which contains the test suite itself.

As you'll see in a little bit, describe calls can be nested. By convention, the outermost call typically has the name of the class under test. The outermost describe call must be invoked as RSpec.describe, since that call starts outside of RSpec's control. Nested calls can use just plain describe, since RSpec manages those calls internally.

The actual spec is defined with the it method, which takes an optional string argument that documents the spec, an optional amount of metadata, and then a block that is the body of the spec. The string argument is not used internally to identify the spec—you can have multiple specs with the same description string. Again, the metadata is used to adjust RSpec's behavior.

RSpec also defines specify as an alias for it. Normally, you'd use it when the method takes a string argument to give the spec a readable natural-language name. (Historically the string argument started with "should," so the name would be something like "it should be valid," but that documentation pattern is no longer considered a good practice.) For single-line tests in which a string description is unnecessary, you can use specify to make the single line read more clearly, such as this:

```
specify { expect(user.name).to eq("fred") }
```

On line 6 you write your first testable expectation about the code:

```
expect(project.done?).to be_truthy
```

The general form of an RSpec expectation is expect(actual_value).to(matcher), with the parentheses around the matcher often omitted in practice. In this case, the expectation would more formally read, expect(project.done?).to(be_truthy). A *matcher* is an RSpec object that takes a value and determines if it matches expectations based on some set of logic. In this example, the matcher is be_truthy.

Let's trace through what RSpec does with this expectation. First is the expect call itself, expect(project.done?). RSpec defines the expect method, which takes in any object as an argument and returns a special RSpec proxy object called an ExpectationTarget.

The ExpectationTarget holds on to the object that was the argument to expect, and itself responds to two messages: to and not_to. (Okay, technically three messages, since to_not exists as an alias.) Both to and not_to are ordinary Ruby methods that expect a single argument, which needs to be an RSpec matcher.

There's nothing special about an RSpec matcher; at base it's just an object that responds to a matches? method. There are several predefined matchers and you can write your own.

In this case, be_truthy is a method defined by RSpec to return the BeTruthy matcher. You could get the same behavior with

```
expect(project.done?).to(RSpec::BuiltIn::BeTruthy.new)
```

but you probably would agree that the idiomatic version is easier to read.

The ExpectationTarget is now holding on to two objects: the object being matched (in this case, project.done?) and the matcher (be_truthy). When the spec is executed, RSpec calls the matches? method on the matcher, with the object being matched as an argument. If the expectation uses to, then the expectation passes if matches? is true. If the expectation uses not_to, then it checks for a does_not_match? method in the matcher. If there is no such method it falls back to passing if matches? is false. This is shown in the following diagram.

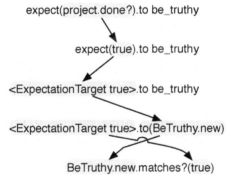

From an RSpec perspective, you're creating an object and asserting an initial condition. What are you doing from a TDD perspective, and why is this useful?

Small as it might seem, you've performed a little bit of design. You're starting to define the way parts of your system communicate with each other, and the tests ensure the visibility of important information in your design.

This small test makes three claims about your program:

- There is a class called Project.
- You can query instances of that class as to whether they are done.
- A brand-new instance of Project qualifies as done.

This last assertion isn't inevitable—you could say that you aren't done unless there is at least one completed task, but that's a choice you're making in the application's business logic.

RSpec Predefined Matchers

Before you run the tests, let's take a quick look at RSpec's basic matchers. RSpec predefines a number of matchers. What follows is a list of the most useful ones; you can find a full list online.[2]

```
expect(array).to all(matcher)
expect(actual).to be > expected       # (also works with <, >=, <=, and ==)
expect(actual).to be_a(type)
expect(actual).to be_truthy
expect(actual).to be_falsy
expect(actual).to be_nil
expect(actual).to be_between(min, max)
expect(actual).to be_within(delta).of(expected)
expect { block }.to change(receiver, message, &block)
expect(actual).to contain_exactly(expected)
expect(range).to cover(actual_value)
expect(actual).to eq(expected)
expect(actual).to exist
expect(actual).to have_attributes(key/value pairs)
expect(actual).to include(*expected)
expect(actual).to match(regex)
expect { block }.to output(value).to_stdout   # also to_stderr
expect { block }.to raise_error(exception)
expect(actual).to satisfy { block }
```

Most of these mean what they appear to say. Some elaborations:

- The all matcher takes a different matcher as an argument and passes if all elements of the array pass that internal matcher, as in expect([1, 2, 3]).to all(be_truthy).

- The change matcher takes a block argument that passes if the value of receiver.message changes when the block is evaluated.

- The contain_exactly matcher is true if the expected array and the actual array contain the same elements, regardless of order.

- The satisfy matcher passes if the block evaluates to true.

- The matchers that take block arguments, output and raise_error, are for specifying a side effect of the block's execution—that it raises an error or that it changes a different value—rather than the state of a particular object.

---

2. https://relishapp.com/rspec/rspec-expectations/v/3-7/docs/built-in-matchers

Any of these matchers except raise_error can be negated by using not_to instead of using to.

RSpec allows you to compose matchers to express compound behavior, and most of these matchers have alternate forms that allow them to read better when composed. Composing matchers allows you to specify, for example, multiple array values in a single statement and get useful error messages.

Here is a contrived example:

```
expect(["cheese", "burger"]).to contain_exactly(
    a_string_matching(/ch/), a_string_matching(/urg/))
```

In this case a_string_matching is an alias for match, and the arguments to contain_exactly are themselves matchers that must match individual elements of the array to allow the entire compound matcher to pass.

Running the Test

Having written your first test, you'd probably like to execute it. Although RSpec provides Rake tasks for executing RSpec, I recommend using the rspec command directly to avoid the overhead of starting up Rake. If you use rspec with no arguments, then RSpec will run over the entire spec directory. You can also give RSpec an individual file, directory, or line to run. For details on those options, see Chapter 16, *Running Tests Faster and Running Faster Tests*, on page 319.

What Happens When the Test Is Run?

It fails. You haven't written any code yet.

That's Funny. What Really Happens—Internally?

When you run rspec with no arguments, RSpec loads every file in the spec directory. The following things happen (this process is slightly simplified for clarity):

1. Each file in the spec directory is loaded. Usually these files will contain just these specs, but sometimes you'll define setup, or extra helper methods or dummy classes that exist just to support the tests.

2. Each RSpec file typically requires the rails_helper.rb file. The rails_helper.rb file loads the Rails environment itself, as well as the spec_helper.rb, which contains non-Rails RSpec setup. In the default Rails configuration the .rspec file automatically loads spec_helper.rb; you could also change the .rspec file to automatically load rails_helper.rb.

3. By default the rails_helper.rb file sets up transactional fixtures. *Fixtures* are a Rails mechanism that defines global ActiveRecord data that is available to all tests. By default fixtures are added once inside a database transaction that wraps all the tests. At the end of the test the transaction is rolled back, allowing the next test to continue with a pristine state. More on fixtures in *Fixtures*, on page 103.

4. Each top-level call to RSpec.describe creates an internal RSpec object called an *example group*. The creation of the example group causes the block argument to describe to be executed. This may include further calls to describe to create nested example groups. The block argument to describe may also contain calls to it. Each call to it results in the creation of an individual test, which is internally called an "example." The block arguments to it are stored for later execution.

5. Each top-level example group runs. By default the order in which the groups run is random. The randomness is to discourage the use of global state that might inadvertently make tests dependent on earlier tests. Before running examples in the example group, run any before(:all) blocks. These blocks allow you to create global setup for all examples in the group. Like anything that contains global setup in tests, they are prone to failure and should be used sparingly.

Running an example group involves running each example that it contains, and that involves a few steps:

1. Run all before(:example) setup blocks. I'll talk about those more in a moment, when they become useful.

2. Run the example, which is the block argument to it. The method execution ends when a runtime error or a failed assertion is encountered. If neither of those happens, the test method passes. Yay!

3. Run all after(:example) teardown blocks. Teardown blocks are declared similarly to setup blocks, but their use is much less common.

4. Roll back or delete the fixtures as described earlier. The result of each example is passed back to the test runner for display in the console or IDE window running the test.

5. After all examples in the file have run, run any after(:all) blocks.

The diagram on page 21 shows the flow.

In your specific case, you have one file, one example group, and one spec, and if you run things, you fail pretty quickly. Here's the slightly edited output.

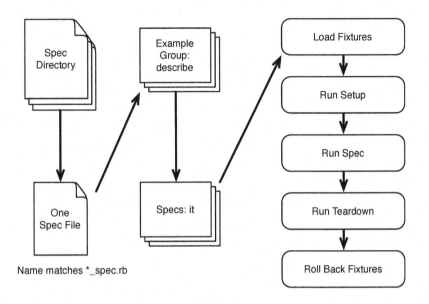

Name matches *_spec.rb

If you have color turned on in your terminal, this output will be conveniently syntax colored:

```
$ rspec
An error occurred while loading ./spec/models/project_spec.rb.
Failure/Error:
  RSpec.describe Project do
    it "considers a project with no tasks to be done" do
      project = Project.new
      expect(project.done?).to be_truthy
    end
  end

NameError:
  uninitialized constant Project
# ./spec/models/project_spec.rb:3:in `<top (required)>'
No examples found.

Finished in 0.00042 seconds (files took 4.75 seconds to load)
0 examples, 0 failures, 1 error occurred outside of examples
```

You're not even getting to the test run; the use of describe Project at the beginning of the test is failing because you haven't defined Project yet.

Making the Test Pass

Now it's time to make the first test pass.

But how?

It seems like a straightforward question, but it has a few different answers.

- The purist way: *Do the simplest thing that could possibly work.* In this case "work" means "minimally pass the test without regard to the larger context." Or it might even mean "write the minimum amount of code to clear the current error without regard to the larger context."

- The "practical" way (scare quotes intended): Write the code you know you need to eventually write, effectively skipping steps that seem too small to be valuable.

- The teaching way: This method is somewhere between the other two and lets me best explain how and why test-driven development works without getting bogged down in details or skipping too many steps.

Ultimately, there isn't a one-size-fits-all answer to the question. The goal is to make the test pass in a way that allows you to best discover the solution to the problem and design your code. In practice, the more complicated the problem is and the less I feel I understand the solution, the more purist I get, taking small steps. It's a funny thing; I rarely regret being too purist, but I sometimes regret being too practical, because it turns out I didn't understand the problem as well as I thought and I've cut a corner I shouldn't have cut.

Let's make this test pass. The first error you need to clear is the uninitialized constant: Project error, so put this in app/models/project.rb:

```
class Project
end
```

This is a minimal way to clear the error. (Well, that's technically not true; I could just declare a constant Project = true or something like that, but even I draw the purist line somewhere.) But the test still doesn't pass. If you run the tests now, you get this:

```
% rspec

Failures:

  1) Project considers a project with no tasks to be done
     Failure/Error: expect(project.done?).to be_truthy

     NoMethodError:
       undefined method `done?' for # <Project:0x007fe9df519cc8>
     # ./spec/models/project_spec.rb:6:in `block (2 levels) in <top (required)>'

Finished in 0.00584 seconds (files took 6.37 seconds to load)
1 example, 1 failure

Failed examples:

rspec ./spec/models/project_spec.rb:4 # Project considers a project with
# no tasks to be done
```

See that last line starting with rspec? That's where RSpec usefully gives you the exact command-line invocation you need to run just the failing spec. This is helpful. Later on, you'll see some other ways to get RSpec to rerun failing specs.

Our error is that you are calling project.done? and the done? method does not exist yet.

That's simple to clear, still in app/models/project.rb:

```ruby
class Project
  def done?
  end
end
```

And when you do this and run rspec again, you finally get a more interesting error:

```
% rspec

F

Failures:

  1) Project considers a project with no tasks to be done
     Failure/Error: expect(project.done?).to be_truthy

       expected: truthy value
            got: nil
     # ./spec/models/project_spec.rb:6:in `block (2 levels) in <top (required)>'
Finished in 0.02281 seconds (files took 5.92 seconds to load)
1 example, 1 failure

Failed examples:

rspec ./spec/models/project_spec.rb:4
    # Project considers a project with no tasks to be done
```

You've now passed out of the realm of syntax and runtime errors and into the realm of assertion failures—the test runs, but the code does not behave as expected. You've expected that the value of project.done? will be truthy, which is to say any Ruby value that evaluates to true. But since your method doesn't return any value, you get nil.

Luckily, that has a simple fix:

```ruby
basics/01/app/models/project.rb
class Project
  def done?
    true
  end
end
```

Which results in this:

```
$ rspec
.

Finished in 0.00392 seconds (files took 5.99 seconds to load)
1 example, 0 failures
```

And the test passes! You're done! Ship it!

Okay, you're not exactly done. You made the test pass, which actually only gets you two-thirds of the way through the TDD cycle. You've done the "red" (failing test) step and the "green" (passing test) step and now you're at the refactoring step. However, you've written almost no code, so you can safely say there are no refactorings indicated at this point.

I suspect that if you're inclined to be skeptical of test-driven development, I haven't convinced you yet. I've gone on for a few pages and you've only written one line of code, and that line of code clearly isn't even final. I reiterate that in practice this doesn't take much time. If I wasn't stopping to discuss each step this would take only a couple of minutes, and some of that time—like setting up the Project class—would need to be spent anyway.

In fact, you haven't exactly done nothing—you've defined and documented a subtle part of how your Project class behaves, and you'll find out immediately if the class ever breaks that behavior. As I've said, though, documentation and regression are only part of what makes test-driven development powerful. You need to get to the design part. And for that, you need to write more tests.

The Second Test

One nice feature of test-driven development is that making one test pass often points the way to the next test. The goal of the next test cycle is to write a test that fails given the current code. At this point the code says that done? is always true, so you should create a case where done? is false:

basics/02/spec/models/project_spec.rb
```
it "knows that a project with an incomplete task is not done" do
  project = Project.new
  task = Task.new
  project.tasks << task
  expect(project.done?).to be_falsy
end
```

This test is similar to the first one, but now you have a second class, Task, and a related attribute of the Project class, tasks. This time you're assuming that a new task is undone, and therefore a project with an undone task is not done. You could write the last line as expect(project.done?).not_to be_truthy, but that seems harder to read. (You'll see an even shorter way to write that line in a little bit.)

The first failure is that the Task constant is missing. You can clear it up easily:

basics/02/app/models/task.rb
```ruby
class Task
end
```

At this point, the next failure is that project.tasks doesn't exist. You can clear that up, and then also clear up the following failure, that project.done? doesn't exist. This leads you to write simple, but still incomplete, done? logic to make the test pass—a project is done if it has no tasks:

basics/02/app/models/project.rb
```ruby
class Project
  attr_accessor :tasks

  def initialize
    @tasks = []
  end

  def done?
    tasks.empty?
  end
end
```

The second test now passes. And you have a clear candidate for the next test—the distinction between complete and incomplete tasks. I'm also starting to think about how you get from that distinction to the more advanced logic of sizing tasks and estimating project due dates.

With the test passing, you now enter the refactoring phase.

If you've done Rails programming before, you may have noticed that I have not yet made Project and Task subclasses of ActiveRecord::Base, meaning I haven't connected them to the database via ActiveRecord.

I have two reasons for this. The first is a purist one—I haven't added any tests that would need ActiveRecord functionality to pass. The second is a teaching-specific one—for the first testing example, I'd like to focus on the testing part, not the Rails boilerplate. Getting caught up in generating migrations and the like is not what I want to talk about here.

And, while there's a pretty good chance that both these classes will become ActiveRecord classes, it's not guaranteed, and if you're using tests to drive design it makes sense not to let the design leap ahead of the tests, but rather to use the tests to suggest the code's structure.

For example, it's not a completely crazy design to say that Projects might never have data of their own and therefore might never need to be ActiveRecord objects. Somewhat more plausibly, the date-projection code that you're writing now might eventually wind up in some kind of dedicated calculator object separate from the ActiveRecord layer. In either case, there's no need for the design to get ahead of the tests.

let and Expectations

In addition to examining code for potential refactoring, it's a good idea to look at the tests for duplication. In this case you have a single line of common setup—namely, project = Project.new, which is shared between the two tests you've already written. You can fix this and turn your tests into slightly more idiomatic RSpec:

`basics/03/spec/models/project_spec.rb`
```
require "rails_helper"

RSpec.describe Project do
  let(:project) { Project.new }
  let(:task) { Task.new }

  it "considers a project with no tasks to be done" do
    expect(project).to be_done
  end

  it "knows that a project with an incomplete task is not done" do
    project.tasks << task
    expect(project).not_to be_done
  end
end
```

This version of the test allows me to show two of my favorite parts of RSpec: the let statement and dynamic matchers.

RSpec's let statement cleans up the creation of test data.

Using let, you can make a variable available within the current describe block without having to place it inside the before block and without having to make it an instance variable. I use let all the time. I like that it separates the definition of each variable, that it encourages concise initializations, and that the word let allows me to pretend I'm writing in Scheme or Elm for a brief moment.

Each let method call takes a symbol argument and a block. The symbol can then be called as if it were a local variable: the first call to the symbol lazily invokes the block and caches the result, and subsequent calls within the same spec return the same result without reinvoking the block. When a new spec starts, the value is cleared and the block is reinvoked.

This example uses let twice, first to describe a project and then to describe a task. You can then use project and task in the body of the specs. Even though task isn't used in the first spec, that's perfectly fine—RSpec invokes the let block only when the variable is used.

In essence, a let call is syntactic sugar for defining a method and memoizing the result, like this:

```
def me
  @me ||= User.new(name: "Noel")
end
```

The main gotcha here is that the let block isn't executed unless it's invoked. That's often a good thing since your test won't spend time creating unused objects. You can get in trouble sometimes if you expect that the object already exists. For a contrived problem case, note that this example will fail since the two let blocks are never invoked:

```
describe "user behavior"
  let(:me) { User.new(:name => "Noel") }
  let(:you) { User.new(:name => "Erin") }
  specify { User.count.should == 2 }
end
```

Luckily, RSpec provides a mechanism in cases where an item must be present even though it is never invoked by name. It's called let!, with a "bang" for "block always needs getting," which I just made up and only makes a tiny amount of sense, but you probably won't forget it.

One of my other favorite bits of RSpec is an implicit matcher that RSpec creates by name-mangling if you give it a matcher it doesn't recognize. Any matcher of the form be_whatever or be_a_whatever assumes an associated predicate method named whatever?—with a question mark—on the object, and calls that predicate method. The predicate method's return value drives the matcher's behavior. If the matcher is called via to, it passes if the predicate method returns a true value. If the matcher is called via not_to, it passes if the predicate method returns a false value.

In the previous examples, you invoked expectations like expect(project.done?).to be_truthy. Since done? is a predicate method, I rewrote those examples to be more direct. This gives us expect(project).to be_done, which almost reads as simple, clear, natural language. Often it's easier to add a predicate method to your object than it is to create a custom matcher in RSpec.

A lot of complexity goes into making RSpec's language clear. In addition to allowing be_a and be_an, if the predicate method is in the present tense, such as matches?, you can write the expectation as be_a_match. In this case RSpec will look for match? and then form matches? if it can't find match?.

Similarly, if the predicate method starts with has, RSpec allows your matcher to start with have for readability (so your tests don't look like they've been written by LOLcats); RSpec allows expect(actual).to have_key(:id) rather than expect(actual).to has_key(:id).

RSpec also allows you to chain multiple matchers using and and or, as in expect(actual).to include("a").and match(/.*3.*/), or expect(actual).to eq(3).or eq(5).

You can also pass matchers as arguments to other matchers, or compose matchers to handle an entire data structure using match. The following two snippets are equivalent:

```
expect(actual[0]).to eq(5)
expect(actual[1]).to eq(7)

expect(actual).to match([an_object_eq_to(5), an_object_eq_to(7)])
```

In the bottom snippet, the elements of the array actual are individually matched against an_object_eq_to(5) and an_object_eq_to(7), which are aliases to eq(5) and eq(7). Most of the built-in matchers have aliases to make them more natural-language-like when used as arguments. (You can see a full list online.[3]) The all matcher, which looks like expect(actual).to all(be_truthy), takes the matcher argument (in this case be_truthy) and applies it to each element in the object being matched (in this case, actual, which should be enumerable).

I love this language inflection because I feel like it allows me to write tests that are succinct and clear. Others find the internal complexity of these features to be too high a price to pay for the natural-language tests. (Some people also really don't like the natural-language syntax.)

Back on Task

What remains of your definition of done? is the distinction between complete and incomplete tasks. Let's start with that, with a test for Task:

basics/03/spec/models/task_spec.rb
```ruby
require "rails_helper"

RSpec.describe Task do
  let(:task) { Task.new }

  it "does not have a new task as complete" do
    expect(task).not_to be_complete
  end
```

---

3. https://relishapp.com/rspec/rspec-expectations/v/3-7/docs/built-in-matchers

```
  it "allows us to complete a task" do
    task.mark_completed
    expect(task).to be_complete
  end
end
```

You have two specs here. The first says that a brand-new task is not complete. The second creates a different task object, marks it as complete, and expects that it is then complete.

This test is entirely at the API level and makes no claim about the underlying mechanism for representing completed tasks. This is great because it means you can change the implementation without breaking tests as long as the API still works. Overreliance on implementation details is a major cause of test fragility, so when you can describe the behavior rather than the implementation, you should do so.

> **Prescription 4** When possible, write your tests to describe your code's behavior, not its implementation.

You can make the test pass with some simple methods in Task:

basics/03/app/models/task.rb
```
class Task
  def initialize
    @completed = false
  end

  def mark_completed
    @completed = true
  end

  def complete?
    @completed
  end
end
```

This implementation probably won't survive long—tasks will probably grow more states—but for now it works.

> **Prescription 5** Keeping your code as simple as possible allows you to focus complexity on the areas that really need it.

You can use a similar test to ensure the project's ability to determine completeness:

basics/04/spec/models/project_spec.rb
```
it "marks a project done if its tasks are done" do
  project.tasks << task
  task.mark_completed
  expect(project).to be_done
end
```

You make the test pass by adding logic to your project's done? method:

basics/04/app/models/project.rb
```
class Project
  attr_accessor :tasks

  def initialize
    @tasks = []
  end

  def done?
    tasks.all?(&:complete?)
  end
end
```

I can't think of an easy way to break the done? method as it currently stands, so it is ... well, done.

Adding Some Math

Moving on. Next, you need to be able to calculate how much of a project is remaining and the rate of completion, and then put them together to determine a projected end date.

The next test is for the project to be able to calculate how much work is remaining.

I like to take a moment before I write a test to think about what the test needs. The typical test structure has three parts:

- Given: What data does the test need? *This test needs a project, at least one complete task, and at least one incomplete task.*

- When: What action is taking place? *I'm calculating the remaining work.*

- Then: What behavior do I need to specify? *The work-calculation result.*

I also like to think about what could make the happy-path test fail; that's more helpful once you get the happy-path test in place and then start looking at it critically.

With that thought exercise over, you write your spec. Actually, there are two assertions and I've split them up. In practice I'd write them one at a time, but I don't think you need to go through all those steps explicitly. To add this to the existing file, I wrapped the specs that were already there in a describe block and added this code as a second describe block:

```
basics/05/spec/models/project_spec.rb
describe "estimates" do
  let(:project) { Project.new }
  let(:done) { Task.new(size: 2, completed: true) }
  let(:small_not_done) { Task.new(size: 1) }
  let(:large_not_done) { Task.new(size: 4) }

  before(:example) do
    project.tasks = [done, small_not_done, large_not_done]
  end
  it "can calculate total size" do
    expect(project.total_size).to eq(7)
  end
  it "can calculate remaining size" do
    expect(project.remaining_size).to eq(5)
  end
end
```

You put the spec in a new describe block in your project_spec.rb file since it has a different setup from the specs you've already written. Each describe block can have its own setup, making it easier to see what setup goes with what spec.

The let statements combined with the before block set up a project with three tasks; the two single-line it blocks have this setup in common. In RSpec, anything in a before(:each) or before(:example) block is executed as part of the setup before each spec.

These specs follow a common RSpec pattern: The "given" data goes in a series of let methods, the "when" action goes in a before block, and then a series of small it statements represent individual assertions.

A couple of minor style choices make the test easier to manage. All the task objects have meaningful names so that at a glance I can tell each object's reason for being in the test. If the tasks had descriptions or names I'd also give them meaningful data so that if the object gets printed to the terminal it's easy to tell which object it is. The specific score numbers that I'm using for each are also a deliberate style choice. Each task has a different score, and neither of the two adds up to the third, which is a very small thing that makes it harder to get a false positive test.

Prescription 6	Choose your test data and test-variable names to make it easy to diagnose failures when they happen. Meaningful names and data that doesn't overlap are helpful.

This test fails first on the creation of Task.new(size: 2, completed: true). Task isn't an ActiveRecord yet, so you don't have the hash argument by default. If this weren't a book example I would bring in ActiveRecord here, but I don't want to stop to define the migrations since they are irrelevant to the current point. I'll cover ActiveRecord when I bring in more Rails features.

basics/05/app/models/task.rb
```ruby
class Task
  attr_accessor :size, :completed

  def initialize(options = {})
    @completed = options[:completed]
    @size = options[:size]
  end

  def mark_completed
    @completed = true
  end

  def complete?
    @completed
  end
end
```

You can then make this pass with a couple more single-line methods in Project:

basics/05/app/models/project.rb
```ruby
class Project
  attr_accessor :tasks

  def initialize
    @tasks = []
  end

  def done?
    tasks.all?(&:complete?)
  end

  def total_size
    tasks.sum(&:size)
  end

  def remaining_size
    tasks.reject(&:complete?).sum(&:size)
  end
end
```

And the test passes.

This time, in the refactoring step you actually have stuff to do. In Project you have two methods that both use a list of incomplete tasks. You can extract that to common code:

basics/06/app/models/project.rb
```ruby
class Project
  attr_accessor :tasks

  def initialize
    @tasks = []
  end

  def incomplete_tasks
    tasks.reject(&:complete?)
  end

  def done?
    incomplete_tasks.empty?
  end

  def total_size
    tasks.sum(&:size)
  end

  def remaining_size
    incomplete_tasks.sum(&:size)
  end
end
```

This doesn't make the code shorter, but it does wrap a slightly opaque functional call containing a negative condition in a method with a semantically meaningful name. And if the definition of completeness changes, you only have to change one location.

There is still potential duplication in the Project class—two methods that call sum(&:size) on a list of tasks. I don't have an obvious place to put that method, though, short of creating a TaskList class. I don't see creating a TaskList as a simplification at this time, so we'll hold off. (A reviewer suggested this might also lead us to question whether the Project class is actually the correct abstraction and if TaskList might be better. Again, I think it's too early to tell.)

The First Date

You've got part of your Project API down; now you need to use that to calculate a projected completion date. The requirement is to calculate the project's end date based on the number of tasks finished in the last three weeks. I'll appropriate the agile term "velocity" to describe the rate of task completion. To make this work, you need to distinguish between tasks that concluded in the last three weeks and tasks that did not.

That means you have to deal with dates.

I'm sorry.

Programming with dates and times is the worst. Time is especially problematic in testing because tests work best when each test run is identical. However, owing to the nature of the universe, the current time inexorably changes from test run to test run. This can lead to all kinds of fun, including tests that fail on or after a particular day or tests that pass only at certain times of day. We'll try to avoid all of that.

You're testing bottom-up, so it's a good idea to start at the smallest unit of code you can think of. In this case, that's having Task instances be aware of whether they have been completed in the three-week window.

In the interest of not showing every tiny step this time around, I'll present the entire set of Task tests. A task completed in the last three weeks counts toward velocity, which implies two negative cases: an incomplete task and a task that was completed longer ago. To be clear, I wrote and passed them one at a time, but I don't think you need to walk through all those steps a second time. Once again, I've wrapped the existing code in a describe block and I'm adding the new specs as their own describe block.

```
basics/07/spec/models/task_spec.rb
describe "velocity" do
  let(:task) { Task.new(size: 3) }

  it "does not count an incomplete task toward velocity" do
    expect(task).not_to be_a_part_of_velocity
    expect(task.points_toward_velocity).to eq(0)
  end

  it "counts a recently completed task toward velocity" do
    task.mark_completed(1.day.ago)
    expect(task).to be_a_part_of_velocity
    expect(task.points_toward_velocity).to eq(3)
  end

  it "does not count a long-ago completed task toward velocity" do
    task.mark_completed(6.months.ago)
    expect(task).not_to be_a_part_of_velocity
    expect(task.points_toward_velocity).to eq(0)
  end
end
```

A couple of changes to the Task class are implied in these specs.

First off, the existing mechanism for completing a task was changed. On lines 16 and 10, the mark_completed call was changed to take an optional date argument indicating the date completed. It'd be nice to do this without touching the existing tests that use mark_completed with no argument. (Though you do have to change the project test that uses completed on a task to use completed_at.)

Two related methods were added to the Task class: part_of_velocity? (implied by the be_part_of_velocity matcher) and points_toward_velocity. According to the requirements, the part_of_velocity? method returns true if the task has been completed in the last three weeks. As a matter of code style, you're naming the method and testing the behavior rather than testing against the specifics of the implementation. By testing against the behavior, hopefully you'll be better able to deal with the inevitable requirements changes.

The points_toward_velocity method is trickier. If the task counts toward velocity, then the size of the task is returned; otherwise the method returns zero. This is an example of designing the class interface via tests. The idea is to keep all the logic for tasks inside the Task class. Specifically, I want a project to be able to determine how much time is remaining without having to query the task twice—once to determine the status of the task and again to determine its size.

There are few interesting design considerations in the specs themselves. Although the order in which you write the specs probably doesn't make a long-term difference, the order in the file above is what you get if you try to write a spec that will break the existing code each time. By that I mean that I wrote the first test and passed it with very basic changes: a part_of_velocity? method that returned false and a points_toward_velocity method that returned 0. Since the third spec has the same outcome, it would pass without further code changes, requiring larger code changes when the remaining spec is added. However, the second spec, where the task is a part of velocity, requires you to add logic specifying that the task must be complete to count toward velocity. Then the third spec says it must have been completed recently. When you think about writing the next spec so that it breaks existing code, it is easier to move in small steps.

As a matter of testing style, notice the way dates are specified on lines 10 and 16 of the test file. I'm using the Rails helpers to concisely specify the dates relative to the current time: 6.months.ago for the out-of-velocity task and 1.day.ago for the in-velocity task. If I had specified an explicit date for yesterday, then eventually the passage of time would push that date beyond the three-week threshold and the test would fail. Using relative dates reduces that problem.

There's a different interesting question about the test design and the dates. Neither six months nor one day is particularly close to the boundary between in-velocity and out-of-velocity tasks. Shouldn't I test more days or test something closer to the boundary? This question reflects the difference between testing as a design aid and testing for verification. In strict TDD you would avoid writing a test that you expect to pass, because a passing test doesn't normally drive you to change the code.

I would write a boundary-condition test only if I had reason to think that my implementation might fail in a boundary condition. That is quite possible for dates and times, and often if I'm dealing with SQL date ranges versus Ruby date ranges or if time zones are involved, I add tests near the boundary to attempt to break the implementation and catch an off-by-one error. I wouldn't write a series of tests for every length of time completed one day through six months ago, since I would expect all those tests to pass. The resulting Task class looks like this:

basics/07/app/models/task.rb

```ruby
class Task
  attr_accessor :size, :completed_at

  def initialize(options = {})
    mark_completed(options[:completed_at]) if options[:completed_at]
    @size = options[:size]
  end

  def mark_completed(date = Time.current)
    @completed_at = date
  end

  def complete?
    completed_at.present?
  end

  def part_of_velocity?
    return false unless complete?
    completed_at > 21.days.ago
  end

  def points_toward_velocity
    part_of_velocity? ? size : 0
  end
end
```

Using the Time Data

With the task tests passing, it's time to switch your attention back to the Project test. You need to make a slight tweak to your project_spec setup so that you have tasks that are in and out of the three-week velocity window:

basics/07/spec/models/project_spec.rb

```ruby
let(:project) { Project.new }
let(:newly_done) { Task.new(size: 3, completed_at: 1.day.ago) }
let(:old_done) { Task.new(size: 2, completed_at: 6.months.ago) }
let(:small_not_done) { Task.new(size: 1) }
let(:large_not_done) { Task.new(size: 4) }

before(:example) do
  project.tasks = [newly_done, old_done, small_not_done, large_not_done]
end
```

Here you added one more completed task, and you're using the ability to pass a completed date to differentiate the two. Note that the total size is now 10 instead of 7 and the total-size test needs to be changed accordingly.

Now the calculations you need for determining the projected project status are straightforward math based on this data:

```
basics/07/spec/models/project_spec.rb
it "knows its velocity" do
  expect(project.completed_velocity).to eq(3)
end

it "knows its rate" do
  expect(project.current_rate).to eq(1.0 / 7)
end

it "knows its projected days remaining" do
  expect(project.projected_days_remaining).to eq(35)
end

it "knows if it is not on schedule" do
  project.due_date = 1.week.from_now
  expect(project).not_to be_on_schedule
end

it "knows if it is on schedule" do
  project.due_date = 6.months.from_now
  expect(project).to be_on_schedule
end
```

You can quibble with some style choices in these tests. Even though the tests are against the Project class, they have a stealth dependency on the Task class also working. That's not ideal, as it makes it harder to determine the cause if the test fails. In Chapter 7, *Using Test Doubles as Mocks and Stubs*, on page 129, I'll go over some strategies for breaking this kind of dependency in tests.

I also use a couple of different strategies for dealing with math. The assertion on line 6 has a mathematical answer expressed as a math expression in the test (1.0 / 7), while the assertion on line 10 does all the math and spits out the final answer (35). The algebraic version is more clear because it describes the way the answer is derived (and, in this case, makes it easier to express a floating-point answer), whereas the numerical version can seem magical—why 35? However, the downside of having code expressions in test assertions is that it encourages using the test to directly describe the final code, by copying and pasting the code from the test. It's usually better to have the implementation code be as independent as possible from the test itself. Also, when comparing floating-point numbers as you are in this case, the implementation is often not precise enough to use equality as the comparison. Using the entire 1.0 / 7 expression in both places should make the spec and the code more likely to be equal; otherwise you can use the RSpec matcher expect(actual).to be_within(delta).of(expected).

The resulting passing code is a bit anticlimactic—you've pushed almost all the conditional logic to the Task, making the Project code straightforward. This is a good sign and implies that you're factoring the code reasonably.

basics/07/app/models/project.rb
```ruby
def completed_velocity
  tasks.sum(&:points_toward_velocity)
end

def current_rate
  completed_velocity * 1.0 / 21
end

def projected_days_remaining
  remaining_size / current_rate
end

def on_schedule?
  (Time.zone.today + projected_days_remaining) <= due_date
end
```

In addition, you need to add attr_accessor :due_date to the Project class.

This passes the tests and moves you into the refactoring phase. I don't see anything in the code that screams for a refactoring (although one reviewer did suggest turning the rate into a Ruby Rational instance). I'm considering extracting the (Time.zone.today + projected_days_remaining) logic to a method called projected_end_date, but you don't need to do that at the moment.

It is also important to look for potentially dangerous special cases to make sure they work—for example, the case where no tasks have been completed. You can put this test, along with the other initialization tests, in the original project_spec.rb file, inside the describe block, for initialization:

basics/08/spec/models/project_spec.rb
```ruby
it "properly handles a blank project" do
  expect(project.completed_velocity).to eq(0)
  expect(project.current_rate).to eq(0)
  expect(project.projected_days_remaining).to be_nan
  expect(project).not_to be_on_schedule
end
```

The first three assertions in this test pass as is; the last one needs some code. The be_nan assertion uses the RSpec dynamic matcher to check against nan?, which is a method on Number that is true if the number is "not a number," which is the somewhat odd construct that division by zero gets you in Ruby. You also need to make sure projected_days_remaining doesn't raise an exception if there are no tasks.

You can use the same predicate in the code to make the on_schedule? assertion pass like this:

basics/08/app/models/project.rb
```ruby
def on_schedule?
  return false if projected_days_remaining.nan?
  (Time.zone.today + projected_days_remaining) <= due_date
end
```

And the tests pass, which brings you to the refactoring phase. The first thing to notice is that you have a duplicated piece of data: the 21-day window for determining whether a task counts toward velocity. This data point is referenced in both Project#current_rate and Task#part_of_velocity?. They are pretty clearly the same bit of data—if I changed the time period to two weeks, I'd have to change it in both places.

That said, it's not clear what to do with this information. To me, the velocity length feels most like a static constant value owned by the Project class, since velocity applied to a single task makes no sense. In code you can do this by implementing the velocity_length_in_days as a class method with a constant return value:

basics/08/app/models/project.rb
```ruby
def self.velocity_length_in_days
  21
end
```

I'm using a method rather than a constant because this seems likely to become dynamic at some point in the future. Using a method preserves the API at no additional complexity cost.

The one usage of velocity length in the Project class changes to this:

basics/08/app/models/project.rb
```ruby
def current_rate
  completed_velocity * 1.0 / Project.velocity_length_in_days
end
```

And the one usage of velocity length in Task is now as follows:

basics/08/app/models/task.rb
```ruby
def part_of_velocity?
  return false unless complete?
  completed_at > Project.velocity_length_in_days.days.ago
end
```

And the tests pass. This structure eliminates the duplicate value, though the way that particular value is needed by both the Project and Task classes makes me wonder if we really just need a VelocityCalculator class.

What You've Done

Using the TDD process of "write a simple test, write simple code to make it pass, and refactor," you started your Rails application by creating some business logic.

What has the TDD process given you? You started with a requirement and it was not immediately clear how to turn it into an algorithm. By using TDD you were able to attack the problem incrementally, choosing to start in a small, well-understood corner and move outward as your understanding of the problem improved. It allowed you to easily change the code structure as you learned more about the solution.

Most important, you wrote better code. The solution you ended up with has short, well-named methods, it has logic in its proper place, and it will be easy to adjust as the requirements change.

Now it's time to integrate this model into an actual web application. Let's do some Rails testing.

CHAPTER 3

Test-Driven Rails

In the previous chapter you created some basic functionality for a project-management application using test-driven development. The title of this book, though, is *Rails 5 Test Prescriptions*, not *Generic Test Prescriptions*. (As with most generics, if that book did exist, it'd probably be cheaper but with less-interesting packaging.)

In this chapter you'll augment your model testing by testing the logic of the entire Rails stack from request to response using *end-to-end* tests. To do this, you'll use a tool called Capybara to help write your end-to-end tests.

A good test suite consists of a few end-to-end tests, a lot of tests that target a single unit, and relatively few tests that cover an intermediate amount of code. By moving logic outside the Rails controller and views, you can turn those harder-to-test parts of Rails tests into code that can be tested with faster and more robust unit tests.

Let's Write Some Rails

To start a test-driven development process, it's important to have some requirements in mind. Without some sense of what your code should be doing, it's hard to write tests to describe behavior.

Requirements-gathering could be an entire book by itself (specifically, this one: *Software Requirements, 2nd Edition [Wie03]*). For purposes of this example, let's assume you're your own client and you're working on a small project, so you don't exactly need military-grade precision. Here's my informal list of the first few things you'll tackle:

- A user can enter a task, associate it with a project, and also see it on the project page.

- A user can create a project and seed it with initial tasks using the somewhat contrived syntax of task name:size.

- A user can change a task's state to mark it as done.

- A project can display its progress and status using the date projection you created in the last chapter.

Let's walk through these one by one, following the basic guideline that any new logic should be driven by a failing test. Let's start with the ability to enter a project.

End-to-End Testing

You'll follow a testing practice called *outside-in testing*, which involves writing an end-to-end test that defines the feature (the "outside"), and augmenting it with a series of unit tests that drive the actual code and design (the "inside").

Capybara will make your end-to-end tests easier to read and write. It allows tests to describe user interaction with the web page and the document object model (DOM).[1] We'll cover Capybara and end-to-end testing in more detail in Chapter 8, *Integration Testing with Capybara and Cucumber*, on page 151.

In Rails 5.1 and higher, Capybara is already included as part of the default project. In older projects, you need to add it to the Gemfile yourself:

```
group :test do
  gem "capybara"
end
```

and reinstall the bundle:

```
% bundle install
```

Then make two more system-setup tweaks that will be useful. First, in the rails_helper file, uncomment the following line:

```
Dir[Rails.root.join("spec/support/**/*.rb")].each { |f| require f }
```

This causes RSpec to autoload any file in spec/support, which lets you keep the RSpec setup clean at a slight setup cost.

Next, put the following in spec/support/system.rb:

---

1.   https://github.com/teamcapybara/capybara

```
test_first/01/spec/support/system.rb
RSpec.configure do |config|
  config.before(:each, type: :system) do
    driven_by :rack_test
  end
end
```

This tells RSpec how to run end-to-end system tests. Specifically, you'll use a tool called rack_test, which is provided by Capybara to simulate a browser DOM tree without JavaScript. Many more details on driven_by may be found in Chapter 8, *Integration Testing with Capybara and Cucumber*, on page 151.

The first test covers the case where a user adds a project to the system. This task will be very close to Rails boilerplate, so your end-to-end test actually won't need much augmentation from unit tests. Later in this tutorial you'll add features that need more business logic.

Let's plan out what this test needs in terms of given/when/then:

- Given: You're starting with empty data, so no setup
- When: Filling out a form with project data and submitting
- Then: Verifying that the new project shows up on your list of projects with the entered tasks attached

This is what the test looks like, using the system tests added in Rails 5.1 and RSpec 3.7:

```
test_first/01/spec/system/add_project_spec.rb
Line 1  require "rails_helper"
   -
   -    RSpec.describe "adding a project", type: :system do
   -      it "allows a user to create a project with tasks" do
   5        visit new_project_path
   -        fill_in "Name", with: "Project Runway"
   -        fill_in "Tasks", with: "Choose Fabric:3\nMake it Work:5"
   -        click_on("Create Project")
   -        visit projects_path
  10        expect(page).to have_content("Project Runway")
   -        expect(page).to have_content(8)
   -      end
   -    end
```

This is called an "outside" test because it works from outside the Rails stack to define functionality. You're simulating user activity and browser requests and evaluating browser responses as HTML. This test is not dependent on your code's structure.

You have no setup in this test (in part because you're not requiring any security or login at this point). The test uses Capybara methods to interact with the application to simulate user interaction.

> **Prescription 7** Using Capybara allows you to simulate user activity for end-to-end tests of your Rails features.

Start by using the Capybara method visit to simulate a request to your application at the URL that matches the route new_project_path. Once it gets to that page, it uses the Capybara method fill_in to put text in a couple of form fields, then it clicks a button labeled Create Project using the click_on method. I'll talk in more detail about the Capybara API in Chapter 8, *Integration Testing with Capybara and Cucumber*, on page 151. Right now it's enough to get the gist of what the test is doing.

Finally, on line 10, you enter the evaluation phase of the test by visiting a route, projects_path, that represents the project index page and asserting that the title of the new task appears on the page, as does the total size of the project. A task of size 3 points and a task of size 5 points means you're looking for a total of 8 points.

You're not making any assumptions about the layout or presentation of the page—only that the new task name is there. Typically, when doing an end-to-end test the goal is to have the success criteria be based on something that is visible in a response rather than checking the database to see if the object is created. Later I'll talk about ways to incorporate assumptions about the layout of the page to help make the test more descriptive of the expected output.

This is a reasonable end-to-end test. It simulates a simple workflow by filling out a form, submitting it, and validating at least part of the resulting data.

There are several reasons why it's valuable to have a test like this one that works from outside the application:

- It makes no assumptions about the structure of the underlying code.
- It forces you to think of your feature in terms of behavior that is visible to a user or client of the application. Not all features have user-facing components, but where they do, being able to specify correct behavior without regard to the implementation is valuable.

- Eventually the unit tests will focus on as small a part of the code as you can manage. Having one test that makes sure all those little pieces correctly pass control between them prevents bugs from living in the gaps between the pieces.

Right now this test will fail—spectacularly. Absolutely none of the component bits are in place. So let's take this tiny step by tiny step, in each case minimally clearing the current error.

Pending Tests

In case it bothers you to see the integration test continue to fail while you write the unit tests that will make it pass, RSpec allows you to specify a test as pending or to skip it altogether. In RSpec, any it method defined without a block is considered to be "pending."

```
it "bends steel in its bare hands"
```

You can temporarily mark an it or describe block as pending by adding :pending as a second argument after the string:

```
it "bends steel in its bare hands", :pending do
  #anything
end
```

Alternatively, you can use the method pending in the spec:

```
it "bends steel in its bare hands" do
  pending "not implemented yet"
end
```

In RSpec all pending specs are actually run if there is code in the block part of the spec. The code is executed, with any failure in the pending spec treated as a pending result rather than a failure result. However, if the code in the pending spec passes, you'll get an error that effectively means, "You said this was pending, but lo and behold, it works. Maybe it's not actually pending anymore; please remove the pending status."

If you want the spec to not run, which means that you do not check for whether the spec passes, employ the preceding syntax but use skip instead of pending. Alternatively, you can prefix the method name with x, as in xit or xdescribe. A skipped test will not run, meaning you won't get any notification if the test suddenly starts to pass.

Making the Test Pass

You can see the first error by running the test using rspec:

```
NameError: undefined local variable or method `new_project_path'
```

Since Project isn't yet a standard ActiveRecord resource with routes, the test (unsurprisingly) can't find new_project_path.

If you were reading the previous chapter and wondering when you would create ActiveRecord models, your time has come—you're going to need to save to the database for the end-to-end test to pass. You'll use the Rails resource generator, which creates a controller, migration, route, and the like, but doesn't put any code in the generated controller. (Honestly, it'll create a bunch of files you're unlikely to use, but we'll let that part slide for now.) When you execute the rails generate command, Rails will interactively ask you if you want to override the model project.rb and the model test project_spec.rb. Don't override! You want to keep your existing code and update the model file by hand.

In the interest of sanity, you'll also update Task now. (Otherwise, keeping the tests for both Task and Project passing while one is an ActiveRecord and the other isn't is a pain.)

Here are the exact commands to use (note that the commands need to be on one command line):

```
% rails generate resource project name:string due_date:date
% rails generate resource task project:references \
  title:string size:integer completed_at:datetime
```

Two attributes are added to the project class: name (which you need for this test) and due_date (which you added in the previous chapter). The Task model tests a title attribute for this test, and size and completed_at attributes from last chapter. Again, don't override the existing files. Rails fans, note that you're using generate resource rather than generate scaffold, meaning you'll get blank controllers and no view files. That's fine since you want to build those via your tests.

Then, change the project.rb file as follows—note that you're removing some code, such as the initialize method, that is no longer needed because ActiveRecord is taking over the functionality. Other methods, such as incomplete_tasks and done?, are still needed:

test_first/01/app/models/project.rb

```ruby
class Project < ApplicationRecord
  has_many :tasks, dependent: :destroy

  def self.velocity_length_in_days
    21
  end

  def incomplete_tasks
    tasks.reject(&:complete?)
  end

  def done?
    incomplete_tasks.empty?
  end

  def total_size
    tasks.sum(&:size)
  end

  def remaining_size
    incomplete_tasks.sum(&:size)
  end

  def completed_velocity
    tasks.sum(&:points_toward_velocity)
  end

  def current_rate
    completed_velocity * 1.0 / Project.velocity_length_in_days
  end

  def projected_days_remaining
    remaining_size / current_rate
  end

  def on_schedule?
    return false if projected_days_remaining.nan?
    (Time.zone.today + projected_days_remaining) <= due_date
  end
end
```

You've added the superclass ApplicationRecord, which Rails defines for your project and which inherits from ActiveRecord::Base. You've also removed the due_date attr_accessor since ActiveRecord now manages attributes. The relationship to Task is now an ActiveRecord has_many.

Similarly, remove the def initialize method and attr_accessor, and replace the references to @completed_at to completed_at. This cleans up the Task class as follows:

```
test_first/01/app/models/task.rb
class Task < ApplicationRecord
  belongs_to :project

  def mark_completed(date = Time.current)
    self.completed_at = date
  end

  def complete?
    completed_at.present?
  end

  def part_of_velocity?
    return false unless complete?
    completed_at > Project.velocity_length_in_days.days.ago
  end

  def points_toward_velocity
    part_of_velocity? ? size : 0
  end
end
```

Run the new migration:

```
% rake db:migrate
```

If you run the tests now, they should still all pass (except for the new integration test), but you'll probably see a couple of pending warnings from boilerplate tests that RSpec puts in the helpers tests. I typically delete these pending warnings on the grounds that the reminder is of low value and high annoyance.

The Days Are Action-Packed

Running the tests now gives a different error since you've defined new_project_path:

```
1) adding a project allows a user to create a project with tasks
     Failure/Error: visit new_project_path

     AbstractController::ActionNotFound:
       The action 'new' could not be found for ProjectsController
```

You need a new action in the Projects controller. Since it is not going to have logic beyond Rails boilerplate, you don't need to test anything more than the existing Capybara test does:

```
test_first/01/app/controllers/projects_controller.rb
class ProjectsController < ApplicationController
  def new
    @project = Project.new
  end
end
```

Running the specs now triggers an error because Rails expects to find a template file at /app/views/projects/new.html.erb. After you create a blank file in that spot, you see a Capybara error:

```
1) adding a project allows a user to create a project with tasks
   Failure/Error: fill_in "Name", with: "Project Runway"

   Capybara::ElementNotFound:
     Unable to find field "Name"
```

Capybara searches for form items by DOM ID, form name, or the text of the associated label, whichever it finds first. You're presumably using the label, but since the view file is blank, it isn't there. You have three form elements to take care of: a text field for the name, a multiline text area for the tasks, and a submit button.

With the understanding that in a real project you would care about things like "design" and "making it not look ugly," just put in a basic form that matches your current needs:

```
test_first/01/app/views/projects/new.html.erb
<h1>New Project</h1>

<%= form_for(@project) do |f| %>
  <%= f.label(:name) %>
  <%= f.text_field(:name) %>
  <br />
  <%= f.label(:tasks) %>
  <%= text_area_tag("project[tasks]") %>
  <br />
  <%= f.submit %>
<% end %>
```

This is boilerplate, with one exception—you're creating the text area for tasks by using a text_area_tag rather than the ActiveRecord data-aware text_area method. This is because you're going to do some processing on the list of tasks, and tasks isn't a basic attribute of Project. If you do use f.text_area :tasks, Rails tries to make the value of the text area the value of the tasks relation, and places in that text area an ugly Ruby string representation of the empty relation, which is not what you want.

At this point the test will submit the form and fail. Now the test is looking for the create method in the controller that is invoked by submitting the form.

Going with the Workflow

Now you need to make some decisions. You have some logic that goes beyond Rails boilerplate—namely, you need to parse that list of tasks and create Task instances out of them when the form is submitted. That code needs to go somewhere, and the unit tests you're about to write against that code need to know where that place is. This is where the design thinking comes in the TDD process.

No matter where you put the actual coding logic, Rails will still insist on the existence of a controller, so you have the separate decision of how (or whether) to test whatever logic winds up in the controller itself.

Let's start with the business logic; I'll come back to the controller.

Three locations are commonly used for business logic that responds to user input beyond the common "pass the params hash to ActiveRecord#create" Rails behavior. Here are the options:

- Put the extra logic in the controller. This is often the Rails core team's preferred method, and if there isn't much logic it works perfectly fine. In my experience this location doesn't work as well for complex logic. It's challenging to test, awkward to refactor, and difficult to share if that becomes an issue. It also becomes confusing if there is more than one complicated action in the controller.

- Put the extra logic in the associated model, often at least partially in a class method. This was my go-to move for years. It's somewhat easier to test, but still kind of awkward to refactor—Ruby class method semantics are a pain. It also makes the model more complicated and doesn't really help manage actions that legitimately span multiple models, as this one does since it's creating a Project and multiple Tasks.

- Create a separate class to encapsulate the logic and workflow. This tends to be my first choice these days. It's the easiest to test and the best able to manage complexity changes as they come. The main downside is you wind up with a lot of little classes, but I don't mind having a lot of little pieces anyway.

> **Prescription 8** Placing business logic outside Rails classes makes that logic easier to test and manage.

So, you're creating a new class. I'll stress here that this design is not the only way to go, and if you feel the complexity of this particular action doesn't warrant its own class, that's fine. There is no consistent generic name for a logic class like this. Let's call it a workflow class. Other names you might see in use for different kinds of logic classes include action, service, context, use case, concern, and factory.

Now I'd like to show how you can use TDD to move logic outside the Rails classes. The workflow class needs to create a project from a name and a list of tasks. Let's start with the name:

```
test_first/01/spec/workflows/creates_project_spec.rb
require "rails_helper"

RSpec.describe CreatesProject do
  it "creates a project given a name" do
    creator = CreatesProject.new(name: "Project Runway")
    creator.build
    expect(creator.project.name).to eq("Project Runway")
  end
end
```

It's a straightforward test, which is the point. Because the logic isn't in the controller, you don't need to do anything fancy to test it. I'm calling the class CreatesProject because I like having action classes that aren't nouns. Alternate naming conventions might include CreateProject, ProjectCreator, or ProjectFactory.

And the passing code looks like this:

```
test_first/01/app/workflows/creates_project.rb
class CreatesProject
  attr_accessor :name, :project

  def initialize(name: "")
    @name = name
  end

  def build
    self.project = Project.new(name: name)
  end
end
```

One thing to notice about the build method is that it creates the project object but does not save it. Often, when I create an action object I try to separate initialization, execution, and persisting the result. One reason to separate these features is that it is much easier to write fast tests of using the workflow object if I can do so without hitting the database. In addition to making testing easier, this comes in handy when I want to create an object and not save the result immediately, which happens more often than you might think.

Here I'm using Ruby keyword arguments in the initializer, as a cheap type check to make sure the arguments passed to the CreatesProject initializer are limited to the ones you want.

Next the string-parsing features are tested. If you're following along, you should write these one at a time, making each test pass before writing the next:

test_first/02/spec/workflows/creates_project_spec.rb

```ruby
require "rails_helper"

RSpec.describe CreatesProject do

  describe "initialization" do
    it "creates a project given a name" do
      creator = CreatesProject.new(name: "Project Runway")
      creator.build
      expect(creator.project.name).to eq("Project Runway")
    end
  end

  describe "task string parsing" do
    it "handles an empty string" do
      creator = CreatesProject.new(name: "Project Runway", task_string: "")
      tasks = creator.convert_string_to_tasks
      expect(tasks).to be_empty
    end

    it "handles a single string" do
      creator = CreatesProject.new(
        name: "Project Runway", task_string: "Start Things")
      tasks = creator.convert_string_to_tasks
      expect(tasks.size).to eq(1)
      expect(tasks.first).to have_attributes(title: "Start Things", size: 1)
    end

    it "handles a single string with size " do
      creator = CreatesProject.new(
        name: "Project Runway", task_string: "Start Things:3")
      tasks = creator.convert_string_to_tasks
      expect(tasks.size).to eq(1)
      expect(tasks.first).to have_attributes(title: "Start Things", size: 3)
    end

    it "handles a single string with size zero" do
      creator = CreatesProject.new(
        name: "Project Runway", task_string: "Start Things:0")
      tasks = creator.convert_string_to_tasks
      expect(tasks.size).to eq(1)
      expect(tasks.first).to have_attributes(title: "Start Things", size: 1)
    end

    it "handles a single string with malformed size" do
      creator = CreatesProject.new(
        name: "Project Runway", task_string: "Start Things:")
      tasks = creator.convert_string_to_tasks
      expect(tasks.size).to eq(1)
      expect(tasks.first).to have_attributes(title: "Start Things", size: 1)
    end
```

```ruby
  it "handles a single string with negative size" do
    creator = CreatesProject.new(
      name: "Project Runway", task_string: "Start Things:-1")
    tasks = creator.convert_string_to_tasks
    expect(tasks.size).to eq(1)
    expect(tasks.first).to have_attributes(title: "Start Things", size: 1)
  end

  it "handles multiple tasks" do
    creator = CreatesProject.new(
      name: "Project Runway", task_string: "Start Things:3\nEnd Things:2")
    tasks = creator.convert_string_to_tasks
    expect(tasks.size).to eq(2)
    expect(tasks).to match(
      [an_object_having_attributes(title: "Start Things", size: 3),
       an_object_having_attributes(title: "End Things", size: 2)])
  end

  it "attaches tasks to the project" do
    creator = CreatesProject.new(
      name: "Project Runway", task_string: "Start Things:3\nEnd Things:2")
    creator.create
    expect(creator.project.tasks.size).to eq(2)
    expect(creator.project).not_to be_a_new_record
  end
 end

end
```

The specs have a progression; each one responds to a limitation of the code at the end of the previous step. In the first spec, an empty string parses to an empty list of tasks. In the next spec, we have a single element with a default size. Next we check for a single element where size is set. Having covered the normal cases, then there are a few specs that test error cases. All those tests call an internal convert_string_to_tasks method that allows you to test string parsing separate from any other feature of the class. These tests use the RSpec has_attributes matcher to allow you to specify multiple attributes of the same object in one line.

In the error tests, test a series of options for how the size is converted to an integer, such that anything empty or below 1 gets converted to 1. Because the integer conversion has been split out to its own method internally, you could also choose to test that method directly, but right now the internal method is in implementation detail. That might change if the conversion logic got more complex and wound up being a service object of its own.

Then test the case where multiple tasks are separated by a \n line separator. This one uses the RSpec matches matcher, which takes a data structure and matches the elements one by one. The alternate name an_object_having_attributes lets you match the attributes of each element. The matcher in the test is equal to expect(tasks[0]).to have_attributes(title: "Start Things", size: 3) and expect(tasks[1]).to have_attributes(title: "End Things", size: 2).

After all that, do a mini integration test where you explicitly call create to ensure that the task creation is picked up as part of the regular API process.

It is important to test save behavior because sometimes Rails associations behave better when all the objects have been saved, since Rails uses ID numbers to track associated objects and IDs are assigned only when objects are saved. In tests I often call the Rails save! method, which throws an exception (and therefore fails the test) immediately if the object is invalid. Failing the test as quickly as possible after an error happens is a good idea—if an object fails to save and causes a problem several lines later, that problem is harder to track down.

And back to the code:

```ruby
test_first/02/app/workflows/creates_project.rb
class CreatesProject
  attr_accessor :name, :project, :task_string

  def initialize(name: "", task_string: "")
    @name = name
    @task_string = task_string
  end

  def build
    self.project = Project.new(name: name)
    project.tasks = convert_string_to_tasks
    project
  end

  def create
    build
    project.save
  end

  def convert_string_to_tasks
    task_string.split("\n").map do |one_task|
      title, size_string = one_task.split(":")
      Task.new(title: title, size: size_as_integer(size_string))
    end
  end

  def size_as_integer(size_string)
    return 1 if size_string.blank?
    [size_string.to_i, 1].max
  end
end
```

You've now separated the string conversion and the task size string conversion into their own methods.

Refactoring to Single-Assertion Specs

There's nothing to refactor in the code right now, but you have a series of tests that have a common setup and a common set of assertions. This duplication can be managed in RSpec in a few different ways—including letting it stay the way it is if you find the tests quite readable in their current structure.

Also, there's a style of coding that prefers to have specs that contain just a single assertion. By default, RSpec ends the spec when the first expectation fails. This means that if there are any expectations later in the spec, you don't know whether they are correct. Sometimes this can lead to the tests giving an inaccurate sense of the status of the code.

The single-assertion style looks a little different than the testing style you've seen so far. It often takes advantage of the lazy nature of RSpec's let to specify the common action and allows each test to specify an input to the action. Here's an example:

```ruby
test_first/03/spec/workflows/creates_project_spec.rb
require "rails_helper"

RSpec.describe CreatesProject do
  let(:creator) { CreatesProject.new(
    name: "Project Runway", task_string: task_string) }

  describe "initialization" do
    let(:task_string) { "" }
    it "creates a project given a name" do
      creator.build
      expect(creator.project.name).to eq("Project Runway")
    end
  end

  describe "task string parsing" do
    let(:tasks) { creator.convert_string_to_tasks }

    describe "with an empty string" do
      let(:task_string) { "" }
      specify { expect(tasks).to be_empty }
    end

    describe "with a single string" do
      let(:task_string) { "Start Things" }
      specify { expect(tasks.size).to eq(1) }
      specify { expect(tasks.first).to have_attributes(
        title: "Start Things", size: 1) }
    end
```

```
    describe "with a single string with size " do
      let(:task_string) { "Start Things:3" }
      specify { expect(tasks.size).to eq(1) }
      specify { expect(tasks.first).to have_attributes(
        title: "Start Things", size: 3) }
    end

    describe "handles a single string with size zero" do
      let(:task_string) { "Start Things:0" }
      specify { expect(tasks.size).to eq(1) }
      specify { expect(tasks.first).to have_attributes(
        title: "Start Things", size: 1) }
    end

    describe "handles a single string with malformed size" do
      let(:task_string) { "Start Things:" }
      specify { expect(tasks.size).to eq(1) }
      specify { expect(tasks.first).to have_attributes(
        title: "Start Things", size: 1) }
    end

    describe "handles a single string with negative size" do
      let(:task_string) { "Start Things:-1" }
      specify { expect(tasks.size).to eq(1) }
      specify { expect(tasks.first).to have_attributes(
        title: "Start Things", size: 1) }
    end

    describe "with multiple tasks" do
      let(:task_string) { "Start Things:3\nEnd Things:2" }
      specify { expect(tasks.size).to eq(2) }
      specify { expect(tasks).to match(
        [an_object_having_attributes(title: "Start Things", size: 3),
         an_object_having_attributes(title: "End Things", size: 2)]) }
    end

    describe "attaches tasks to the project" do
      let(:task_string) { "Start Things:3\nEnd Things:2" }
      before(:example) { creator.create }
      specify { expect(creator.project.tasks.size).to eq(2) }
      specify { expect(creator.project).not_to be_a_new_record }
    end
  end

end
```

This version also splits the assertions into separate specs, using specify as an alias for it for test blocks that don't have (or need) a descriptive comment. The specs work a little differently in this version. At the top of the describe block, RSpec's let is used to define creator in terms of a CreatesProject object and an as-yet-undefined task_string. Then another let is used to define tasks in terms of creator.

Each individual test case is now its own describe. Each one uses a let to define the task_string that the creator object is looking for.

The individual assertions are now wrapped in specify calls since the assertion is (arguably) expressive enough not to need another text description. When each assertion references tasks, RSpec calls the let block for tasks, which references creator, lazily triggering that let block—which in turn references task_string, which triggers the let block in that particular test case.

This setup allows each test case to very clearly identify what makes it different from the other cases—the different task_string. In the previous version that information was buried in the noise of the common creation steps. The downside is that the nesting and indirection make it harder to trace execution, especially if you're unfamiliar with this testing style.

Another downside is that the setup is running more frequently, which means the tests will be slower if the setup is doing anything at all complicated.

If you *really* like the single-assertion style, then I recommend the rspec-given gem,[2] which allows you to replace the let and specify blocks with Given, When, and Then. The nicest part of the rspec-given syntax is that you can replace something like specify { expect(tasks.size).to eq(1) } with the somewhat more direct Then { tasks.size == 1 }.

In case you'd like to keep the speed benefits of having multiple assertions in a spec but would also like the benefit of seeing errors past the first one, RSpec offers the :aggregate_failures metadata setting. When applied to any describe or it block, as in RSpec.describe CreatesProject, :aggregate_failures, RSpec won't stop after the first failure, but will show all failures in the spec. (RSpec will still stop on an error.) You can also set :aggregate_failures to be the default in the RSpec configuration, but I don't recommend that, as integration tests, in particular, are kind of annoying and verbose if all their failures are displayed.

> **Prescription 9** Use :aggregate_failures to get the best features of single-assertion and multiple-assertion tests.

Who Controls the Controller?

All of the new tests pass, so let's take stock. You still have one test pending—your end-to-end test still doesn't like that the create action can't be found in the ProjectsController. Now you have all the pieces you need to write that action.

---

2.   https://github.com/rspec-given/rspec-given

The next question is, are you going to write any tests specifically to target the logic in the controller? And the answer, perhaps surprisingly, is "no." Or at least "not with the tools already discussed."

Controller tests, which have been a feature of Rails from the beginning, have increasingly been seen as lower-value tests in a couple of different ways.

If you write Rails applications the way that the Rails core team writes Basecamp (their flagship application) and follow the process and structures as espoused by Rails founder David Heinemeier Hansson, then regardless of how your controllers are structured, controller tests feel like duplicates of integration tests. Since there has been a lot of work in Rails 5 to make integration tests faster, controller tests become less valuable.

If you do more aggressive test-driven development, or you like moving application logic to separate workflow objects, then the controller doesn't have much functionality of its own, and you're concerned with a controller test duplicating model or workflow tests.

In either case, it's tricky to write a controller test that covers the controller logic without duplicating other tests. When I talk about test doubles in Chapter 7, *Using Test Doubles as Mocks and Stubs*, on page 129, I'll discuss a strategy that might help. Also, Rails and RSpec still provide some features for testing controllers, which I'll discuss in Chapter 11, *Testing Rails Display Elements*, on page 217.

Since you've put the business logic in the workflow object, the controller doesn't have much logic, but it does have some. Specifically, the controller sends data both to the workflow object and onward to the view layer. In the current test structure, these functions are controlled by the system test. Notice that responsibilities are separated here—almost nothing that the controller does is dependent on the logic of creating and saving projects.

Although I haven't stressed the point, the controller also needs to do something in case the action object errors or does something else unexpected. I don't normally like to test error conditions in system tests—too slow. I try to create the error conditions at the unit level.

The code to clear the controller-specific lines in the integration test looks like:

```
test_first/03/app/controllers/projects_controller.rb
class ProjectsController < ApplicationController
  def new
    @project = Project.new
  end
```

```
  def create
    @workflow = CreatesProject.new(
      name: params[:project][:name],
      task_string: params[:project][:tasks])
    @workflow.create
    redirect_to projects_path
  end
end
```

There is nothing complicated in the controller action itself; you create an action object, invoke it, and redirect. Since you're explicitly extracting specific values from the params hash, Rails's strong parameters are not an issue here.

That clears the "create action not found" error, but now the redirect to index fails. Let's wrap that up.

A Test with a View

Let's look at that end-to-end test again:

test_first/03/spec/system/add_project_spec.rb
```
require "rails_helper"

RSpec.describe "adding a project", type: :system do
  it "allows a user to create a project with tasks" do
    visit new_project_path
    fill_in "Name", with: "Project Runway"
    fill_in "Tasks", with: "Choose Fabric:3\nMake it Work:5"
    click_on("Create Project")
    visit projects_path
    expect(page).to have_content("Project Runway")
    expect(page).to have_content(8)
  end
end
```

So far this test passes up to where the code completes the controller create action. At the end of that action, it redirects to projects_path—which you didn't know when you started the end-to-end test, and it might mean that you don't need to explicitly visit projects_path in the test. Either way, projects_path triggers a visit to the path /projects, which is routed to the index method of the ProjectController. Since there isn't an index method, the current error is The action 'index' could not be found for ProjectsController.

You'll need the index method:

test_first/04/app/controllers/projects_controller.rb
```
class ProjectsController < ApplicationController
  def new
    @project = Project.new
  end
```

```
  def index
    @projects = Project.all
  end

  def create
    @workflow = CreatesProject.new(
      name: params[:project][:name],
      task_string: params[:project][:tasks])
    @workflow.create
    redirect_to projects_path
  end
end
```

And now you have an action without a view, resulting in the error message that starts with ActionView::MissingTemplate: Missing template projects/index,.... To get past this error, create a blank view file at app/views/projects/index.html.erb.

Now the error is on the following line of the test:

```
adding projects allows a user to create a project with tasks
    Failure/Error: expect(page).to have_content("Project Runway")
      expected to find text "Project Runway" in ""
 # ./spec/system/add_project_spec.rb:11:in `block (2 levels) in <top (required)>'
```

At this point, the Capybara test is evaluating the HTML response from your application. You're asking the test to have_content, which is defined by Capybara and which passes if the response either literally contains a string argument or matches a regular-expression argument. Specifically, you're asserting that the output contains the string Project Runway (which is the name of the newly created project) and the string 8 (which is its size).

This is a weak test. There are all kinds of ways, for example, that the number 8 could appear in the response HTML. To pick one unlikely scenario, the user could be journalist and author Jennifer 8. Lee.[3] The struggle when view-testing is to find a balance between a test that validates something meaningful about the output and one that isn't so tied to the markup that it will break when a designer looks at the page cross-eyed.

Let's make the test pass first, then explore how you can strengthen the test. Passing the test requires a straightforward Rails view:

---

3. http://en.wikipedia.org/wiki/Jennifer_8._Lee

```
test_first/04/app/views/projects/index.html.erb
<h1>All Projects</h1>
<table>
  <thead>
    <tr>
      <td>Project Name</td>
      <td>Total Project Size</td>
    </tr>
  </thead>
  <tbody>
    <% @projects.each do |project| %>
      <tr>
        <td><%= project.name %></td>
        <td><%= project.total_size %></td>
      </tr>
    <% end %>
  </tbody>
</table>
```

Don't be concerned with making this pretty; in a production application, presumably the markup would be more complex.

When this executes, your newly entered project gets its own table row—complete with its name and size.

And your end-to-end test finally passes.

That puts you in a refactoring phase. You didn't write much code in this step, but I'd like to take the opportunity to refactor the last couple of lines of the end-to-end test using the Capybara-Rails has_selector matcher. This is a really common work pattern for me. Sometimes I have trouble seeing the shape of a view before I write it, so I write a very loose test and then tighten the test once I see what pieces of the view will exist for me to hook onto.

The has_selector method takes as its argument a jQuery-style selector, with the usual # representing a DOM ID, and a dot (.) representing a DOM class. The assertion passes if the page contains a DOM element that matches the selector. You can also specify a text: option that means the matching DOM element must also contain particular text (or match a particular regular expression).

With has_selector, you can rewrite the test as follows:

```
test_first/05/spec/system/add_project_spec.rb
require "rails_helper"
RSpec.describe "adding a project", type: :system do
  it "allows a user to create a project with tasks" do
    visit new_project_path
    fill_in "Name", with: "Project Runway"
    fill_in "Tasks", with: "Choose Fabric:3\nMake it Work:5"
    click_on("Create Project")
    visit projects_path
    @project = Project.find_by(name: "Project Runway")
    expect(page).to have_selector(
      "#project_#{@project.id} .name", text: "Project Runway")
    expect(page).to have_selector(
      "#project_#{@project.id} .total-size", text: "8")
  end
end
```

In the final two lines you're testing for the same text as you did in the previous example, but now you're forcing it to appear on a specific part of the page. You want each bit of text to be associated with a DOM ID representing the project item—using the Rails-blessed pattern <class>_<id> and then a DOM class representing type. This gives you a stronger test: no longer would a random 8 somewhere on the page cause a pass—now the 8 specifically has to be associated with the size of this project.

However, the test isn't completely brittle—nothing specifies, for example, that the elements are table rows and cells. So if you go off and redesign this page using more modern markup, as long as the size element is subordinate to the project element, the test will still pass. The view needs only minor changes to make this test pass:

```
test_first/05/app/views/projects/index.html.erb
<h1>All Projects</h1>
<table>
  <thead>
    <tr>
      <td>Project Name</td>
      <td>Total Project Size</td>
    </tr>
  </thead>
  <tbody>
    <% @projects.each do |project| %>
      <tr class="project-row" id="<%= dom_id(project) %>">
        <td class="name"><%= project.name %></td>
        <td class="total-size"><%= project.total_size %></td>
      </tr>
    <% end %>
  </tbody>
</table>
```

You've only added a few DOM IDs and DOM classes.

And with that the test passes again, and I think you've got this feature in the books. Almost.

Testing for Failure

Failure, of course, is always an option, so you need to test for it. I prefer to do failure-path testing in unit tests rather than end-to-end tests. Success requires the entire system to work in concert. A failure response can usually be isolated to one component. That said, it's often useful to have one end-to-end failure test, especially in cases where the failure is easily causable and visible to a typical user.

I haven't yet talked about the tools that will allow you to fake failure—that requires a mock object package. (See Chapter 7, *Using Test Doubles as Mocks and Stubs*, on page 129.) But in this case it's not hard to create a real failure by adding a validation that you can then not fulfill.

Let's first see what an end-to-end failure test might look like, by seeing what would happen if you allow a user to create a project without a name:

```
test_first/06/spec/system/add_project_spec.rb
it "does not allow a user to create a project without a name" do
  visit new_project_path
  fill_in "Name", with: ""
  fill_in "Tasks", with: "Choose Fabric:3\nMake it Work:5"
  click_on("Create Project")
  expect(page).to have_selector(".new_project")
end
```

This test is similar to the original feature test, except that the name field is "filled in" with an empty string. You could just not include that line, but I find it's better to explicitly show that you're setting the name field to blank rather than hope the default works and is readable. In the validation section, you're looking for a .new_project class, which is the DOM class for the new project form. In other words, you're checking that you redirect back to something that allows you to reenter the project.

The test fails because you don't have anything catching the failed save. What you want is for the workflow to indicate that saving the project was not successful and then for the controller to redisplay the form on failure rather than display the index page.

Let's also create a test for this condition at the workflow level. Usually I would not write both of these error tests for a condition that was so simple. If I had other failure cases that might cause the workflow to return failure, I would not write an end-to-end test for each one because the controller behavior remains the same.

This test has a workflow with empty strings and checks an as-yet-nonexistent success? method to determine if the workflow has failed:

```
test_first/06/spec/workflows/creates_project_spec.rb
describe "failure cases" do
  it "fails when trying to save a project with no name" do
    creator = CreatesProject.new(name: "", task_string: "")
    creator.create
    expect(creator).not_to be_a_success
  end
end
```

(At this point, you could also refactor the tests to change the original let block for creator to take the name as something defined by later let calls, the same way you already do for task_string, so as to keep this test in line with the pattern of other tests.)

You now have two failing tests. And if you'll indulge a quick side note, there's an easy way to get RSpec to focus on just running the failures, which can be very helpful in a situation like this.

Uncomment the following line in the spec/spec_helper.rb:

```
config.example_status_persistence_file_path = "spec/examples.txt"
```

This tells RSpec to persist runtime information at spec/examples.txt. You'll also want to add that file to your .gitignore listing.

Now, if you rerun RSpec it generates the file spec/examples.txt. Here are the first few lines of that file:

```
| example_id                                | status | run_time        |
|:------------------------------------------|:-------|:----------------|
| ./spec/features/add_project_spec.rb[1:1]  | passed | 0.17632 seconds |
| ./spec/features/add_project_spec.rb[1:2]  | failed | 0.06486 seconds |
| ./spec/models/project_spec.rb[1:1:1]      | passed | 0.00191 seconds |
```

It's a list of every spec in the system, whether it most recently passed or failed, and the amount of time it took to run the last time it ran. The numbers for each spec are the order of the spec in its example group. You'll notice here that the first line, which is the first test in the feature spec that successfully creates a project, is much, much slower than the other tests.

Anyway, now that you have this information, you have two useful command-line options for RSpec. You can run your tests as rspec --only-failures, and RSpec will run only the specs listed as failing in the examples.txt file—in this case bypassing the slower successful test, which is handy. You also have rspec --next-failure, which also runs the failing tests but stops after the first test that is still failing. RSpec guarantees that the run order will be the same for a series of successive rspec --next-failure runs, so this can be a good way to work through a bunch of failed tests.

Back to making the test pass. Add a validation to the Project model:

```
test_first/06/app/models/project.rb
validates :name, presence: true
```

Now, use that information in the workflow to determine failure. One thing I like to do in this kind of workflow is start with the assumption of failure and only show success when I know that the workflow has succeeded:

```
test_first/06/app/workflows/creates_project.rb
def initialize(name: "", task_string: "")
  @name = name
  @task_string = task_string || ""
  @success = false
end

def success?
  @success
end

def build
  self.project = Project.new(name: name)
  project.tasks = convert_string_to_tasks
  project
end

def create
  build
  result = project.save
  @success = result
end
```

Here an @success instance variable is added with an initial value of false. It is set to true only if the result of saving the project in the create method is true. This causes the workflow test to pass, because the no-name project will fail the validation, causing the result of saving to be false and causing success? of the workflow to also be false. Additionally, you have an easy mechanism to support other possible failure modes when they arise.

Next, update the controller to know about the possibility of failure:

```
test_first/06/app/controllers/projects_controller.rb
def create
  @workflow = CreatesProject.new(
    name: params[:project][:name],
    task_string: params[:project][:tasks])
  @workflow.create
  if @workflow.success?
    redirect_to projects_path
  else
    @project = @workflow.project
    render :new
  end
end
```

After you ask the workflow to create, check for success. If successful, redirect to the index URL as before. If not successful, take the project that was built but not saved, set it to the instance variable @project, and render the new action. By setting @project, any information that was entered into the form will still display when the form is rerendered.

What You've Done

You've written an entire (albeit small) piece of Rails functionality, starting with an end-to-end integration test and moving down to unit tests to make each part of the feature work. And it took only one chapter. It goes a lot faster when you don't stop to explain every line of code.

In the next few chapters you'll look at model testing, controller testing, and view testing, covering the libraries discussed in this chapter in more detail. You'll also learn about related topics, such as placing data in tests, testing for security, and testing JavaScript. After that you'll tackle some wider topics: how to test legacy code, how to keep your tests from becoming legacy code, how to test external services, and the like.

First, though, let's step back for a second and talk about what makes automated testing effective.

CHAPTER 4

What Makes Great Tests

As the Rails community has matured, Rails developers have become much more likely to work with codebases and test suites that contain many years' worth of work. As a result, there has been a lot of discussion about design strategies to manage complexity over time.

There hasn't been nearly as much discussion about what practices make tests and test suites continue to be valuable over time. As applications grow, as suite runs get longer, as complexity increases, how can you write tests that will be useful and not impede future development?

In this chapter I'll discuss various ways you can evaluate whether you're writing tests that provide value and that minimize cost.

The Big One

This is the best general piece of advice I can give about the style and structure of automated tests: Your code is verified by your tests, but your tests are verified by nothing. Having your tests be as clear and as manageable as possible is the best way to keep them honest.

> **Prescription 10** Your tests are also code. Specifically, your tests are code that does not have tests.

In practice this means avoiding complex metaprogramming or loops in test code that might make it challenging to understand and evaluate test failure. One thing you might be tempted to do from time to time is invoke RSpec it methods inside a loop. This is a bad idea. Even though handling very similar logic in separate tests seems like more code, giving each test a unique line of code for failure reporting makes it much easier to determine what's going on and much easier to isolate in individual test failure.

If a programming practice or tool is successful, following or using it will make it easier to

- add the code you need in the short term.
- continue to add code to the project over time.

All kinds of gems in the Ruby and Rails ecosystem help with the first goal (including Rails itself). Testing is normally thought of as working toward the second goal. That's true, but often people assume the only contribution testing makes toward long-term application health is verification of application logic and prevention of regressions. In fact, over the long term, test-driven development tends to pay off as good tests lead toward modular designs.

Cost and Value

Tests have costs and tests have value. The goal of testing is to minimize the cost of doing testing and maximize the value. This leads to the question of what the costs are and what the value is.

The cost is easier to see and define. The cost of a test includes the following:

- The time it takes to write the test
- The time it takes to run the test every time the suite runs
- The time it takes to understand the test
- The time it takes to fix the test if it breaks and the root code is okay
- In some cases, the time it takes to change the code to make it testable

The currency I'm using here is time. Tests cost time. Eventually every programming decision costs time. When people talk about code quality making it easier or harder to make changes, they are inevitably talking about the amount of time it takes to change the code.

How can writing a test save time? Here's an incomplete list:

- The act of writing the test makes it easier to define the structure of the code.
- Running an automated test is frequently faster than manually going through elaborate integration steps.
- The test can provide efficient proof that code is working as desired.
- The test can provide warning that a change in code has triggered a change in behavior.
- The test can make it easier to locate and fix bugs.

Both the cost and the value of the test are scattered over the entire life cycle of the code. The cost starts in a burst when the test is written, but continues to add up as the test is read and executed. The cost really increases if the test fails when there is no underlying problem with the code.

The value can come when the test is written if it is part of a process to create the correct code more quickly. The value can also come as a replacement for manual testing, and the value can be added later on when the test fails in a case where it indicates a real problem with new code. Longer term, tests can add value if they encourage a design style that makes code change easier.

Let's look at some example tests. The Shoulda gem provides a series of matchers of the form <Class> should belong_to :users.[1] That's the whole test. This test is low cost. It takes very little time to write, it's easy to understand, and it executes quickly. But it's also low value—it's tied to the database, not the code logic, so it doesn't say much about the design of the code. It's also very unlikely to fail in isolation. If the association with users goes away, many tests are likely to fail, so the failure of this test probably isn't telling you anything that you don't already know about the state of the code.

Conversely, imagine an end-to-end system test written with Capybara, similar to the ones you wrote in the last chapter. This test is high cost. It requires a lot of data, a number of testing steps, and complex output matching. At the same time, the test could be high value. It might be your only way to find out if all the different pieces collaborating in the checkout are communicating correctly, which is to say a test like this might find errors that no other test in the system will flag. It might also be faster to run the test by itself when developing than to walk through the checkout manually.

So the goal in keeping your test suite happy over the long haul is to minimize the costs of tests and maximize the value.

Here are some concrete steps you can take:

- Instead of thinking about what will make a test pass, think about what will make it fail. If there's no way to make the test fail that won't make an existing test fail, maybe you don't need the test.

- Think of integration tests that will help you automate a series of actions that are useful while developing the code, so you get time savings from running the integration test.

- For unit tests, write the test so that it invokes the minimal amount of code needed to make the test fail. For example, as you'll see in Chapter 7, *Using Test Doubles as Mocks and Stubs*, on page 129, error cases often

---

1. https://github.com/thoughtbot/shoulda

can be set up as unit tests with test doubles rather than much slower and harder-to-set-up integration tests.

- Try to avoid high-cost activities like calling external libraries and saving a lot of objects to a database. In testing, a good way to avoid this is to use test doubles to prevent unit tests from having to use real dependencies.

- If you find that a single bug makes multiple tests fail, think about whether all those tests are needed. If the failure is in setup, think about whether all those tests need all that setup.

- Sometimes tests that are useful during development are completely superseded by later tests. These tests can be deleted.

- If it takes a lot of setup to write a unit test, consider the possibility that the test is trying to tell you that the design of the code could be improved to minimize dependencies.

> **Prescription 11** Think about both the short-term and long-term cost of tests as you write them.

SWIFT: The Five Qualities of Valuable Tests

A valuable test saves time and effort over the long term, while a poor test costs time and effort. I've focused on five qualities that tend to make a test save time and effort. The absence of these qualities is often a sign that the test could be a problem in the future. I've even managed to turn them into an acronym that is only slightly contrived: SWIFT:

- Straightforward
- Well defined
- Independent
- Fast
- Truthful

Let's explore those in more detail.

Straightforward

A test is *straightforward* if its purpose is immediately understandable.

Straightforwardness in testing goes beyond just having clear code. A straightforward test is also clear about how it fits into the larger test suite. It should test something different from the other tests, and that purpose should be easy to discern from reading the test. That purpose is usually tied to what condition would make the test fail, not what condition would make the test pass.

Here is a test that is not straightforward:

```
## Don't do this
it "should add to 37" do
  expect(User.all_total_points).to eq(37)
end
```

Where does the 37 come from? It's part of the global setup. If you were to peek into this fake example's user fixture file, you'd see that somehow the totals of the points of all the users in that file add up to 37. The test passes. Yay?

There are two relevant problems with this test:

- The 37 is a magic literal that apparently comes from nowhere.
- The test's name is utterly opaque about whether this is a test for the main-line case, a test for a common error condition, or a test that exists only because the coder was bored and thought it would be fun.

Combine these problems, and it quickly becomes next to impossible to fix the test a few months later when a change to the User class or the fixture file breaks it.

Naming tests is critical to being straightforward. Creating data locally and explicitly also helps. With most factory tools (see *Factories*, on page 109), default values are preset, so the description of an object created in the test can be limited to defining only the attributes that are important to the behavior being tested. Showing those attributes in the test is an important clue to the programmer's intent. Rewriting the preceding test with a little more information might result in this:

```
it "rounds total points to the nearest integer" do
  User.create(:points => 32.1)
  User.create(:points => 5.3)
  expect(User.all_total_points).to eq(37)
end
```

It's not poetry, but at the very least an interested reader now knows where that pesky 37 comes from and where the test fits in the grand scheme of things. The reader might then have a better chance of fixing the test if something breaks. The test is also more independent since it no longer relies on global fixtures—making it less likely to break.

Long tests or long setups tend to muddy the water and make it hard to identify the critical parts of the test. The same principles that guide refactoring and cleaning up code apply to tests. This is especially true of the general coding guideline that a method should only do one thing, which here means splitting up test setups into semantically meaningful parts, as well as keeping each test focused on one particular goal.

On the other hand, if you can't write short tests, consider the possibility that it is the code's fault and you need to do some redesign. If it's hard to set up a short test, that often indicates the code has too many internal dependencies.

Brian W. Kernighan and P.J. Plauger state in *The Elements of Programming Style [KP78]*, "Debugging is twice as hard as writing the code in the first place. Therefore, if you write the code as cleverly as possible, you are, by definition, not smart enough to debug it." Because tests don't have their own tests, this quote suggests that you should keep your tests simple to give yourself cognitive room to understand them.

In particular, this guideline argues against using clever tricks to reduce duplication among multiple tests that share a similar structure. If you find yourself starting to metaprogram to generate multiple tests in your suite, you'll probably find that complexity working against you at some point. You never want to have to decide whether a bug is in your test or in the code. And when—not if—you do find a bug in your test suite, it's easier to fix if the test code is simple.

At some point in your testing career, you'll have a series of key/value pairs to test, and you'll be tempted to do something like this (this example is deliberately simplified):

```ruby
DATA = {admin: 5, super_admin: 20, user: 3}

DATA.each_pair do |key, value|
  it "correctly determines the threshold for #{key} users" do
    user = User.new(role: key)
    expect(user.threshold).to eq(value)
  end
end
```

This will work; RSpec is flexible enough to programmatically create it blocks inside a loop. And while this is "good code" according to normal code metrics—it removes duplication while maintaining a single assertion—it's also a little opaque, especially if the body of the loop or the data gets more complicated. When this code fails, it's a little harder to see what happens. Specifically, RSpec will give you a failure message with a line number and it will be hard to tell from that information which iteration of the loop has failed, and hard to run that iteration without running all of the others.

You can put the loop inside a single it, which removes the extra metaprogramming but keeps the line-number problem. If a line of test code is executed multiple times, it's hard to see which iteration of the line caused failure.

My inclination would be to unroll the loop and write separate specs for each key/value pair. If you're concerned for some reason about how much space that takes up, it's worth mentioning that if the setup is that simple, you can write the code quite compactly:

```
describe "correctly determines threshold values" do
  specify { (User.new(role: :admin).threshold).to eq(5) }
  specify { (User.new(role: :super_admin).threshold).to eq(20) }
  specify { (User.new(role: :user).threshold).to eq(3) }
end
```

I think this is more clear and more likely to give useful information in the case of test failure.

I'll talk more about clarity issues throughout the book. In particular, the issue will come up when I discuss factories versus fixtures as ways of adding test data, in Chapter 6, *Adding Data to Tests*, on page 101.

Well Defined

A test is *well defined* if running the same test repeatedly gives the same result. If your tests are not well defined, the symptom will be intermittent, seemingly random test failures (sometimes called Heisenbugs, Heisenspecs, or Rando Calrissians).

Three classic causes of repeatability problems are time and date testing, random numbers, and third-party or Ajax calls. These all have the same root cause, which is that it is basically impossible to ensure that each test is run in a consistent environment. Dates and times have a nasty habit of never staying the same—the time is continually increasing, while random data stubbornly insists on being random. Similarly, tests that depend on a third-party service or even test code that makes Ajax calls back to your own application can vary from test run to test run, causing intermittent failures.

Dates and times tend to lead to intermittent failures when certain magic time boundaries are crossed. You can also get tests that fail at particular times of day or when run in certain time zones. Random numbers, in contrast, make it somewhat hard to test both the randomness of the number and that the arbitrary number is used properly in whatever calculation requires it.

The test plan is similar for dates, randomness, and external services—really, it applies to any constantly changing dataset. The key is to make the test data replicable and consistent. You can do this with a combination of encapsulation and test doubles. You encapsulate the data by creating a service object that wraps around the changing functionality. By mediating access to the changing functionality, you make it easier to stub or mock the output values. Stubbing the values provides the consistency you need for testing—you provide the exact value that will be used in the test.

You might create a RandomStream class that wraps Ruby's rand() method:

```ruby
class RandomStream
  def next
    rand()
  end
end
```

This example is a little oversimplified—normally you'd be encapsulating RandomStream. With your own wrapper class, you can provide more specific methods tuned to your use case—something like def random_phone_number. First you unit-test the stream class to verify that the class works as expected. Then any class that uses RandomStream can be provided mock random values to allow for easier and more stable testing.

The exact mix of encapsulation and mocking varies. The Rails ActiveSupport gem has methods that stub the time and date classes with no encapsulation, allowing you to specify an exact value for the current time for testing purposes.

In Chapter 14, *Testing External Services*, on page 285, I'll discuss this pattern for wrapping a potentially variable external service in more detail. I'll cover mock objects in Chapter 7, *Using Test Doubles as Mocks and Stubs*, on page 129, and I'll talk more about debugging intermittent test failures in Chapter 15, *Troubleshooting and Debugging*, on page 303.

Independent

A test is *independent* if it doesn't depend on any other tests or external data to run. An independent test suite gives the same results no matter the order in which the tests are run, and tends to limit the scope of test failures to only tests that cover a buggy method.

In contrast, a very dependent test suite could trigger failures throughout your tests from a single change in one part of an application. A clear sign that your tests are not independent is if you have test failures that happen only when the test suite is run in a particular order—in fully independent tests, the order in which they are run should not matter. Another sign is a single line of code breaking multiple tests. You can also uncomment the generated line config.order = :random in the spec_helper.rb file to mandate random ordering of specs and to shake out potentially subtle test dependencies. Or you can use order --random on the RSpec command line to ensure random ordering.

The biggest impediment to independence in the test suite itself is the use of global data. Rails fixtures are not the only possible cause of global data in a Rails test suite, but they are a common cause. Somewhat less common in a Rails context is using a tool or third-party library in a setup and not tearing it down.

If you believe you have an intermittent test failure in RSpec that is triggered by the order of testing, the rspec --bisect option will attempt to discover the minimal set of specs that trigger the failure. I cover this in Chapter 15, *Troubleshooting and Debugging*, on page 303.

Outside the test suite, if the application code is not well encapsulated it may be difficult or impossible to make the tests fully independent.

Fast

It's easy to overlook the importance of pure speed in the long-term maintenance of a test suite or a TDD practice. In the beginning it doesn't make much difference. When you have only a few methods under test, the difference between one second per test and one-tenth of a second per test is almost imperceptible. The difference between a one-minute suite and a six-second suite is easier to discern.

From there, the sky's the limit. I worked in one Rails shop where nobody really knew how long the tests ran in development because they farmed out the test suite to an external server setup that was more powerful than most production web servers I've seen. This is bad.

Slow test suites hurt you in a variety of ways.

There are startup costs. In the sample TDD session you walked through in Chapter 2, *Test-Driven Development Basics*, on page 11, and Chapter 3, *Test-Driven Rails*, on page 41, you went back and forth to run the tests a lot. In practice I went back and forth even more frequently. Over the course of writing that tutorial, I ran the tests dozens of times. Imagine what happens if it takes even 10 seconds to start a test run. Or a minute, which is not out of the question for a larger Rails app. I've worked on JRuby-based applications that took well over a minute to start.

TDD is about flow in the moment, and the ability to go back and forth between running tests and writing code without breaking focus is crucial to being able to use TDD as a design tool. If you can check Twitter while your tests are running, you just aren't going to get the full value of the TDD process.

Tests get slow for a number of reasons, but the most important in a Rails context are as follows:

- Startup time

- Dependencies within the code that require a lot of objects to be created to invoke the method under test

- Extensive use of the database or other external services during a test

Not only do large object trees slow down the test at runtime, but setting up large amounts of data makes writing the tests more labor-intensive. And if writing the tests becomes burdensome, you aren't going to do it.

Speeding tests up often means isolating application logic from the Rails stack so that logic can be tested without loading the entire Rails stack or without retrieving test data from the database. As with a lot of good testing practices, this isolation results in more robust code that is easier to change moving forward.

Since test speed is so important for successful TDD, throughout the book I'll discuss ways to write fast tests. In particular, the discussion of creating data in Chapter 6, *Adding Data to Tests*, on page 101, and the discussion of testing environments in Chapter 16, *Running Tests Faster and Running Faster Tests*, on page 319, will be concerned with creating fast tests.

Truthful

A *truthful* test accurately reflects the underlying code—it passes when the underlying code works, and fails when it doesn't. This is easier said than done.

A frequent cause of brittle tests is targeting assertions at surface features that might change even if the underlying logic stays the same. The classic example along these lines is view testing, in which you base the assertion on the creative text on the page (which will frequently change even though the basic logic stays the same):

```
it "shows the project section" do
  get :dashboard
  expect(response).to have_selector("h2", :text => "My Projects")
end
```

It seems like a perfectly valid test right up until somebody determines that "My Projects" is a lame header and decides to go with "My Happy Fun-Time

Projects," breaking the test. You're often better served by testing something that's slightly insulated from surface changes, such as a DOM ID:

```
it "shows the project section" do
  get :dashboard
  expect(response).to have_selector("h2#projects")
end
```

The basic issue here is not limited to view testing. There are areas of model testing in which testing to a surface feature might be brittle in the face of trivial changes to the model (as opposed to tests that are brittle in the face of changes to the test data itself, which I've already discussed).

The other side of truthfulness is not just a test that fails when the logic is good, but a test that stubbornly continues to pass even if the underlying code is bad—a tautology, in other words.

Speaking of tautologies, mock objects have their own special truthfulness issues. It's easy to create a tautology by using a mock object. It's also easy to create a brittle test because a mock object often creates a hard expectation of what methods will be called on it. If you add an unexpected method call to the code being tested, you can get mock-object failures simply because of that unexpected call. I've had changes to a login filter cause hundreds of test failures because mock users going through the login filter bounced off the new call.

What You've Done

In this chapter you learned about writing effective and valuable test suites. Writing effective test suites is hard. The complexity and runtime of a typical test suite increases slowly, and often you don't realize you have a serious problem until it's too late. Paying attention to detail in keeping individual tests simple and fast will pay off over time.

The goal of your test suite is to allow you to use tests to improve the design and for the existing tests to empower you to make changes with less fear of introducing new bugs. If your test suite is slow, complicated, or fragile, then you make your tests unable to help you with either of these goals. In the worst case, you can find yourself still needing to maintain a test suite but having that test suite slow down development because of how hard it is to keep the tests synchronized with the code.

Being strict about writing tests first, writing tests against behavior and not implementation, and taking time to make the tests simple and fast will all help keep your test suite useful and healthy over the course of a long project.

CHAPTER 5

Testing Models

A standard Rails application uses a design pattern called *MVC*, which stands for model-view-controller. Each of the three sections in the MVC pattern is a separate layer of code, which has its own responsibilities and communicates with the other layers as infrequently as possible. In Rails, the model layer contains both business logic and persistence logic, with the persistence logic being handled by ActiveRecord. Typically, all of your ActiveRecord objects will be part of the model layer, but not everything in the model layer is necessarily an ActiveRecord object. The model layer can include various services, value objects, or other classes that encapsulate logic and use ActiveRecord objects for storage.

I'll start the tour of testing the Rails stack with the model layer because model tests have the fewest dependencies on Rails-specific features and are often the easiest place to start testing your application. Standard Rails model tests are very nearly vanilla RSpec. Features specific to Rails include a few new matchers and the ability to set up initial data.

I'll also talk about testing ActiveRecord features such as associations and models. And I'll talk about separating logic from persistence and why that can be a valuable practice for both testing and application development.

What Can You Do in a Model Test?

An RSpec file in the spec/models directory is automatically of type: :model, which gives you ... not a whole lot of new behavior, actually. An add-on gem called rspec-activemodel-mocks,[1] which is maintained by the RSpec core team, includes some mock-object tools specific to use with ActiveModel.

---

1. https://github.com/rspec/rspec-activemodel-mocks

What Should You Test in a Model Test?

Models. Next question?

Okay, Funny Man, What Makes a Good Set of Model Tests?

There are a lot of different, sometimes conflicting, goals for tests. It's hard to know where to start your TDD process, how many tests to write, and when you're done. The classic description of the process—"write a simple test, make it pass, then refactor"—doesn't provide a lot of affirmative guidance or direction for the larger process of adding a feature.

A TDD Metaprocess

The following diagram illustrates a metaprocess that reflects how I write a new business-logic feature. (I handle view logic a little differently.) This process is more of a guideline than a hard-and-fast checklist. As the logic gets more complex, and the less I know about the implementation when I start, the closer I stick to this process and the smaller the steps I take.

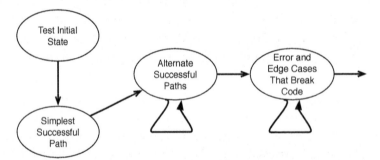

Often the best place to start is with a test that describes an initial state of the system, without invoking logic. This is especially useful if you're test-driving a new class, so the first test just sets up the class and verifies the initial state of instance variables. If you're working in an existing class, this step may not be necessary.

Next, determine the main cases that drive the new logic. Sometimes there will be only one primary case, like "calculate the total value of a user's purchase." Sometimes there will be many; "calculate tax on a purchase" might have lots of cases based on the user's location or the items being purchased.

Take that list and write tests for the main cases one at a time. I do not recommend writing multiple failing tests simultaneously—that turns out to be confusing. It can be helpful to use comments or pending tests to at least note what the future tests will be. Ideally these tests are small—if they need a lot of setup, you probably should be testing a smaller unit of code.

As you saw in the first few chapters, sometimes you'll pass the first test by putting in a solution that is deliberately specific to the test, like a one-line method that only returns the exact value that makes the test pass. Gary Bernhardt of Destroy All Software calls this technique *sliming*.[2] This can be helpful in keeping your code close to the tests—again, especially when the algorithm is complex.

> **Prescription 12** If you find yourself writing tests that already pass given the current state of the code, that often means you're writing too much code in each pass.

The goal in these tests is to first make the test pass quickly without worrying much about niceties of implementation. Once each test passes, look for opportunities to refactor. (I'll talk more about that in the next section.) When the main cases are done, you try to think of ways to break the existing code. Sometimes you'll notice something as you're writing code to pass a previous test, like, "Hey, I wonder what would happen if this argument were nil?" Write a test that describes what the output should be and make it pass. Refactoring gets increasingly important here because special cases and error conditions tend to make code complex, and managing that complexity becomes really important to future versions of the code. The advantage of waiting to do special cases at the end is that you already have tests to cover the normal cases, so you can use those to check your new code each step of the way.

When you can no longer think of a way to break your code, you're likely done with this feature and ready to move on to the next. If you haven't been doing so, run the entire test suite to make sure you didn't inadvertently break something else. Then take one further look at the code for larger-scale refactoring.

Refactoring Models

In a TDD process, much of the design takes place during the refactoring step. A lot of this design happens under the guise of cleanup—looking at parts of the code that seem overly complicated or poorly structured and figuring out how best to rearrange them.

Just because the refactoring step includes cleanup doesn't mean you can skip this step when you're in a hurry. Don't do that. Refactoring is not a luxury.

---

2.   http://www.destroyallsoftware.com

Refactoring is where you think about your code and how best to structure it. Skipping refactoring will slowly start to hurt, and by the time you notice the problem, it'll be much harder to clean up than if you had addressed it early.

> **Prescription 13** Refactoring is where a lot of design happens in TDD, and it's easiest to do in small steps. Skip it at your peril.

At the most abstract level, you're looking for three things: complexity to break up, duplication to combine, and abstractions waiting to be born.

Break Up Complexity

Complexity will often initially manifest itself as long methods or long lines of code. If you're doing a "quick to green" first pass of the code to make the tests pass, there will often be a line of code with lots of method chaining or the like. It's almost always a good idea to break up long methods or long lines by extracting part of the code into its own method. In addition to simplifying the original method, you have the opportunity to give the method you're creating a name that is meaningful in the domain and that can make your code self-documenting.

Booleans, local variables, and inline comments are almost always candidates for extraction:

- Any compound Boolean logic expression goes in its own method. It's much harder than you might think for people to understand what a compound expression does. Give people reading your code a fighting chance by hiding the expression behind a name that expresses the code's intent, such as valid_name? or has_purchased_before?.

- Local variables are relatively easy to break out into methods with the same name as the variable—in Ruby, code that uses the variable doesn't need to change if the variable becomes a method with no arguments. Having a lot of local variables is a huge drag on complex refactorings. You'll be surprised at how much more flexible your code feels if you minimize the number of local variables in methods. (I first encountered this idea, along with a lot of other great refactoring ideas, in *Refactoring: Improving the Design of Existing Code [FBBO99]*.)

- In long methods, sometimes a single-line comment breaks up the method by describing what the next part does. This nearly always is better extracted to a separate method with a name based on the comment's contents. Instead of one twenty-five-line method, you wind up with a five-line method that calls five other five-line methods, each of which does one thing and each of which has a name that is meaningful in the context of the application domain.

> **Prescription 14** Try to extract methods when you see compound Booleans, local variables, or inline comments.

Combine Duplication

You need to look out for three kinds of duplication: duplication of fact, duplication of logic, and duplication of structure.

Duplication of fact is usually easy to see and fix. A common case would be a "magic number" used by multiple parts of the code, such as a conversion factor or a maximum value. You saw this in an earlier example with the 21 days that you used to calculate velocity. Another common example is a status variable that has only a few valid values, and the list of those values is duplicated:

```
validates :size, numericality: {less_than_or_equal_to: 5}

def possible_sizes
  (1 .. 5)
end
```

The remedy for duplication of fact is also usually simple—make the value a constant or a method with a constant return value, like this:

```
MAX_POINT_COUNT = 5

validates :size, numericality: {less_than_or_equal_to: MAX_POINT_COUNT}

def possible_sizes
  (1 .. MAX_POINT_COUNT)
 end
```

Or, alternatively, like this:

```
VALID_POINT_RANGE = 1 .. 5
validates :size, inclusion: {in: VALID_POINT_RANGE}
```

The key metric is how many places in the code would need to change if the underlying facts change, with the ideal number being 1. That said, at some point the extra character count for a constant is ridiculous and Java-like in the worst way. For string and symbol constants, if the constant value is effectively identical to the symbol (as in ACTIVE_STATUS = :active), I'll often leave the duplication. I'm not saying I recommend that; I'm just saying I do it.

I also often make the constant value an instance method with a static return value rather than a Ruby constant, like this:

```ruby
def max_point_count
  5
end
```

I do this because then max_point_count has the same lookup semantics as any other instance value, and it often reads better to make a value owned by the instance rather than the class. It's also easier to change if the constant turns out to be less than constant in the future.

Duplication of logic is similar to duplication of fact, but instead of looking for simple values, you're looking for longer structures. This often includes compound Boolean statements used as guards in multiple methods (in the task-manager example, this might be something about whether a task has been completed) or simple calculations that are used in multiple places (such as converting task size to time based on the project's rate of completion).

In this example, the same Boolean test is applied twice and it's easy to imagine it being used many more times:

```ruby
class User
  def maximum_posts
    if status == :trusted then 10 else 5 end
  end

  def urls_in_replies
    if status == :trusted then 3 else 0 end
  end
end
```

One way to mitigate this is to move the duplicated logic into its own method and call the method from each location (in this case, def trusted?). I recommend being aggressive about this—you'll sometimes see advice that you should just notice duplication on the second instance and refactor on the third instance. In my experience, that just means you wind up with twice as much duplication as you should have. (See the next section for other ideas about reused Booleans.)

Keep in mind that not every piece of logic that is spelled the same in Ruby is actually duplication. It's possible for early forms of two pieces of logic to look similar but eventually evolve in separate directions. A great example of this is Rails controller scaffolding. Every RESTful controller starts with the same boilerplate code for the seven RESTful actions. And there have been innumerable attempts to remove that duplication by creating a common abstraction. Most of those attempts eventually wind up in a tangle of special case logic because each controller eventually needs to have different features.

Find Missing Abstractions

Duplication of structure often means there's a missing abstraction, which in Ruby generally means you can move some code into a new class.

One symptom is a set of instance attributes that are always used together—especially if the same group of attributes is being passed to multiple methods. Use of a common set of variables often indicates that you want a new class with those friendly attributes as the instance attributes.

Another common symptom is a group of methods that all share a prefix or a suffix, such as logger_init, logger_print, and logger_read. Often this means you need a class corresponding to the common word.

In ActiveRecord, one side effect of discovering friendly attributes is the creation of value objects, which are immutable instances that represent parts of your data. For example, a start_date and end_date are often used together and could easily be combined into a DateRange class. Also, how often do you write something like this?

```ruby
class User < ActiveRecord::Base
  def full_name
    "#{first_name} #{last_name}"
  end
  def sort_name
    "#{last_name}, #{first_name}"
  end
end
```

You could try this:

```ruby
class Name
  attr_reader :first_name, :last_name
  def initialize(first_name, last_name)
    @first_name, @last_name = first_name, last_name
  end
  def full_name
    "#{first_name} #{last_name}"
  end
  def sort_name
    "#{last_name}, #{first_name}"
  end
end

class User < ActiveRecord::Base
  delegate :full_name, :sort_name, to: :name
  def name
    Name.new(first_name, last_name)
  end
end
```

If you have existing tests on User in that situation, those tests should continue to pass.

Normally I don't change tests when I refactor—the goal is to test functionality, not implementation. I will sometimes make an exception to this rule if I move the code to a new class, especially if I expect the new class to be shared often.

When you break out related attributes into their own class, as in this Name example, you'll often find it's much easier to add complexity when you have a dedicated place for that logic. When you need middle names or titles, it's easier to manage those in a separate class than it would be if you had a half implementation of names in multiple classes.

You'll also find that these small classes are easy to test because Name no longer has a dependency on the database or any other code. Without dependencies, it's easy to set up and write fast tests for name logic:

```
it "generates sortable names" do
  name = Name.new("Noel", "Rappin")
  expect(name.sort_name).to eq("Rappin, Noel")
end
```

The tests for the new Name class are quick to write and to run. The easier it is to write tests, the more tests you'll write.

Also look out for repeated if statements or other conditionals that switch on the same values. A common example is continually checking for a nil value. Another is frequent checking against a status variable. The task tracker, for example, might have a lot of methods that do this:

```
if status == :completed
  calculate_completed_time
else
  calculate_incompleted_time
end
```

Every program needs the occasional if statement. But if you're continually checking an object's state to determine what to do next, consider the possibility that you have a new set of classes. For example, the preceding snippet implies the existence of something like CompleteTask and IncompleteTask. (Or maybe completeness and incompleteness affect only part of the class functionality, so you get something like CompleteTaskCalculator and IncompleteTaskCalculator.)

Once you've separated functionality into separate classes, an object-oriented program is supposed to switch based on class, using message passing and polymorphism:

```
def calculator
  if complete?
    CompleteTaskCalculator.new(self)
  else
    IncompleteTaskCalculator.new(self)
  end
end

def calculate
  calculator.calculate_time
end
```

In the most recent example there is still an if statement about the logic between complete and incomplete tasks, but only one. Any further difference between complete and incomplete tasks is handled in the difference between the two calculator classes. If you're testing for completion in many places, separating functionality into classes can be more clear.

Since these classes typically don't depend on the database, it's easy to write fast tests for them, and you'll often find these classes attracting behavior. Once they exist, it's easier to see what behavior belongs there.

A Note on Assertions per Test

You'll often find that a common setup results in multiple assertions in a test. This is particularly true of integration tests. For example, when you wrote your initial test to add tasks back in Chapter 3, *Test-Driven Rails*, on page 41, you made several assertions about the existence of the project and its relationship with the tasks you'd just created.

There are two contrasting styles for writing tests with multiple assertions. In one style, the setup and all the assertions are part of the same test. If you were trying to test changes when you mark a task complete, then having all the assertions in the same test might look like this:

```
it "marks a task complete" do
  task = tasks(:incomplete)
  task.mark_complete
  expect(task).to be_complete
  expect(task).to be_blocked
  expect(task.end_date).to eq(Date.today.to_s(:db))
  expect(task.most_recent_log.end_state).to eq("completed")
end
```

In contrast, you could put each assertion in a separate test and put the common setup in a setup block. Using the same set of assertions in separate tests looks like the following:

```
describe "task completion" do
  let(:task) {tasks(:incomplete)}
  before(:example) { task.mark_complete }
  specify { expect(task).to be_complete }
  specify { expect(task).to be_blocked }
  specify { expect(task.end_date).to eq(Date.today.to_s(:db)) }
  specify { expect(task.most_recent_log.end_state).to eq("completed") }
end
```

You've already seen this pattern a bit, where the variable is defined in a let method, with some additional configuration happening in a before method.

The tradeoff is pretty plain: The one-assertion-per-test style has the advantage that each assertion can fail independently—when all the assertions are in a single test, the test bails on the first failure. In the all-in-one test, if expect(task).to be_complete fails, you won't even get to the check for expect(task).to be_blocked. If all the assertions are in separate tests, everything runs independently, but it's harder to determine how tests are related. There are two significant downsides to the one-assertion style. First, there can be a significant speed difference since the one-assertion-per-test version will run the common setup multiple times, and second, the one-assertion style can become difficult to read, especially if the setup and test wind up with some distance between them.

Often I compromise by making my first pass at TDD in the one-assertion-per-test style, which forces me to work in baby steps and gives me a more accurate picture of what tests are failing. When I'm confident in the correctness of the code, I consolidate related assertions, giving me the speed benefit moving forward. Another compromise is the use of compound RSpec matchers or the has_attributes matcher to create a single assertion out of what might otherwise be multiple assertions.

Recent versions of RSpec make this tradeoff significantly easier to manage with the :aggregate_failure metadata tag. When used, :aggregate_failure causes RSpec to no longer exit on the first failure in a spec, but to keep going and combine all the failures when reporting. (An error, like a missing method, still ends the spec.)

So, you can now have the speed or clarity advantage of a multiple-assertion test and still have the reporting fidelity of the single-assertion test:

```
it "marks a task complete", :aggregate_failures do
  task = tasks(:incomplete)
  task.mark_complete
  expect(task).to be_complete
  expect(task).to be_blocked
  expect(task.end_date).to eq(Date.today.to_s(:db))
  expect(task.most_recent_log.end_state).to eq("completed")
end
```

You can specify :aggregate_failure in an it method or a describe method. If you use aggregate_failure in a describe block, it applies to every spec inside the block. You can even specify aggregate_failure in the configuration to apply to all specs. That can cause problems, though, especially in integration tests where early failures often mean late code can't pass or might even be problematic to run.

No matter how you handle your specs, expectations that genuinely cover different branches of the application logic should be handled in separate specs. Avoid changing local variables inside a spec just to test different logic in the same test. That means you would want to keep these specs separate.

| Prescription 15 | Expectations that cover different branches of the application logic should be handled in separate specs. |

```
it "knows full names" do
  user = User.create(:first_name => "Fred", :last_name => "Flintstone")
  expect(user.full_name).to eq("Fred Flintstone")
end

it "knows full names with a middle initial" do
  user = User.create(:first_name => "Fred", :last_name => "Flintstone"
      :middle_initial => "D")
  expect(user.full_name).to eq("Fred D. Flintstone")
end

it "knows full name where there's no first name" do
  user = User.create(:last_name => "Flintstone")
  expect(user.full_name).to eq("Flintstone")
end
```

Continually changing the value of user to put all those assertions in the same branch makes for a test that is very hard to read and understand.

Testing What Rails Gives You

Rails provides built-in functionality for associations and validations, which leads to questions about how to effectively and usefully test those features in your application.

The answer in both cases is similar, and goes back to the basic principle that we're testing functionality and not implementation. Although I do not normally write tests just to show the existence of a particular association or validation, I do sometimes write tests that show those features in action. For associations, this means showing the association in use. For validations, it means testing the overall logic of what makes an instance valid.

The testing gem shoulda-matchers defines matchers that specifically test for the existence of validations and associations,[3] like so:

```
describe Task do
  it { should belong_to(:project) }
  it { should belong_to(:user) }
  it { should ensure_length_of(:name) }
end
```

Tests like that are not particularly valuable for a TDD process because they aren't about the design of new features. If you're doing the TDD process, you shouldn't start from the idea that your Task belongs to a Project. Rather, as you describe features, the relationship is implied from the feature tests you're writing. More operationally, this means that in a good TDD process, any condition in the code that would cause a direct test like those Shoulda matchers to fail would also cause another test to fail. In which case, what's the point of the Shoulda matcher?

To briefly and halfheartedly argue the other side, you often don't need to go through a whole TDD process to know that a relationship or a validation should exist, and these tests don't cost very much to write. And to rebut myself, part of doing the TDD process is to force you to examine the things you think you know and prove that they are really necessary. In particular, if I see a lot of those should belong_to lines of code in a test suite, rightly or wrongly I'm going to be worried about the test suite's effectiveness.

Validations are a little different since the validity of a piece of data is often a legitimate and complex piece of business logic and the Rails helpers cover only a set of common cases. I think you can make validations in your code work efficiently with the TDD process if you focus on the functional part—"this object is or is not valid"—rather than the "I'm using a Rails numerical validator" part. Also, consider using a Rails database-blocking validation only as a last resort when you sincerely believe it's worth potentially raising an exception rather than having this data in your database.

I would typically test for the functional effect of an invalid object rather than the implementation fact of the existence of a Rails validation. The functional effect is often along the lines of an object or objects not saving to the database. If you wanted to augment your project tracker's project creation to require that all the tasks for the new project have a size, you might try something like this:

---

3.   https://github.com/thoughtbot/shoulda-matchers

```
it "doesn't allow  creation of a task without a size" do
  creator = CreatesProject.new(name: "Test", task_string: "size:no_size")
  creator.create
  expect(creator.project.tasks.map(&:title)).to eq(["size"])
end
```

In this test, you're validating that the second task, with the clever name no size, does not get added to the project. This test works whether the size limitation is implemented as a Rails validation or as some kind of filter that the CreatesProject class manages. Again, you're testing the behavior, not the implementation. This strategy works for all kinds of Rails validations, including uniqueness (create two objects and validate that the second one doesn't save). When I create a custom validator, though, as either a method or a separate class, it goes through the same TDD process as any other method.

Testing ActiveRecord Finders

ActiveRecord provides a rich set of methods that are wrappers around SQL statements sent to your database. These methods are collectively referred to as *finders*. One great feature of ActiveRecord finders is that they can be composed, allowing you to express a compound statement like "bring me the most recently completed five large tasks" as Task.where(status: completed).order("completed_at DESC").where("size > 3").limit(5).

You can even compose the finders if you extract them to their own methods in pieces:

```
class Task < ActiveRecord::Base

  def self.completed
    where(status: :completed)
  end

  def self.large
    where("size > 3")
  end

  def self.most_recent
    order("completed_at DESC")
  end

  def self.recent_done_and_large
    completed.large.most_recent.limit(5)
  end
end
```

Being able to compose this logic is awesome. But finder methods occupy an awkward place between methods you might write and Rails core features, leading to the question of how best to test them.

Here are some guidelines.

Be aggressive about extracting compound finder statements to their own methods, in much the same way and for much the same reason as I covered for compound Boolean logic in *Break Up Complexity*, on page 82. The methods are easier to understand and reuse if they are bound together behind a method name that defines the intent of the method. When I talk about test doubles you'll also see that having finders called behind other methods makes it much easier to avoid touching the database when you don't need to.

If a finder is extracted during refactoring and an existing test already covers its functionality, you may not need a new test to cover it. Like any other method extracted in refactoring, you aren't adding logic. Again, though, if the finder method winds up in a different class than that covered by the existing test, consider transferring the test logic.

If you're test-driving the finder method directly, you have two issues in tension. On one hand, you need to create enough objects to feel confident that the finder method is being tested. On the other, ActiveRecord finder methods need to touch the database, which makes the test slow, so you want to create as few objects as possible. Don't shy away from creating ActiveRecord objects when you're legitimately testing database retrieval behavior, but don't create more objects than you need to.

If you're testing a method that finds objects based on criteria, start with a test that creates two objects—that's one object you expect the method to find and one that you do not, which allows you to cover the logic from both sides:

```ruby
it "finds completed tasks" do
  complete = Task.create(completed_at: 1.day.ago, title: "Completed")
  incomplete = Task.create(completed_at: nil, title: "Not Completed")
  expect(Task.complete.map(&:title)).to eq(["Completed"])
end
```

The test creates two objects and asserts that the Task.complete method finds only one of them. The last line of the test does something that is a little idiosyncratic but that I've found useful. Specifically, it converts the list of ActiveRecord objects (Task.complete) to a list of strings (map.(&:title)).

Generally, I'm converting a complex object to a simple one for purposes of testing. This is for increased readability—to some extent in the test, but more so in the test output. If this test fails as written, the output will look something like this:

```
 1) Failure:
Expected: ["Completed"]
  Actual: []
```

Had I not converted the last line, the error would be more like this:

```
-[#<Task id: 980190963, project_id: nil, title: "Completed",
size: nil, completed_at: "2013-12-14 21:47:22",
created_at: "2013-12-15 21:47:22",
updated_at: "2013-12-15 21:47:22">]
+[]
```

I submit the first error message makes it easier to determine what's going on.

Another option, using recent RSpec parlance, is to use a *compound matcher*:

```
it "finds completed tasks" do
  complete = Task.create(completed_at: 1.day.ago, title: "Completed")
  incomplete = Task.create(completed_at: nil, title: "Not Completed")
  expect(Task.complete).to match(
    [an_object_having_attributes(title: "Completed")])
end
```

In this case, the match matcher expects the structure of Task.complete to be a one-element array where that one element has a title attribute with the value "completed." This style can be very readable and allows RSpec to create very useful error messages when it fails. Whether you use this style is a matter of preference. I find it quite readable in many cases; sometimes it's more clear to write the expectation using multiple matchers.

Once you've written your initial two-object test, write another test only if you can think of another pair of objects that would fail given the current code, such as if your finder had compound logic. If you were writing a method to find tasks that were both "completed" and "large," you might start with a test that has one object with both of those criteria and one with neither, and then write a second test that has an object with both criteria and an object that has only one of the two criteria.

I'm trying to avoid a combinatorial explosion where you create 16 objects to test a finder with four elements. Going two at a time and creating new pairs only if there's still a potential failure keeps each test small and easy to understand.

If you're testing for sort logic, you have to work around the fact that the order in which you add data to the database in setup is the order in which you get the objects back when you don't explicitly specify an order (because the default order is ascending by ID). If you input your data in the same order as the expected output, then the test passes before you do anything. That is bad.

If I need to test sort behavior, I create three objects: expected middle value first, expected high value second, and expected low value third. This pattern is out of order no matter which way you go, so a test for sorting will correctly fail until the logic is in place.

Testing Shared Modules and ActiveSupport Concerns

Often multiple models in your application share some kind of common feature set. For example, you may have multiple object types that can be purchased, tagged, or commented on. You can use standard Ruby classes and modules for this shared behavior. If the shared behavior has both class and instance methods, Rails provides ActiveSupport::Concern, which allows you to easily use a common pattern to mix multiple kinds of behavior from one module.

Testing this shared behavior can be a challenge. You don't want to have to rewrite the shared behavior specs for each class that shares the mixed-in module. At the same time, if the shared feature depends on data being available in each class, that dependency is testable logic.

RSpec has a powerful mechanism for sharing specs across multiple objects that have common functionality, simply called the *shared example*. You can use shared examples to run the same set of specs in multiple describe blocks, whether the common feature is encapsulated in a module or not.

Shared examples in RSpec have two parts: the definition and the usage. Shared examples must be defined before they're used. In a Rails context, the easiest way to do that is to put the shared examples inside a spec/shared directory and then add this line to the Rails rails_helper.rb file to load everything in that directory before any specs are run:

```
Dir[Rails.root.join("spec/shared/**/*.rb")].each { |f| require f }
```

Let's create a contrived example, suggesting we want projects and tasks to respond to a similar set of adjectives about their size. Here a shared group is created, with the method shared_examples taking a string argument and a block:

```
model/01/spec/shared/size_group.rb
RSpec.shared_examples "sizeable" do
  let(:instance) { described_class.new }

  it "knows a one-point story is small" do
    allow(instance).to receive(:size).and_return(1)
    expect(instance).to be_small
  end

  it "knows a five-point story is epic" do
    allow(instance).to receive(:size).and_return(5)
    expect(instance).to be_epic
  end
end
```

The block inside the shared_examples method is similar to a describe block. Inside, you can use let to define variables or it to define specs. The only unusual thing about this block is that rather than create an object explicitly, the let statement at the top creates a generic instance using the described_class, which is the class referenced by the innermost describe whose argument is a class. Most of the time this will be the initial RSpec.describe. We're also "setting" the size via a mock on the theory that while tasks have a setter for their size, projects don't.

To use the shared example group, all you need to do is declare it. RSpec defines multiple equivalent methods for doing so (and even allows you to define your own), one of which is it_should_behave_like followed by the name of the group. Here's what that looks like in the task_spec file:

model/01/spec/models/task_spec.rb
```ruby
RSpec.describe Task do

  it_should_behave_like "sizeable"
```

When task_spec is executed, the shared group is invoked with Task as the described_class, and the test will look for the small? and epic? methods to pass the test. To make the code pass, you need to add the concern:

model/01/app/models/concerns/sizeable.rb
```ruby
module Sizeable
  extend ActiveSupport::Concern

  def small?
    size <= 1
  end

  def epic?
    size >= 5
  end
end
```

And then include it in the Task class:

model/01/app/models/task.rb
```ruby
class Task < ApplicationRecord
  include Sizeable
```

With that in place you can quickly add both the spec and the feature to the project class (assuming you rename the project method from total_size to size):

model/01/spec/models/project_spec.rb
```ruby
RSpec.describe Project do

  it_should_behave_like "sizeable"
```

and

```
model/01/app/models/project.rb
class Project < ApplicationRecord
  include Sizeable
```

There are a couple of other ways to invoke a shared example group—RSpec defines synonymous methods include_examples and it_behaves_like. You can also use RSpec metadata, which I'll discuss in Chapter 16, *Running Tests Faster and Running Faster Tests*, on page 319.

When invoking the group, you can also have the it_should_behave_like method take a block argument. Inside that block, you can use let statements to define variables, which are then visible to the shared example specs. In other words, an alternative to creating an instance with described_class is to place the burden on the calling spec to create a variable and give it an appropriate name in a let block, like this:

```
it_should_behave_like "sizable" do
  let(:instance) { Project.new }
end
```

Writing Your Own RSpec Matchers

RSpec's built-in matchers are flexible, but sometimes you have behavior patterns you specify multiple times in your code and the existing matchers don't quite cover it. Sometimes this is because the specification requires multiple steps, and sometimes it's because the generic matcher doesn't quite match the code's intent.

RSpec provides tools for creating your own custom matchers to cover just such an eventuality. A basic matcher is really simple. Let's say you wanted a custom matcher to measure project size in points. Rather than say expect(project.size).to eq(5) you'd say expect(project).to be_of_size(5). It's a little contrived, but work with me.

Normally custom matchers are placed in the spec/support folder, which can be imported when RSpec starts. To import your matcher, you need to explicitly require the custom matcher file in your rails_helper file. RSpec 3.1 contains a commented line in the rails_helper that you can uncomment in your setup to have the entire spec/support directory loaded automatically. You can also choose to directly import individual matcher files at the beginning of the spec files that use them.

Here's an example of converting the size comparisons to an RSpec custom matcher:

```
model/02/spec/support/size_matcher.rb
RSpec::Matchers.define :be_of_size do |expected|
  match do |actual|
    actual.size == expected
  end
end
```

The definition starts with a call to RSpec::Matchers.define, passing it the name of the matcher and a block. The block takes an argument that will eventually be the expected value—the value passed to the matcher when called.

Inside the block, the match method is called with a block. That block takes one argument, actual, which is the value passed to expect when the matcher is invoked. The block is expected to do something with the expected and actual values and return true if they match according to the definition of the matcher being written. In this case, you're calling size on the actual value, presumably a Project, and comparing it to the expected value for an equality match. If the matcher takes multiple expected arguments, then the outer block definition should name all the arguments: define :have_sizes do |first, second|.

Remember: The expected value is the value defined by the test, and the actual value is the value defined by the code. Here is the form in which the matcher gets called:

```
expect(actual_value).to be_of_size(expected_value)
```

You can then use this in a test, just like any other matcher:

```
model/02/spec/models/project_spec.rb
it "can calculate total size" do
  expect(project).to be_of_size(10)
  expect(project).not_to be_of_size(5)
end
```

In the first call, 10 is the expected value and project is the actual value. In the second call, not_to is used to negate the matcher, and 5 is the expected value.

There are, of course, additional options. You can call other methods inside the define block to further specify behavior. For instance, you can override the messages RSpec will use when the matcher is displayed:

```
model/03/spec/support/size_matcher.rb
RSpec::Matchers.define :be_of_size do |expected|
  match do |actual|
    actual.size == expected
  end

  description do
    "have tasks totaling #{expected} points"
  end

  failure_message do |actual|
    "expected project #{actual.name} to have size #{expected}, was #{actual}"
  end

  failure_message_when_negated do |actual|
    "expected project #{actual.name} not to have size #{expected}, but it did"
  end
end
```

Three different customizations are used here: description takes no arguments and returns a string used by RSpec formatters that display the matcher's description. The other two are displayed by RSpec when the matcher fails, with failure_message being printed when a to match fails, and failure_message_on_negation being printed when a not_to match fails. You can also adjust the failure message by calling the method diffable in the matcher block—no arguments, no block. Effectively, you're declaring the matcher to be diffable, which means that on failure the expected and actual arguments are displayed in a diff format. RSpec uses this in the built-in string and array matchers.

If you want to be able to chain additional methods after the initial matcher to specify further arguments, then you use the chain method inside the matcher block:

```
model/04/spec/support/size_matcher.rb
RSpec::Matchers.define :be_of_size do |expected|
  match do |actual|
    size_to_check = @incomplete ? actual.remaining_size : actual.size
    size_to_check == expected
  end

  description do
    "have tasks totaling #{expected} points"
  end

  failure_message do |actual|
    "expected project #{actual.name} to have size #{expected}, was #{actual}"
  end

  failure_message_when_negated do |actual|
    "expected project #{actual.name} not to have size #{expected}, but it did"
  end
```

```
chain :for_incomplete_tasks_only do
    @incomplete = true
  end
end
```

The chain method takes an argument and a block, with the argument being the name of the method you want to chain. Any arguments to that method become arguments to the block—in this case the method has no arguments. Typically, inside a chained method you set instance variables, which are then referenced inside the match method to affect the match. The for_incomplete_tasks_only method sets a flag used to determine how to query the project for the size being tested.

The new method can then be chained onto the matcher:

model/04/spec/models/project_spec.rb
```
it "can calculate total size" do
  expect(project).to be_of_size(10)
  expect(project).not_to be_of_size(5)
end

it "can calculate remaining size" do
  expect(project).to be_of_size(5).for_incomplete_tasks_only
end
```

What You've Done

In this chapter you learned about strategies for dealing with Rails models and looked at a way of driving the TDD process to add a particular feature. Once the process is added, the next step is refactoring, and you looked at how to mitigate complexity, duplication, and missing abstractions. You also looked at testing Rails features such as associations and validations, and at how to create your own RSpec matchers if the built-in ones aren't expressive enough.

The guidelines discussed in this chapter should give you some direction as you test-drive new business logic in your Rails application. Every test you write, however, depends on some data to run. Getting useful data into the test cleanly and quickly turns out to be kind of complicated. In the next chapter you'll look at several ways of managing test data.

CHAPTER 6

Adding Data to Tests

Creating test data sounds like it should be the easiest thing ever. I mean, we already have ActiveRecord#create; isn't that enough? Not quite. To be useful, the data you generate for your tests needs to support the goals of testing. You should be able to create the data quickly and easily, both in the amount of typing it takes to create data and the speed at which the test runs. The data should be the same every time you generate it, should be specific to a set of tests, and should be an accurate representation of the objects that will be used when the code runs outside of tests.

Nothing against ActiveRecord#create, but if it's the only way you get data into your tests, you're going to have some problems. These problems include tests with a lot of extraneous details, slow tests, and tests that are brittle against future changes to your model's definition.

In this chapter I'll discuss two techniques that are in wide use in the Rails community for creating data: fixtures and factories. Defined by the Rails framework, *fixtures* are used to rapidly create global data. As you'll see, fixtures solve some of the problems of creating test data, but cause different ones. Specifically, fixtures are fast and easy to use but are global to all tests.

The Rails community has created a set of *factory* tools, which use some variant on the factory design pattern to create data. Factories' strengths overlap with but are slightly different from fixtures' strengths; factories are also easy to create but can be slow to run.

In the next chapter you'll explore a completely different way to think about your test's inputs when I talk about *test doubles*.

As with many testing decisions, no one answer works for all situations; there's a variety of tools with different strengths that can be used well or poorly.

What's the Problem?

What's the big deal if I want to use normal, ordinary ActiveRecord#create in my tests? I use it in my code. What could go wrong?

Since you asked ...

I'll start with a simple test involving two users:

```
it "can tell which user is older" do
  eldest_user = User.create(date_of_birth: '1971-01-22')
  youngest_user = User.create(date_of_birth: '1973-08-31')
  expect(User.eldest).to eq(eldest_user)
  expect(User.youngest).to eq(youngest_user)
end
```

That test is deliberately simple so as not to distract from the data-creation issue. The only weird thing here is that I'm testing a hypothetical finder method, eldest, that goes into the database, so for the test it's necessary that the objects I create come from the database.

You make the test pass and forget about it. The test silently continues to pass every time you run your test suite.

And then ...

You add authentication. And even though this test has nothing to do with authentication, it fails. Instead of returning eldest_user, the eldest call in the first assertion returns nil.

The problem is that adding authentication adds two new validations: requirements that a user must have an email address and a password. The test data no longer matches those requirements, so the objects aren't saved to the database, and therefore the finder methods can't find them—hence the nil.

With a heavy sigh, I add the required fields to the test:

```
it "can tell which user is older" do
  eldest_user = User.create!(date_of_birth: '1971-01-22',
    email: "eldest@example.com", password: "password")
  youngest_user = User.create!(date_of_birth: '1973-08-31'
    email: "youngest@example.com", password: "password")
  expect(User.eldest).to eq(eldest_user)
  expect(User.youngest).to eq(youngest_user)
end
```

Okay, that's not horrible. It's not great, either, but life marches on. I've switched to create! so now at least any further validation will fail at the point of creation, which makes diagnosing the failure much easier.

Some time later, the marketing department insists on obtaining full demographic data for all your users, including height in centimeters, zip code, and handedness. (Handedness? Sure, let's say your company makes golf clubs.) And the database administrator insists that means that all demographic categories must be required in the database. Now the test looks like this:

```
it "can tell which user is older" do
  eldest_user = User.create!(date_of_birth: '1971-01-22',
    email: "eldest@example.com", password: "password",
    height: 185, zip_code: "60642", handedness: "left")
  youngest_user = User.create!(date_of_birth: '1973-08-31'
    email: "youngest@example.com", password: "password",
    height: 178, zip_code: "60642", handedness: "ambidextrous")
  expect(User.eldest).to eq(eldest_user)
  expect(User.youngest).to eq(youngest_user)
end
```

This is starting to get out of control. Now you need to type three lines of text in a test just to create a single user; additionally, it's nearly impossible to pick out of this data the one attribute—date of birth—that is relevant for the test.

Not only that, but this problem happens every time a user is created in a test and every time a new validation is added to users. In other words, all the time.

I'd like a way to specify a known valid object so that there is at most one place to update when new validations get created. Fixtures and factories are two different mechanisms for solving this problem.

Fixtures

Rails has always made it easy to manage a database just for test data, which is automatically cleared between tests. (While there's no denying this is tremendously useful, it has also lulled all of us into feeling that a test that touches the database—a huge third-party dependency—is somehow a *unit* test.) One of the most valuable ways in which Ruby on Rails has supported automated testing is through the use of easily created data that is accessible to all the tests in your system, no matter when or where you write those tests, using *fixtures* specified in a YAML file. (YAML is a file format. The acronym stands for *YAML Ain't Markup Language*.[1]) It's sometimes hard for an experienced Rails programmer to remember just how exciting the YAML fixtures used to seem. You can just set up data once? In an easy format? And it's always there? Amazing.

---

1. http://www.yaml.org

Over time, the infatuation with fixtures has dimmed, but they are still a quick and easy way to get data into your tests.

What's a Fixture?

Generically, a fixture is any known baseline state that can be made to exist at the beginning of a test. The existence of a fixed state makes it possible to write tests that make assumptions based on that particular set of data. In Rails, the term "fixture" refers to a specific mechanism baked into the framework to easily define a set of objects that will exist globally for all tests. These fixtures are defined in a set of YAML files that are automatically written to the database and converted to ActiveRecord objects at the beginning of each test run.

Each ActiveRecord model in your application can have an associated fixture file. That fixture file is named after the plural version of the model. So, if you wanted fixtures for your Projects and Task models, they would go in spec/fixtures/projects.yml and spec/fixtures/tasks.yml, respectively. (If you're using Minitest, the directory would be test/fixtures/.) If you use Rails generators to create your model, then a fixture file is created for you, with some boilerplate values for each attribute.

The fixture file is in YAML format, a data-description format often used as an easier-to-type alternative to XML. The details of YAML syntax are both way outside the scope of this book and largely irrelevant to fixtures. YAML contains a number of advanced features that don't concern us here.

Each entry in a fixture file starts with an identifier, with the attributes for that entry subordinate to the identifier. Here's a sample for Project:

```
runway:
  name: Project Runway
  due_date: 2016-12-18

book:
  name: Write the book
  due_date: 2017-04-14
```

YAML syntax is somewhat reminiscent of Python, both in the colon used to separate key/value pairs and in the use of indentation to mark the bounds of each entry. The fact that the line book: is outdented two spaces indicates to the YAML parser that a new entry has begun. Strings do not need to be enclosed in quotation marks (except for strings the YAML parser would find ambiguous, such as if the string value also contains a colon and a space). It doesn't hurt to add the quotation marks if you find it more readable, though.

You can specify a multiline string by putting a pipe character (|) on the line with the attribute name. The multiline string can then be written over the next set of lines; each line must be indented relative to the line with the attribute name. Once again, outdenting indicates the end of the string:

```
runway:
  name: Project Runway
  due_date: 2016-12-18
  description: |
    The awesomest project ever.
    It's really, really great.
```

The Rails fixture-creation process uses information in your database to coerce the values to the proper type. I write dates in SQL format (yyyy-mm-dd), though any format readable by Ruby's Date.parse() will work.

The identifier that introduces each record is then used to access the individual fixture entry within your tests. Assuming that this is the Project class, you'd be able to retrieve these entries throughout your test suite as projects(:runway) and projects(:book), respectively. Unless you like trying to figure out what's special about projects(:project_10), I recommend meaningful entry names, especially for entries that expose special cases, like this: projects(:project_with_no_due_date).

The YAML data is converted to a database record directly in SQL, without using ActiveRecord#new or ActiveRecord#create. (To be clear, when you use the data in your tests, the objects you get are ActiveRecord models—ActiveRecord is bypassed only when the fixture is first converted to a database record.) This means you can't use arbitrary methods of the model as attributes in the fixture the way you can in a create call.

Fixture attributes have to be either actual database columns or ActiveRecord associations explicitly defined in the model. They can not be arbitrary setter methods defined in the model's code. Removing a database column from your model and forgetting to take it out of the fixtures results in your test suite erroring out when loaded. The fixture-loading mechanism also bypasses any validations you've created on your ActiveRecord, meaning there is no way to guarantee the validity of fixture data on load, short of explicitly testing each fixture yourself.

You do not need to specify the id for a fixture (although you can if you want). If you do not specify an id explicitly, the id is generated for you based on the entry's YAML identifier name. If you allow Rails to generate these ids, you get a side benefit: an easy way of specifying relationships between fixture objects. If your two model classes have an explicitly defined ActiveRecord relationship, you can use the fixture identifier of one object to define the relationship in the other object. In this snippet from a potential tasks.yml, I'm defining the task as having a relationship with the project defined as projects(:book):

```
chapter:
  title: Write a chapter
  project: book
```

If the relationship is has_many, the multiple values in the relationship can be specified as a comma-delimited list. This is true even if the two objects are in a has_and_belongs_to_many relationship via a join table, although a has_many :through relationship does need to have the join model entry explicitly specified.

Fixture files are also interpreted as ERB (Embedded Ruby) files, which means you can have dynamic attributes like this:

```
runway:
  name: Project Runway
  due_date: <%= 1.month.from_now %>
```

Or you can specify multiple entries dynamically, like this:

```
<% 10.times do |i| %>
task_<%=i%>:
  name: "Task <%= i %>"
<% end %>
```

In the second case, notice that the identifier still needs to be at the leftmost column; you can't indent the inside of the block the way normal Ruby style would suggest. Try not to loop inside fixture files; it gets confusing really quickly, largely because the record names are generated dynamically, making the file hard to read. (The only exception would be if you don't intend to refer to any individual record directly, only via finders; then the naming confusion is less of an issue.) If you find yourself needing dynamic data functionality like this, you're probably better off with a factory tool.

Loading Fixture Data

By default, all your defined fixtures are loaded into the database once at the beginning of your test run. Rails starts a database transaction at the beginning of each test. At the end of each test the transaction is rolled back, restoring the initial state very quickly.

The transactional behavior of fixtures is a problem if you're trying to test transactional behavior in your application. In that case the fixture transaction will overwhelm the transaction you're trying to test. If you need less-aggressive transaction behavior, you can go into the spec/spec_helper.rb file and add the line config.use_transactional_fixtures = false. There's no way to change this behavior to be fine-grained enough to use the nontransactional behavior for only a single spec. Again, if you need to test transactional behavior, fixtures may not be your best bet.

Why Fixtures Are Great

Fixtures have a bad reputation in some circles, but they do have their good points. Used judiciously, fixtures are a fast way to create background static data.

Fixtures Are Fast

One reason to use fixtures in a modern Rails application is how fast they are. They add overhead only when the Rails framework is loaded; there's no real cost to having fixtures persist between tests, so there's no particular downside to having a lot of objects defined in fixture files.

Well, there's *one* downside: sometimes you might write a test that assumes the database table is blank, so you'd test something that's supposed to create an object and then test that there's exactly one object in the database. The existence of fixture data will break that test because you'll start with objects in the database. One workaround is to explicitly test the change between the initial state and the ending state rather than assuming the start state is an empty table.

Fixture speed makes fixtures ideal for setting up reasonably complicated object-relationship trees that you might use in your tests. That said, if you're truly unit-testing, you likely don't need complicated object-relationship trees. (If you're acceptance-testing, on the other hand … hold that thought.)

Fixtures Are Always There

You can count on fixtures always being available anywhere in your test suite. In many unit-testing situations that's not a big deal because you don't create a lot of data for each test.

However, some applications rely on the existence of some kind of mostly static data that's stored in the database. Often this is metadata, product types, user types, or categories of some kind. It's stored in the database to make it easy to modify, but most of the time it's static data. If your application assumes that kind of data will always be there, setting that data up via fixtures will be faster and easier than re-creating the data for each test.

| Prescription 16 | Fixtures are particularly useful for global semistatic data stored in the database. |

Why Fixtures Are a Pain

As great as fixtures are when you're starting out, using them long term on complex projects exposes problems. Here are some things to keep an eye on.

Fixtures Are Global

There is only one set of fixtures in a default Rails application, so the temptation to add new data points to the fixture set every time you need a corner case is overwhelming. The problem is that every time you add a user to test what happens when a left-handed user sends a message to a user who has a friend relationship and lives in Fiji (or whatever oddball scenario you need), every other test has to deal with that data point being part of the test data.

Fixtures Are Spread Out

Fixtures live in their own directory, and each model has its own fixture file. That's fine until you start needing to manage connections, and a simple setup of a user commenting on a post related to a given article quickly spans across four fixture files, with no easy way to trace the relationships. I'm a big fan of "small and plentiful" over "large and few" when it comes to code structure, but even I find fixtures too spread out sometimes.

Fixtures Are Distant

If you're doing a complex test based on the specific fixture lineup, you'll often wind up with the end data being based on the fixture setup in such a way that, when reading the test, it's not clear exactly how the final value is derived. You need to go back to the fixture files to understand the calculation.

Fixtures Are Brittle

Of course, once you add that left-handed user to your fixture set, you're guaranteed to break any test that depends on the exact makeup of the entire user population. Tests for searching and reporting are notorious culprits here. There aren't many more effective ways to kill your team's enthusiasm for testing than having to fix 25 tests on the other side of the project every time you add new sample data.

Sounds grim, right? It's not. Not only are fixtures perfectly suitable for simple projects, but the Rails community has responded to the weaknesses of fixtures by creating factory tools that can replace them in creating test data.

Factories

Generically, the factory pattern refers to a class or module in your application whose sole purpose is to safely and correctly create other objects in your application. Outside of tests, factories are frequently used to encapsulate complex object-creation logic. Inside of Rails tests, factories are used to provide templates for creating valid objects.

Rather than specifying all the test data exactly, the factory tool provides a blueprint for creating a sample instance of your model. When you need data for a specific test, you call a factory method, which gives you an object based on your blueprint. You can override the blueprint to identify any specific attribute values required to make your test work out. Calling the factory method is simple enough to make it feasible to set up a useful amount of data in each test.

The most common factory tools used for Rails testing are factory_bot and its Rails library, factory_bot_rails.[2] [3] The current version as I write this is 4.8.2. Until quite recently this gem was called factory_girl, so you'll likely see many references to it under that name.

Let's talk first about how to set up and use factory_bot, and once you have the basics down I'll talk about how to use it effectively.

Installing factory_bot

To install factory_bot in a Rails project, include the following in the Gemfile in the development and test group:

```
gem 'factory_bot_rails'
```

In a Rails project, factory files are automatically loaded if they are in spec/factories.rb or spec/factories/*.rb. (In Minitest-land, that would be test/factories.rb or test/factories/*.rb.) Factories defined in any other place need to be explicitly required into the program.

There's one optional configuration, which is to place the following line inside the configuration definition in spec/rails_helper.rb or some other file that is loaded as part of the RSpec setup:

---

2.   https://github.com/thoughtbot/factory_bot
3.   https://github.com/thoughtbot/factory_bot_rails

```
data/01/spec/support/factory_bot.rb
RSpec.configure do |config|
  config.include FactoryBot::Syntax::Methods
end
```

If the FactoryBot::Syntax::Methods are included, you can use the factory_bot creation methods without the FactoryBot prefix—this will make more sense in a little bit.

Basic Factory Definition

All the definitions of your factories go inside a call to the method FactoryBot.define, which takes a block argument. Inside that block, you can declare factories to define default data. Each factory declaration takes its own argument in which you can define default values on an attribute-by-attribute basis.

A simple example for the task builder might look like this for tasks:

```
data/01/spec/factories/tasks.rb
FactoryBot.define do
  factory :task do
    title "Thing to do"
    size 1
    completed_at nil
  end
end
```

and this for projects:

```
data/01/spec/factories/projects.rb
FactoryBot.define do
  factory :project do
    name "Project Runway"
    due_date 1.week.from_now
  end
end
```

Note the absence of equals signs—these are not assignments. Technically they are method calls, so if it makes it more readable to write the lines like name("Project Runway"), go for it.

Factory_bot assumes there is an ActiveRecord class with the same name as the one you give the factory. When the factory is invoked, the resulting object is of that class.

If you want to have the factory refer to an arbitrary class, you can specify the class when the factory is defined (some of these examples are not in the sample codebase):

```
FactoryBot.define do
  factory :big_project, class: Project do
    name "Big Project"
  end
end
```

In the previous factory, all the values are static and are determined when the factory file is loaded. If you want a dynamic value to be determined when an individual factory object is created, pass a block instead of a value. The block will be evaluated when each new factory is called:

```
FactoryBot.define do
  factory :project do
    name "Project Runway"
    due_date { Date.today - rand(50) }
  end
end
```

You can also refer to a previously assigned value later in the factory:

```
FactoryBot.define do
  factory :project do
    name "Project Runway"
    due_date { Date.today - rand(50) }
    slug { "#{name.downcase.gsub(" ", "_")}" }
  end
end
```

What's nice about this is that the factory will always use the value in the name attribute to calculate the slug, even if you pass the name in yourself rather than use the default value. So this factory could be used as follows:

```
it "uses factory_bot slug block" do
  project = Factorybot.create(:project, name: "Book To Write")
  expect(project.slug).to eq("book_to_write")
end
```

If you used the include FactoryBot::Syntax::Methods call alluded to previously, then you could write the first line as project = create(:project, name: "Book To Write"). In the past I preferred the explicit reminder that factory_bot is being used, but based on what I see in code these days, I've kind of lost that battle.

Inside the factory, you can call any attribute in the model that has a setter method. Unlike with fixtures, any virtual attribute in the model (such as the unencrypted password attribute of a secure user model) is fair game.

Basic Factory Creation

Factory_bot provides four ways of turning a factory into a Ruby object. For the project factory we were just looking at, the four ways are as follows:

- build(:project), which returns a model instance that has not been saved to the database.

- create(:project), which returns a model instance and saves it to the database.

- attributes_for(:project), which returns a hash of all the attributes in the factory that are suitable for passing to ActiveRecord#new or ActiveRecord#create. This method is most often useful for creating a hash that will be sent as params to a controller test.

- build_stubbed(:project), which is almost magical. Like build, it returns an unsaved model object. Unlike build, it assigns a fake ActiveRecord ID to the model and stubs out database-interaction methods (like save) such that the test raises an exception if they are called.

Your existing project_spec uses basic Project and Task instances. You can rewrite it as follows:

```
data/01/spec/models/project_spec.rb
describe "without a task" do
  let(:project) { FactoryBot.build_stubbed(:project) }
  it "considers a project with no tasks to be done" do
    expect(project).to be_done
  end

  it "properly estimates a blank project" do
    expect(project.completed_velocity).to eq(0)
    expect(project.current_rate).to eq(0)
    expect(project.projected_days_remaining).to be_nan
    expect(project).not_to be_on_schedule
  end
end

describe "with a task" do
  let(:project) { FactoryBot.build_stubbed(:project, tasks: [task]) }
  let(:task) { FactoryBot.build_stubbed(:task) }

  it "knows that a project with an incomplete task is not done" do
    expect(project).not_to be_done
  end

  it "marks a project done if its tasks are done" do
    task.mark_completed
    expect(project).to be_done
  end
end
```

Here the build_stubbed strategy is used to create your project. The first spec group uses the factory as is, whereas the second group uses a key/value pair to set the associated tasks. (Very subtle note: you have to set the tasks attribute on Project rather than the project ID on Task because you're accessing it via the project, and build_stubbed only sets the association in one direction. You'll see more on this in a moment.)

All four of these build strategies allow you to pass key/value pairs to override the factory value for a given attribute. You can use this, for example, to create tasks with different sizes:

```
data/01/spec/models/project_spec.rb
describe "estimates" do
  let(:project) { FactoryBot.build_stubbed(:project,
    tasks: [newly_done, old_done, small_not_done, large_not_done]) }
  let(:newly_done) { FactoryBot.build_stubbed(:task,
    size: 3, completed_at: 1.day.ago) }
  let(:old_done) { FactoryBot.build_stubbed(:task,
    size: 2, completed_at: 6.months.ago) }
  let(:small_not_done) { FactoryBot.build_stubbed(:task, size: 1) }
  let(:large_not_done) { FactoryBot.build_stubbed(:task, size: 4) }

  it "can calculate total size" do
    expect(project).to be_of_size(10)
    expect(project).not_to be_of_size(5)
  end

  it "can calculate remaining size" do
    expect(project).to be_of_size(5).for_incomplete_tasks_only
  end
```

In this example, you're overriding the size and completed_at attributes of your tasks and assigning them to the project. Remember the last version of this code; you've gotten rid of the before hook, because you're now specifying the tasks as part of the factory.

When building the object from the factory, I consider it useful to explicitly list any attribute whose value is essential to the test. I do this even if the attribute has the same value as the factory default because I like having the explicit value in the test, where it can easily be seen. So, in this case, I might specify completed_at: nil for the not-done tasks in the setup.

All the build strategies will also yield the new object to a block in case you want to do more custom processing:

```
project = FactoryBot.build_stubbed(:project) do |p|
  p.tasks << FactoryBot.build_stubbed(:task)
end
```

I don't use this form very much, though I think it would be helpful if you had additional creation logic on a new test object.

This is the strategy by which I determine which of these methods to use:

- Use attribute_for only in the specialized case of needing a valid set of hash attributes. Again, in my experience that's most likely in a controller test.

- Use create only if the object absolutely must be in the database. Typically, this is because the test code must be able to access it via an ActiveRecord finder. Sometimes this is because the objects are in an ActiveRecord relationship and it is much easier to specify that with create. However, create is much slower than any of the other methods, so it's also worth thinking about whether there's a way to structure the code so that persistent data is not needed for the test.

- Use build in some cases where you don't actually need items in the database but Rails wants to force things to be saved (like associations). Factory_bot gets snippy about stubbed objects not being able to access the database, and this can cause problems testing objects with associations. Sometimes, though, it's better to rewrite the spec to add the association in the setup, as you did in the recent examples.

- In all other cases, use build_stubbed, which does everything build does, plus more. Because a build_stubbed object has a Rails ID, you can build up real Rails belongs_to associations and still not have to take the speed hit of saving to the database.

> **Prescription 17** Your go-to build strategy for factory_bot should be build_stubbed unless there is a need for the object to be in the database during the test.

In case you need to create a set of objects together, all the build strategies have two special forms: *_pair and *_list. The pair methods, like create_pair(:project) and build_stubbed_pair(:project), create exactly two objects of the given factory. You can still pass key/value pairs to the method, in which case the attribute overrides are applied to both objects. The list methods create an arbitrary number of items, denoted by an integer argument after the name of the factory, as in create_list(:project, 5), which creates five projects. As with the pair methods, key/value pairs can be passed in and are applied to the entire list. As far as I can tell, there's no way to specify in the call to the *_pair or *list method that the attributes should be different in different instances of the object. The same key/value pairs are applied to each instance.

Associations and Factories

Factory_bot has a powerful set of features for adding associations to factories. I'll talk about them because they are so powerful, and you might see code that uses them. Then I'll talk about why you should be careful about using them.

The simplest case is also a common one: the class being created has a belongs_to association with the same name as a factory. In that case, you just include that name in the factory (these code snippets aren't in the code sample, for reasons you'll learn by the end of this section):

```
FactoryBot.define do
  factory :task do
    title "Do Something"
    size 3
    project
  end
end
```

In this case, calling task = FactoryBot.create(:task) would also implicitly call task.project = FactoryBot.create(:project).

If you want to explicitly specify the project when calling the task factory, you can do so the same way you would for any other attribute—namely, via task = FactoryBot.create(:task, project: Project.new). If the association is specified in the factory definition but you don't want any value in the test, you need to explicitly set the association to nil, as in: task = FactoryBot.create(:task, project: nil).

If the association name doesn't match the factory name or if you want to specify default attributes of the associated object, you can explicitly use the association method in the factory definition:

```
FactoryBot.define do
  factory :task do
    title "Do Something"
    size 3
    project
    association :doer, factory: :user, name: "Task Doer"
  end
end
```

The syntax is association, followed by the name of the association in the ActiveRecord model and then a bunch of key/value pairs, with the factory key being used by factory_bot to determine which factory to use to create the associated object.

The way in which the subordinate object is built depends on the build strategy used for the parent object. The problem lies in the way ActiveRecord manages associations. The associated object needs an ID so that the parent object can link to it, and in Rails you get an ActiveRecord ID only when an ActiveRecord instance is saved to the database, meaning that a true association can exist only if the subordinate object is in the database and has an ID.

The easiest way to manage subordinate objects is by using build_stubbed to create the parent. Since the build_stubbed strategy assigns an ID to the objects being created, using build_stubbed sidesteps the whole issue. If a factory with associations is instantiated using build_stubbed, then by default all the associations are also invoked using build_stubbed. That solves the problem as long as you always use build_stubbed.

Calling the parent factory (in this case Task) with create causes the associated factory (in this case Project) to also be instantiated using create.

Where it gets tricky is if you use the build strategy. By default, even if you call the parent factory with build, the subordinate factory is still called with create. This is necessary to make sure the subordinate object has a Rails ID.

As a result, even if you use the build strategy specifically to avoid slow and unnecessary database interaction, if the factory has associations you'll still save objects to the database. Since those associated factories may themselves have associations, if you aren't careful you can end up saving a lot of objects to the database, resulting in prohibitively slow tests.

It's exactly this characteristic of factory_bot that has made it unwelcome in some circles, particularly if the people in those circles have to maintain large, unwieldy test suites. Factory-association misuse can be a big cause of a slow test suite, as tests create many more objects than they need to because of factory_bot associations.

However, if you use the longer form of specifying the association, you can explicitly specify the build strategy:

```
FactoryBot.define do
  factory :task do
    title: "To Something"
    size: 3
    project
    association :doer, factory: :user, strategy: :build
  end
end
```

If you go this route, you may have problems because the associated object won't have an ID. In this specific case, for example, the Task object will have its user attribute set but not its user_id. If your code is expecting the user_id to be set—for example, because user_id is faster to access than user—this may cause problems in your tests. (I suppose you can have an ID as one of the key/value pairs when creating the subordinate object. I've never tried that myself, but it could work.)

My preferred strategy is to not specify attributes in factories at all. If I need associated objects in a specific test, I explicitly add them to the test at the point they're needed.

Why?

- The surest way to keep factory_bot from creating large object trees is to not define large object trees.

- Tests that require multiple degrees of associated objects often indicate improperly factored code. Making it harder to write associations in tests nudges me in the direction of code that can be tested without associations.

> **Prescription 18** Avoid defining associations automatically in factory_bot definitions. Set them test by test, as needed. You'll wind up with more manageable test data.

The only downside is that there's a little more typing involved in some tests. Especially in Rails 5, where by default belongs_to associations are required, when saving data you may need to create objects just to make ActiveRecord happy. That's another argument against saving data unless you need to.

Managing Duplication in Factories

Once you have more than a couple of factories in your application, you want to make sure you can manage complexity and duplication. Factory_bot has a number of features to allow you to do just that.

Sequences

A common problem is the creation of multiple objects that require unique values. This most often happens with unique user attributes such as a login or email address. To allow the easy creation of unique attributes, factory_bot allows you to define an attribute as part of a sequence of values. The short version of the syntax looks like this:

```
FactoryBot.define do
  factory :task do
    sequence(:title) { |n| "Task #{n}" }
  end
end
```

Calling sequence inside a factory takes one argument (which is the attribute whose values are being sequenced) and a block. When the factory is invoked, the block is called with a new sequential value and the block's return value is set to be the value of the attribute. The start value is 1 by default, but a second argument to sequence can be used to specify an arbitrary value, which is usually a number but can be any object that responds to next.

When a sequence is defined inside a factory, it can be used in only that one place; however, sequences can also be defined outside of factories and reused:

```
FactoryBot.define do
  sequence :email do |n|
    "user_#{n}@test.com"
  end

  factory :user do
    name "Fred Flintstone"
    email
  end
end
```

The use of email inside the factory is a shortcut that assumes the sequence and the attribute have the same name. If so, the sequence is triggered and the next value becomes the value of the attributes. If the sequence and the attribute have different names, then you need to invoke the sequence explicitly by calling generate inside an attribute's block:

```
factory :task do
  title "Finish Chapter"
  user_email { generate(:email) }
end
```

Inherited Factories

Often you'll need to create multiple factories from the same class—a classic example is the ability to create different kinds of users, such as regular users versus administrators.

The most direct way to create slightly different factories in the same class is via factory_bot's inheritance feature. If you define a factory as having another factory as a parent, it takes all the attributes set in that parent but then allows you to override those attributes in the child factory. Effectively, factory _bot inheritance allows you to group common attributes so they can be reused:

```
FactoryBot.define do
  factory :task do
    sequence(:title) { |n| "Task #{n}" }
  end
```

```
  factory :big_task, parent: :task do
    size 5
  end

  factory :small_task, parent: :task do
    size 1
  end
end
```

In the preceding set of factories, big_task and small_task share the sequence being used to generate unique titles, but they each define their own size value.

In addition to explicitly setting the parent, you can achieve the same effect by nesting the child factories inside the parent definition, like so:

```
FactoryBot.define do
  factory :task do
    sequence(:title) { |n| "Task #{n}" }

    factory :big_task do
      size 5
    end

    factory :small_task do
      size 1
    end
  end
end
```

In case creating a parent factory and child factories seems a little backward to you, factory_bot also allows you to group a set of common attributes into a single chunk, called a *trait*, which can be used inside other factories. This makes sense if you have groups of attributes with values that are orthogonal to each other.

Traits can be used as though they were single attributes. Creating a noncontrived example is tricky without making the sample classes much more complex than they currently are—just realize that each trait could hold multiple attributes here:

```
data/02/spec/factories/tasks.rb
FactoryBot.define do
  factory :task do
    sequence(:title) { |n| "Task #{n}" }
    size 3
    completed_at nil

    trait :small do
      size 1
    end
```

```
  trait :large do
    size 5
  end

  trait :soon do
    due_date { 1.day.from_now }
  end

  trait :later do
    due_date { 1.month.from_now }
  end

  trait :newly_complete do
    completed_at { 1.day.ago }
  end

  trait :long_complete do
    completed_at { 6.months.ago }
  end

  factory :trivial, class: Task, traits: %i[small later]
  factory :panic, class: Task, traits: %i[large soon]
  end

end
```

The last couple of factories can be written slightly differently:

```
factory :trivial do
  small
  later
end

factory :panic do
  large
  soon
end
```

You can then rewrite the test that created a bunch of tasks to use these traits:

data/02/spec/models/project_spec.rb
```
describe "estimates" do
  let(:project) { FactoryBot.build_stubbed(:project,
    tasks: [newly_done, old_done, small_not_done, large_not_done]) }
  let(:newly_done) { FactoryBot.build_stubbed(:task, :newly_complete) }
  let(:old_done) { FactoryBot.build_stubbed(
    :task, :long_complete, :small) }
  let(:small_not_done) { FactoryBot.build_stubbed(:task, :small) }
  let(:large_not_done) { FactoryBot.build_stubbed(:task, :large) }

  it "can calculate total size" do
    expect(project).to be_of_size(10)
    expect(project).not_to be_of_size(5)
  end
```

```
it "can calculate remaining size" do
  expect(project).to be_of_size(6).for_incomplete_tasks_only
end
```

Having just one attribute per trait doesn't show the feature in its best light, but you have the basic tradeoff of verbose versus succinct. Traits take some extra definition but give meaningful names to groups of attributes that you might reuse. The good side is the meaningful name; the downside is the extra typing and added complexity of the factory, and that there are more details in the factory file that you might have to look up. I find traits most useful where there is a clear definition and set of attributes that would get set together, the classic example being setting up the permissions for an administrative user.

As factories get even more complex, factory_bot offers a few other techniques to manage them, including the ability to have postcreation callbacks, create custom build strategies, and have dummy attributes that are used only to control the factory creation. I suspect that these are useful only in somewhat specialized cases, so I won't go into them in more detail. The factory_bot documentation can help you if you're curious.[4]

Verifying Factories

The idea behind using factories is that the factory creates a valid object that can just be dropped into a test and used. Over time, though, you might add a new validation or drop an attribute or do something that will make the factories invalid. If you then run your test suite, every test that tries to save a factory object will fail. This can be a lot of failed tests and can be somewhat irritating to wade through.

Factory_bot allows you to verify all the defined factories, testing that they create valid objects. The method to call is FactoryBot.lint, but since calling the method on its own may create some objects in your database, the factory_bot docs recommend ensuring that you run it in the test environment so as not to interfere with your development data. There are a few ways to do this. Here's one that uses the Database Cleaner gem in a script you can run from the command line:[5]

---

4. https://github.com/thoughtbot/factory_bot/blob/master/GETTING_STARTED.md
5. https://github.com/DatabaseCleaner/database_cleaner

```
data/02/bin/factory_bot.rb
ENV["RAILS_ENV"] ||= "test"
require File.expand_path("../../config/environment", __FILE__)
begin
  DatabaseCleaner.start
  FactoryBot.lint(traits: true)
ensure
  DatabaseCleaner.clean
end
```

For this to work, you need to add gem "database_cleaner" in the :test group of the Gemfile. The first two lines of this code are exactly what RSpec does to force execution in the test environment: set the environment variable and load the config/environment.rb file. The FactoryBot.lint call is set with traits: true so that it will verify all traits—in isolation, it won't build up a combinatorial explosion of combined traits. Also, surround it with Database Cleaner calls to make sure anything it saves to the database goes away.

If you run this from the command line with

```
$ ruby bin/factory_bot.rb
```

you get three validation fails, which is impressive given that you have only two factories:

```
* task - Validation failed: Project must exist (ActiveRecord::RecordInvalid)
* trivial - undefined method `due_date=' for #<Task:<ID>> (NoMethodError)
* panic - undefined method `due_date=' for #<Task:<ID>> (NoMethodError)
```

The first failure in task is because in Rails these days, the belongs_to association in Task sets up a validation, which makes sense in production but somewhat goes against the association usage guidelines I listed earlier. You can fix this by adding a project to the Task factory—as long as Tasks are created with build_stubbed it won't really be an issue, but when you use create it's the first step toward slower specs.

The other two fails are embarrassing. due_date isn't an attribute of Task at the moment; it's an attribute of Project, but that's the kind of thing we run linters to find out, I suppose. Fix it by either moving the traits to Project or by adding the attribute to Task.

Preventing Factory Abuse

The initial temptation when using factories is to continue to build large trees of objects—this is particularly true if you're converting a project that was using fixtures. The best way to use factories is to create only the smallest amount of data needed to expose the issue in each test. This practice speeds up the tests, makes the issue easy to see rather than burying it among dozens of fixtures, and makes the correctness of the tests themselves easier to verify.

Dates and Times

Date and time logic has a well-deserved reputation as some of the most complex and irritating logic in any application. Testing calendar logic—including time-based reports, automatic logouts, and "1 day ago" text displays—can be a particular headache, but you can do a couple of things to simplify the time-logic beast.

Part of the Problem

You have a test that uses factories. You'd like to test some time-based code that might be used in a search or report result. This goes in spec/unit/project_spec.rb:

```ruby
let(:runway) { create(:project, name: "Project Runway",
  start_date: "2018-01-20" }
let(:greenlight) { create(:project, name: "Project Greenlight",
  start_date: "2018-02-24" }
let(:gutenberg) { create(:project, name: "Project Gutenberg",
  start_date: "2018-01-31" }

it "finds recently started projects" do
  actual = Project.find_recently_started(6.months)
  expect(actual.size).to eq(3)
end
```

Here's code that makes the test pass, from app/models/project.rb:

```ruby
def self.find_recently_started(time_span)
  old_time = Date.today - time_span
  all(conditions: ["start_date > ?", old_time.to_s(:db)])
end
```

On January 20, 2018, the test passes. And on January 21 it will pass, and it will pass the day after that....

Six months later, about June 20 (when you've probably long forgotten about this test, this sample data, and maybe even this entire project), the test will fail. And you'll spend way too much time trying to figure out what happened, until you remember the date issue and realize that the project with a January 20 date is no longer within the six-month time span specified in the test. Of course, changing all the dates just pushes the problem forward and gives us time to forget all about it again.

This issue may sound silly, but like many of the more ridiculous examples in the book, this happened to me and can end up costing a lot of time. I've seen tests that fail at a particular time of day (because time zones used inconsistently push part of the code into the next day). I've seen tests that pass in Chicago but fail in California. I've seen tests that fail on the first day of a new month and a new year—and, of course, tests that fail on the boundary in and out of daylight savings time. Most of this can be prevented.

When I was young and got paid to write Java, I solved this problem by adding an optional argument to every method that had a default value of Date.today, allowing an optional time to explicitly be passed to the method for testing. This is a lot of work (although, interestingly, I think the Ruby community is coming back to allowing this kind of optional argument injection as a regular practice). Here are a few other options for dealing with date and time data.

Using Relative Dates

Using relative dates in your test data is often a way to work around date and time weirdness. You can do this with fixtures, factories, or just the objects you create in your tests.

You can adjust the test to use dates relative to now:

```
let(:runway) { create(:project, name: "Project Runway",
  start_date: 1.week.ago }
let(:greenlight) { create(:project, name: "Project Greenlight",
  start_date: 1.month.ago }
let(:gutenberg) { create(:project, name: "Project Gutenberg",
  start_date: 1.day.ago }

it "finds recently started projects" do
  actual = Project.find_recently_started(6.months)
  expect(actual.size).to eq(3)
end
```

Since Rails fixture files are evaluated as ERB files before loading, you can specify dynamic dates in fixture files, as well:

```
runway:
  name: Project Runway
  start_date: <%= 1.month.ago %>

greenlight:
  name: Project Greenlight
  start_date: <%= 1.week.ago %>

gutenberg:
  name: Project Gutenberg
  start_date: <%= 1.day.ago %>
```

With fixtures written like this, the previous test will always work since the start_date of the projects will never fall out of the six-month range.

You can do something similar in factory_bot:

```
factory :project do
  name "Project Runway"
  start_date { 1.week.ago }
end
```

Although this technique works quite well for keeping test data a consistent relative distance from the test time, it's less helpful if you're trying to test based on the exact value of one of the dates—for example, if you're testing an output value or format. With the first, static set of fixture data, you could write the following:

```
it "displays project date in this goofy format" do
  expect(projects(:runway).goofy_start_date).to eq("2018 1 January")
end
```

This test is a lot more difficult to write if you don't explicitly know the value of the project's start_date.

Stubbing Time

Another option for managing date logic in tests is to "freeze" time by using a stub to explicitly specify what time Ruby reports when you ask for the current time. Rails has also added support for this feature with the methods ActiveSupport::Testing::TimeHelpers#travel and ActiveSupport::Testing::TimeHelpers#travel_to. In the past I've used the Timecop gem,[6] but in the interest of keeping things in house, as it were, I'll use the newer ActiveSupport syntax.

The travel_to method is effectively a superspecific mock-object package: it stubs out Date.today and Time.now, allowing you to explicitly set the effective date for your tests. Using this, the original test could be rewritten as follows:

```
it "finds recently started projects" do
  travel_to(Date.parse("2018-02-10"))
  actual = Project.find_recently_started(6.months)
  expect(actual.size).to eq(3)
end
```

The travel_to method stubs the current date and time methods to the date passed as the argument: in this case, February 10, 2018. Time does not move for the duration of the test.

A separate method, travel, allows you to specify the duration of the time change rather than the absolute target, as in travel 1.month. This is particularly useful when you need time to pass during the course of a test, as in loan calculations.

6. https://github.com/travisjeffery/timecop

The method travel_back resets time to its original state.

It's sometimes useful to put the following line in a setup method:

```
travel_to(Date.today)
```

and then the other half in the teardown method:

```
travel_back
```

This ensures that the current time doesn't change for the duration of each test. Again, with certain timing-related issues, that consistency eliminates a possible source of intermittent test failures or just plain confusion.

The argument to travel_to is a Date, Time, DateTime, or anything that accepts the message to_time. The argument to travel is an integer number of seconds that is added to the current time.

Both methods also take blocks such that the fake time is good only for the duration of the block:

```
it "reports based on start date" do
  travel_to(Date.parse("2015-02-10")) do
    actual = Project.find_started_in_last(6.months)
    expect(actual.size).to eq(3)
  end
end
```

The time-travel methods can be in your setup or in an individual test. You can use travel to change the time in the middle of a test to speed up an ongoing process:

```
it "knows if the project is over" do
  p = Project.new(:start_date => Date.today,
      :end_date = Date.today + 8.weeks)
  expect(p).not_to be_complete
  travel(10.weeks)
  expect(p).to be_complete
end
```

These methods let you keep explicit dates in your test data without causing problems later. The only downside is that if you have many tests setting time to different days, it can get somewhat confusing in the aggregate. It's easier if you use the same start date consistently. (On a solo project, you might use your birthday, for instance, but that's probably overly cute for a team project.) A more minor problem is that the line at the end of your test runs that indicates how long the test suite took may be hopelessly messed up because of the continued tweaking of Time.now.

Comparing Time

Ruby, not content with a simple date-and-time system, has three separate classes that manage date and time data. The Time class is a thin wrapper around the same Unix C library that pretty much every language exposes. (Motto: "Annoying programmers since 1983!") The Ruby-specific classes Date and DateTime are more flexible and have a more coherent API but are slower.

For Rails testing purposes, the relevant points are that ActiveRecord uses Date and DateTime (depending on the specifics of the underlying database column). Comparing a Date to a DateTime instance will always fail, as will trying to add or subtract them. And most of the Rails ActiveSupport methods (such as 5.days.ago) return DateTime. In testing this can lead to a lot of annoying failures, especially when you have a Date column with no time information—which is recommended if the time is not important.

In general, it's a good idea to compare dates and times by converting them using to_s(:db). It avoids the irritating question of object equality and you get more readable tests and error messages. When the exact time of the time object is in question, try to force the issue by using the Rails ActiveSupport methods to_date, to_time, and to_datetime. At worst, this means something like 5.days.ago.to_date.to_s(:db), which may read a touch awkwardly but is a robust test with a decent error message on failure.

Setting Rails Timestamps

One trick when testing dates is to explicitly set your ActiveRecord model's created_at attribute. Normally created_at is a timestamp automatically generated by Rails, and it's often used for the kind of time-based reporting alluded to in the rest of this section. Since it's automatically created at the current time, you can get into some weird situations if the other dates in the test are explicitly set in the past. Even without that complication, you may still need to explicitly set created_at to use the attribute to test time-based features.

You can set created_at in the fixture file, just like any other attribute; specify it in ActiveRecord::create, ActiveRecord::new, or a factory blueprint or just reset with an assignment or update method.

Setting updated_at is trickier. Under normal circumstances, if you try to explicitly set updated_at Rails will automatically reset it on save, which defeats the purpose. To change this behavior, set the class variable for your class with code like Project.record_timestamps = false, using the name of your class as the message receiver sometime before you save the object with a modified update time. After the save, reset things to normal with Project.record_timestamps = true.

What You've Done

In this chapter you saw how Rails provides fixtures as an exceptionally simple way to create a set of test data that can be shared across multiple tests. However, fixtures are so simple that they tend to not be adaptable to more complex product needs. Factory tools, which take a little bit more initial setup, allow for more flexibility at some cost in test performance. The two structures are not mutually exclusive. One pattern for combining them is to create a complex scenario in fixtures for use in integration or complex controller tests, and to use factories for unit tests or simpler controller tests.

Fixtures and factory tools allow you to get test data into your database to create a known baseline for testing. However, in some cases you may not want to place data in the database. Using the database in a test may be undesirable for performance reasons, for philosophical reasons (some people don't consider it reasonable to touch the database in a "unit" test), or where logistical reasons make objects hard to create. In the next chapter you'll explore test doubles, which allow tests to proceed by faking not the data but rather the method calls that produce the data.

CHAPTER 7

Using Test Doubles as Mocks and Stubs

You have a problem. You want to add credit-card processing to your project application so that you can make money. Testing the credit-card functionality presents immediate difficulties. For one thing, you don't want to accidentally make a credit-card purchase during testing—that would be bad. But even if the purchase gateway provides a test sandbox, you still don't want to depend on it for your unit tests to run. That network call is slow and you don't want your passing tests to depend on the status of a remote server.

Or, you might have a different problem. You'd like to build your code using a modular design. In doing so, you'd like your tests to be as isolated as possible from dependencies on other parts of the code. For example, you might have business logic that calls a model but that you want to test without depending on the model. You want your workflow test to work even if the model is broken—even if the model code does not yet exist.

The solution to both of these problems is a *test double*. A test double is a "fake" object used in place of a "real" object for the purposes of automated testing. By "fake," I mean that the object doesn't have a real implementation, but might instead have canned values that it can return in response to specific messages.

You might use a double when the real object is unavailable or difficult to access from a test environment. Or you might use a double to create a specific application state that would otherwise be difficult to trigger in a test environment. Database or network failures, for example, might depend on program states that are nondeterministic or otherwise hard to replicate in testing.

Doubles can also be used strategically to limit a test's execution to the object and method specifically under test, or to specify the interface of an object or part of an object that does not yet exist. Doubles can be used to support a different style of testing, where the test is verifying the behavior of the system during the test rather than the state of the system at the end of the test.

Test doubles can be a bit of a contentious issue, with different people giving conflicting advice about the best way to use them when testing. I'd like to give you enough information to make informed decisions about who to agree with. (Though I hope you'll agree with me.) I'll start by looking at the mechanics of test doubles, using the rspec-mocks library. Then I'll discuss different ways to use doubles to solve both of the testing issues described at the start of this chapter. Later, in Chapter 12, *Minitest*, on page 241, I'll cover the basics of the Mocha mocking library for use with Minitest.

Test Doubles Defined

One complicating factor in dealing with test doubles is that pretty much everybody who creates a tool feels perfectly free to use slightly different naming conventions than everybody else. Here are the names I use, which are—of course—also the correct ones. (This naming structure is the creation of Gerard Meszaros in *xUnit Test Patterns [Mes07]*.)

The generic term for any object used as a stand-in for another object is *test double*, by analogy to "stunt double" and with the same connotation of a cheaper or more specialized replacement for a more expensive real object. Colloquially, *mock object* is also sometimes used as a generic term but, confusingly, is also the name of a specific type of test double.

A *fake* is typically an ordinary Ruby object that you define that is designed to be used only in tests. The fake matches the API of an object but has vastly simplified or canned internals. Fakes are not typically created using a test-double library, but might be custom-created for use in a specific context. A good example is the Fake Stripe gem,[1] which creates a fake instance of the Stripe server to intercept API calls in a test situation.

A *stub* is a fake object that returns a predetermined value for a method call without calling the actual method on an actual object. A stub can be a new object created only to be a stub, which you can create in RSpec using the double method. Alternatively, you can create a partial stub by stubbing a specific method on an existing object:

```
allow(thing).to receive(:name).and_return("Fred")
```

---

1.   https://github.com/thoughtbot/fake_stripe

That line of code says that if you call thing.name, you'll get Fred as a result. Crucially, the thing.name method is (by default) not touched, so whatever value the "real" method would return is not relevant; the Fred response comes from the stub, not the actual object. If thing.name is not called in the test, nothing happens.

A *mock* is similar to a stub, but in addition to returning the fake value, a mock object sets a testable expectation that the method being replaced will be called in the test. If the method is not called, the mock object triggers a test failure. You can write the following snippet to create a mocked method call instead of a stub, using expect instead of allow:

```
expect(thing).to receive(:name).and_return("Fred")
```

If you use the mock then call thing.name in your test, you still get Fred and the thing.name method is still untouched. But if you don't call thing.name in the test, the test fails with an unfulfilled-expectation error.

In other words, setting a stub on a method is passive and says, "Ignore the real implementation of this method and return this value," while setting a mock on a method is aggressive and says, "This method will return this value, and you better call the method, or else!"

Setting an expectation on whether a method is called allows you to test an object's behavior rather than its final state. Once you've stubbed a method, it makes no sense to write an assertion like this one:

```
allow(thing).to receive(:name).and_return("Fred")
expect(thing.name).to eq("Fred")
```

This test can't fail; you're just testing that the stub works as advertised. But if you do this:

```
expect(thing).to receive(:name).and_return("Fred")
```

the code is required to behave a certain way—namely, it has to call thing.name to pass the test.

A *spy* is a slight twist on a mock or stub. Generically, all that declaring a spy means is that the test-double package is watching the method. However, once you've declared a spy, you can then specify a testable expectation later in the test. Typically you would place the body of the test in between the declaration and the expectation. In RSpec, you can declare a spy the same way you would declare a stub:

```
allow(thing).to receive(:name).and_return("Fred")
# body of test
expect(thing).to have_received(:name)
```

In this test, the first line defines the stub and the last line sets the expectation. In RSpec, the method being spied on must be declared as a stub before you check to see if it has been received.

Using spies mitigates a common criticism of using test doubles, which is that mock expectations are implicit. It can be difficult to look at a test that sets mock expectations and understand what behavior is being tested. More to the point, it can be difficult to see why a test has failed. The spy explicitly declares the expected behavior. Spies are also more consistent with the given/when/then test structure you've used elsewhere, allowing the stub to be declared in the "given" section and the expectation to be set separately in the "then" part of the test.

Creating Stubs

A stub is a replacement for all or part of an object that prevents a normal method call from happening and instead returns a value that is preset when the stub is created. In RSpec, there are two kinds of stubs. You can create entire objects that exist only to be stubs, which we'll call *full doubles*, or you can stub specific methods of existing objects, which we'll call *partial doubles*.

A partial double is useful, for example, when you want to use a "real" ActiveRecord object but you have one or two dangerous or expensive methods you want to bypass. A full double is useful when you're testing that your code works with a specific API rather than a specific object. By passing in a generic object that responds to only certain methods, you make it hard for the code to assume anything about the structure of the objects being used by the code under test.

> Prescription 19   Use partial doubles when you want to ensure most of your real object behavior. Use full doubles when the behavior of the stubbed object doesn't matter—only its public interface does.

Full Doubles

In RSpec, you create full doubles with the double method, which is available anywhere. The double method takes an optional string argument, which is a name for the double, and then key/value pairs representing messages that can be sent to the double. Since Ruby uses duck typing—which is to say it cares not about the type of objects but only about whether objects respond to the messages sent to them—a stub object created in such a way can be inserted into your application as a replacement for a real object:

```
it "can create doubles" do
  twin = double(first_name: "Paul", weight: 100)
  expect(twin.first_name).to eq("Paul")
end
```

The assertion in the last line of the snippet is true because the stub has been preset to respond to the name message with "Paul." This spec is a bad way to use stubs. You've set up a nice little tautology and haven't learned anything about any larger system around this test.

The double method takes an optional hash argument, the keys being messages the stub will respond to and the values being the return values of those messages. These are stubbed methods, meaning that failure to use them will not trigger an error. Alternatively, you can use the same allow and expect methods on the double that you can on any other object. The following are equivalent:

```
twin = double(first_name: "Paul", weight: 100)
twin = double
allow(twin).to receive(first_name).and_return("Paul")
allow(twin).to receive(weight).and_return(100)
```

By default RSpec doubles are "strict," meaning that if you call the stub with a method that is not in the hash argument, RSpec will return an error. If that's not the behavior you want, RSpec provides the as_null_object method, which instead returns the double itself for methods not in the hash argument. Using as_null_object makes sense in the case where there's a large number of potential methods to be stubbed but where the values make so little difference that specifying them reduces the test's readability.

Null-object test doubles automatically spy on all methods, which is useful enough when using spies that RSpec provides spy(name) as an alternative method of writing double(name).as_null_object.

A common problem when using doubles is for the double and the object it is standing in for to drift apart. If the method name or signature changes in the real object, a test that only interacts with a double might not know, and no longer provides an accurate mirror of the real code. For this case, when you know your double needs to mimic a specific object, RSpec provides the concept of a *verifying* double. A verifying double checks to see whether messages passed to the double are real methods in the application. RSpec has a few methods to allow you to declare what to verify the double against:

```
instance_twin = instance_double("User")
instance_twin = instance_double(User)
class_twin = class_double("User")
class_twin = class_double(User)
object_twin = object_double(User.new)
```

Each of these three methods behaves slightly differently. The instance_double method takes a class or a string that is the name of a class. The resulting double only responds to methods that could be passed to an instance of that class. If you attempt to send the resulting double a method that is not implemented by that class, the test will error with a message that says something like "User does not implement method." The class_double method is similar but verifies against class methods on the existing class (or module), rather than instance methods. (Note that instance_double will not recognize methods defined via method_missing. When matching, instance_double uses method_defined? while class_double uses respond_to? on the class itself.)

If you want to verify against a class that has methods dynamically defined with method_missing, you can use object_double, which has an instance of the class as an argument and therefore allows RSpec to call respond_to? on that instance to determine whether the call to the stub is valid.

In addition to verifying the existence of the method, RSpec double verification ensures that the arguments passed to the method are valid. The doubled method will also have the same public/protected/private visibility as the original method.

If you use the string version of a constant name and the constant doesn't exist, RSpec will ignore the string and treat the double like a normal, unverified double. If you'd like a failure if you use a string constant name that doesn't exist, add the line mocks.verify_doubled_constant_names = true to the appropriate section in the spec_helper.rb file. (By default the section that manages mocks is wrapped in a multiline comment; you'll need to remove the comment lines.)

All three of these methods have spy forms—instance_spy, class_spy, and object_spy—which add as_null_object to the double, giving you verification that a method passed to the spy exists without having to specify a return value.

Partial Stubs

You might use a full double object to stand in for an entire object that is unavailable or prohibitively expensive to create or call in the test environment. You can also take advantage of the way Ruby allows you to open up existing classes and objects to add or override methods. It's easy to take a "real" object and stub out only the methods you need. This is extraordinarily useful when it comes to actual uses of stub objects.

In RSpec partial stubs are managed with the allow method:

```
          mocks/01/spec/models/project_spec.rb
Line 1    it "stubs an object" do
   2        project = Project.new(name: "Project Greenlight")
   3        allow(project).to receive(:name)
   4        expect(project.name).to be_nil
   5      end
```

This test passes. Line 3 sets up the stub, and the stub intercepts the project.name call in line 4 to return nil and never even gets to the project name. Note this is not a smart test; you're just verifying that the stubbing works.

If mocks.verify_partial_doubles = true is set in the spec_helper.rb configuration file, which should be the default, then partial doubles will also be verified, meaning the test will fail if the double is asked to stub a method the object doesn't respond to.

Having a stub that always returns nil is pointless, so RSpec allows you to specify a return value for the stubbed method using the following syntax:

```
          mocks/01/spec/models/project_spec.rb
Line 1    it "stubs an object again" do
   2        project = Project.new(name: "Project Greenlight")
   3        allow(project).to receive(:name).and_return("Fred")
   4        expect(project.name).to eq("Fred")
   5      end
```

Line 3 is doing the heavy lifting here, tying the return value Fred to the method :name. The allow method returns a proxy to the real object, which responds to a number of methods that let you annotate the stub. The and_return method is an annotation message that associates the return value with the method.

Since classes in Ruby are really just objects themselves, you can stub classes just like you can instance objects:

```
          mocks/01/spec/models/project_spec.rb
Line 1    it "stubs the class" do
   2        allow(Project).to receive(:find).and_return(
   3          Project.new(name: "Project Greenlight"))
   4        project = Project.find(1)
   5        expect(project.name).to eq("Project Greenlight")
   6      end
```

In this test, the class Project is being stubbed to return a specific project instance whenever find is called. In the last line of the spec the find method is, in fact, called, and returns that object.

Let's pause here and examine what you've done in this test. You're using the find method to get an ActiveRecord object. And because you're stubbing find, you're not touching the actual database. Using the database is, for testing purposes, slow. Very slow. Using test doubles to stub database access is one strategy for avoiding the database for the purpose of speeding up tests. In the meantime, remember that this stub shouldn't be used to verify that the find method works; it should be used by other tests that need the find method along the way to the logic that is under test. For instance, this can be used to ensure that a controller that is accessing the database gets an instance that is controlled by the test.

That said, in practice you also should avoid stubbing the find method because it's part of an external library—you might be better off creating a model method that has a more meaningful and specific behavior and stubbing that method.

On a related note, if you wanted to create multiple partial stubs from the same class and have them all behave the same way, you could do so with the method allow_any_instance_of, as you see here:

```
allow_any_instance_of(Project).to receive(:save).and_return(false)
```

This snippet causes any instance of Project that is created to return false when saved. In other words, it simulates a failure condition.

You should use allow_any_instance_of very sparingly, as it often implies you don't really understand what the underlying code is doing or where objects might come from. However, when you're testing legacy code you may genuinely not know where the object comes from, and allow_any_instance_of might be a lesser evil. Also, sometimes framework concerns in Rails make using allow_any_instance_of easier than managing the set of objects that might be returned by some distant method. In either case, though, consider the possibility of refactoring the code or test to avoid allow_any_instance_of. The RSpec docs explicitly recommend not using this feature if possible, since it is "the most complicated feature of rspec-mocks, and has historically received the most bug reports."

> **Prescription 20** The use of the allow_any_instance_of stub modifier often means the underlying code being tested could be refactored with a more useful method to stub.

A common use of stub objects is to simulate failure and exception conditions. If you want your stubbed method to raise an exception, you can use the and_raise method, which takes an exception class and an optional message:

```
allow(stubby).to receive(:user_count).and_raise(Exception, "oops")
```

Mock Expectations

A mock object retains the basic idea of the stub—returning a specified value without actually calling a live method—and adds the requirement that the specified method must be called during the test. A mock is like a stub with attitude, expecting—nay, demanding—that its parameters be matched in the test or else you get a test failure.

In RSpec, you use the expect method to create mock expectations. This can be applied to full or partial doubles:

```ruby
it "expects stuff" do
  mocky = double("Mock")
  expect(mocky).to receive(:name).and_return("Paul")
  expect(mocky).to receive(:weight).and_return(100)
  expect(mocky.name).to eq("Paul")
end
```

This test fails:

```
Failures:
  1) Project expects stuff
     Failure/Error: expect(mocky).to receive(:weight).and_return(100)
       (Double "Mock").weight(any args)
           expected: 1 time with any arguments
           received: 0 times with any arguments
```

The test sets up two mock expectations, mocky.name and mocky.weight, but only one of those two mocked methods is called in the test. Hence, it's an unsatisfied expectation. To make the test pass, add a call to mocky.weight:

```ruby
it "expects stuff" do
  mocky = double("Mock")
  expect(mocky).to receive(:name).and_return("Paul")
  expect(mocky).to receive(:weight).and_return(100)
  expect(mocky.name).to eq("Paul")
  expect(mocky.weight).to eq(100)
end
```

This also works for existing objects:

mocks/01/spec/models/project_spec.rb
```ruby
it "mocks an object" do
  mock_project = Project.new(name: "Project Greenlight")
  expect(mock_project).to receive(:name).and_return("Fred")
  expect(mock_project.name).to eq("Fred")
end
```

All the modifiers you've seen so far, such as and_return and and_raise, as well as ones you haven't seen, such as with, can be added to a mock just like they can to a stub.

By default, the expects method sets a validation that the associated method is called exactly once during the test. In case that does not meet your testing needs, RSpec has methods that let you specify the number of calls to the method. These methods are largely self-explanatory:

```
proj = Project.new
expect(proj).to receive(:name).once
expect(proj).to receive(:name).twice
expect(proj).to receive(:name).at_least(:once)
expect(proj).to receive(:name).at_least(:twice)
expect(proj).to receive(:name).at_least(n).times
expect(proj).to receive(:name).at_most(:once)
expect(proj).to receive(:name).at_most(:twice)
expect(proj).to receive(:name).at_most(n).times
expect(proj).not_to receive(:name)
```

In practice, the default behavior is good for most usages (I'd worry if I started needing these decorators a lot), though not_to is sometimes useful to guarantee that a particular expensive method is not called. Note that a stub is equivalent to a mock expectation defined with at_least(0).times.

Using Mocks to Simulate Database Failure

A common use case for test doubles in Rails is to simulate database failures. Let's look at how you might do that.

In the past, I would have suggested testing for failure at the controller level. However, Rails has basically deprecated controller tests for reasons I'll talk about in Chapter 11, *Testing Rails Display Elements*, on page 217, and so I'd like to stay within the bounds of Rails community behavior.

Let's look at the project-creation functionality you wrote at the beginning of the book. You wrote a controller:

```
mocks/01/app/controllers/projects_controller.rb
def create
  @workflow = CreatesProject.new(
    name: params[:project][:name],
    task_string: params[:project][:tasks])
  @workflow.create
  if @workflow.success?
    redirect_to projects_path
```

```
    else
      @project = @workflow.project
      render :new
    end
  end
end
```

The controller largely defers to a workflow object that does the actual work:

```
mocks/01/app/workflows/creates_project.rb
class CreatesProject
  attr_accessor :name, :project, :task_string

  def initialize(name: "", task_string: "")
    @name = name
    @task_string = task_string || ""
    @success = false
  end

  def success?
    @success
  end

  def build
    self.project = Project.new(name: name)
    project.tasks = convert_string_to_tasks
    project
  end

  def create
    build
    result = project.save
    @success = result
  end

  def convert_string_to_tasks
    task_string.split("\n").map do |one_task|
      title, size_string = one_task.split(":")
      Task.new(title: title, size: size_as_integer(size_string))
    end
  end

  def size_as_integer(size_string)
    return 1 if size_string.blank?
    [size_string.to_i, 1].max
  end
end
```

Now you have two different pieces of point-of-failure logic to deal with:

- In the event of a database failure, the workflow object should behave gracefully and return the fact that the creation did not succeed.

- In the event the workflow doesn't succeed, the controller redirects to redisplay the form.

The interesting thing here is that in theory, the workflow could fail for a variety of reasons (most likely in this case a validation failure or a networking error reaching the database), but no matter how the workflow fails, the controller responds in basically the same way: redirect and display an error message.

Because the controller's response is consistent—you only need to test at the controller level for one error response—you can test for different error cases at the workflow level. This is great because the workflow test is likely to be much faster than the integration test, so having multiple workflow tests is better for the system's runtime.

```
mocks/01/spec/workflows/creates_project_spec.rb
describe "mocking a failure" do
  it "fails when we say it fails" do
    project = instance_spy(Project, save: false)
    allow(Project).to receive(:new).and_return(project)
    creator = CreatesProject.new(name: "Name", task_string: "Task")
    creator.create
    expect(creator).not_to be_a_success
  end
end
```

Let's think about this test from a given/when/then perspective:

- Given: The test needs some way to simulate failure. In the earlier tutorial, you used a set of form values that were invalid. In this case you'll use a stub. The tricky part is that you need to make sure your stubbed project is the actual project instance that gets used in the workflow. Since the workflow creates its own instance, this is a little tricky, which is why you need to both create an instance_spy for the project and stub the Project class to return the spy when it receives a new message. Another way to do this would be to use allow_any_instance_of(Project). You also might see the use of *dependency injection*, where the behavior of CreatesProject creating an instance of Project would be set as a variable at runtime—usually something like def initialize(initialize(name: "", task_string: "", class_to_create: Project). Allowing the class to be specified dynamically allows the use of a class double or fake class in testing.

- When: The "when" action in this test is the create call on the workflow. When the ActiveRecord save happens inside the CreatesProject object, you need to simulate a save failure.

- Then: The temptation is to test that new objects are not created and existing objects are not updated. It makes no sense to test that the spy doesn't get saved. It can't get saved; it's not an ActiveRecord model. Instead, the test needs to make sure the workflow correctly returns its lack of success. Implicitly, you're also testing that the database failure doesn't trigger another error.

The feature spec has the same basic structure, but actually fills out a form. I should say here that you need to be careful about using test doubles with integration tests. The whole point of integration tests is that they cover how objects fit together, so using test doubles potentially weakens the tests. There are cases, though, where an error condition is just easier to simulate with a test double than with user activity. For example, this test simulates a failure of the CreatesProject workflow:

```
mocks/01/spec/system/add_project_spec.rb
it "behaves correctly in the face of a surprising database failure" do
  workflow = instance_spy(CreatesProject,
    success?: false, project: Project.new)
  allow(CreatesProject).to receive(:new)
    .with(name: "Real Name",
          task_string: "Choose Fabric:3\r\nMake it Work:5")
    .and_return(workflow)
  visit new_project_path
  fill_in "Name", with: "Real Name"
  fill_in "Tasks", with: "Choose Fabric:3\nMake it Work:5"
  click_on("Create Project")
  expect(page).to have_selector(".new_project")
end
```

You do the same dance here, setting up a spy to sit in for the workflow object and making sure that the new method returns it. The spy sets success? to fail, and specifies a return value project, since for Rails-internal reasons, the form on the "new" page needs an actual ActiveRecord. You also use the with modifier to make sure the controller is sending the right values to the workflow. If you specify allow and with on a method, and you send arguments that don't match the with arguments and the test fails, you don't fall through to the original method.

As you find other error conditions, try to specify them in the workflow-level test, because workflow errors should not leak out of the workflow object other than to have the workflow object report that it was not successful.

Using Mocks to Specify Behavior

In addition to merely replacing expensive method calls, test doubles enable a different style of testing where you validate the application's behavior rather than its ending state. In most of the tests you've seen throughout the book, the test validates the result of a computation: it's testing whether something is true at the end of an action. When using doubles, however, you have the opportunity to test the process's behavior during the test rather than the outcome.

Often, this kind of test makes sense given a relatively complex set of object interactions. You don't exactly have that here, but you can use your controller as a reasonable stand-in. Some features of controller tests are deprecated in Rails 5, but you won't touch any of the deprecated features and you'll test the controller as its own unit, without dependencies on any other code. I think using test doubles is still a potentially valid way of unit-testing logic in controllers.

Traditional controller tests—the deprecated kind—often test whether the controller is setting a particular instance variable to pass off to the view and giving it a value matching the incoming data. However, given the way you've written the controller, the specific values are the workflow's responsibility. The controller is acting as merely a conduit. Its job is to get the value from some data source and pass it on. Using the controller test to verify the workflow or view behavior leads to brittle tests.

What is the controller's responsibility? The controller is just a traffic cop. If you test that the controller sets an instance variable, you're testing the output of the conduit. The input of the conduit, though, is verified not by the state of the variable at the end of the controller call, but by the way that value is obtained. In other words, the controller's responsibility is to meet a contract on both ends —it's responsible for setting a particular value to satisfy the view, and it's responsible for calling some other place in the system to acquire data.

Specifically, the controller calls CreatesProject.new and then calls create on the resulting action. Leave the responsibility of verifying that CreatesProject accurately creates a project to the tests for that object (tests you wrote when you added the CreatesProject functionality). All you need to do here is specify that the controller calls the appropriate methods.

Enter mocks. Mock objects are used to set an expectation for the controller's behavior during the user action. This will look similar to the failure test from the last section, but I'm going to emphasize a different part of the test:

mocks/01/spec/controllers/projects_controller_spec.rb
```ruby
require "rails_helper"

RSpec.describe ProjectsController, type: :controller do

  describe "create" do
    it "calls the workflow with parameters" do
      workflow = instance_spy(CreatesProject, success?: true)
      allow(CreatesProject).to receive(:new).and_return(workflow)
```

```
    post :create,
      params: {project: {name: "Runway", tasks: "start something:2"}}
    expect(CreatesProject).to have_received(:new)
      .with(name: "Runway", task_string: "start something:2")
  end

 end

end
```

On the first two lines the doubles are created. You need to do this in two steps because the controller both instantiates a CreatesProject object and calls create on it. The power of this test is in the mock expectations. You're validating all of the following:

- That the controller calls CreatesProject.new

- That the call passes a name and a task_string as key/value pairs based on the incoming parameters

- That the controller calls create on the return value of CreatesProject.new

That's a fairly detailed description of the controller's responsibilities.

This test makes only a minimal attempt to validate the objects outside of the controller. The use of instance_double to create the test double guarantees the test will fail if the controller calls a method on the action item that doesn't exist, but makes no other claim about what the action item does. That's great in that a bug in CreatesProject will trigger only one test failure, making it easier to track down. But it's terrifying in that it's possible for this test to pass without the underlying code working.

Because it is possible to have tests pass due only to mismatches between the API and the test double, generally I do this kind of testing based on setting mock expectations only if there is a separate integration test tying together all the small, focused unit tests.

A plus for this test, however, is speed. Since it doesn't contact the model layer, it's probably going to be fast.

A downside is readability. It can be hard to look at a mocked test and determine exactly what is being validated. Using spies can help here because spies force you to be explicit about the expectations you're claiming in the test at the end of the test, where you normally see test expectations.

Finally, an elaborate edifice of mocked methods runs the risk of causing the test to depend on very specific details of the method structure of the object being mocked. This can make the test brittle in the face of refactorings that might change the object's methods. Good API design and an awareness of this potential problem go a long way toward mitigating the issue.

You could easily have made this test far more brittle if you'd started to worry about tasks being part of projects:

```
it "don't do this" do
  fake_action = double(create: true,
    project: double(name: "Fred", tasks: [double(title: "Start", size: 2)]))
    # and so on …
```

In this snippet, fake_action isn't merely concerned with reporting success; it also wants to stub the project and have the project stub the array of tasks. This is where test doubles become a pain. The preceding snippet is hard to set up, it's hard to read, and it's brittle against changes to object internals. If you find yourself needing to write nested mocks like this, try to restructure your code to reduce dependencies.

> **Prescription 21**
>
> A stubbed method that returns a stub is usually okay. A stubbed method that returns a stub that itself contains a stub probably means your code is too dependent on the internals of other objects.

More Expectation Annotations

RSpec allows a number of different annotations to the expectation part of declaring a test double. You can specify more complex return values or a variety of arguments to the stubbed method.

Stubbing Return Values

A couple of advanced usages of returns might be valuable now and again. If you've multiple return values specified, the stubbed method returns one at a time:

```
mocks/01/spec/models/task_spec.rb
it "stubs with multiple return values" do
  task = Task.new
  allow(task).to receive(:size).and_return(1, 2)
  assert_equal(1, task.size)
  assert_equal(2, task.size)
  assert_equal(2, task.size)
end
```

The return values of the stubbed method walk through the values passed to and_return. Note that the values don't cycle; the last value is repeated over and over again.

RSpec can do a couple of other useful things with return values. If the method being stubbed takes a block and you want to cause the stubbed method to yield a particular set of arguments to the block, you can do so with and_yield:

```
`allow(project).to receive(:method).and_yield("arg")`
```

The expectation is that some method takes a block argument, and you want to pass through method and send arg to the block.

You can also cause the original method to be called as normal with and_call_original. You might use and_call_original if you're just spying on the method to see if it is called but you want the original return value for some reason. Alternatively, you can use it in conjunction with with to specify default behavior for most arguments and special behavior for some arguments. More rarely, there's and_wrap_original, which takes a block argument and runs the return value of the original method through the block before continuing.

Finally, you can pass a block to receive, in which case the block is executed to be the method's value:

```
first_name = "Noel"
last_name = "Rappin"
allow(project).to receive(:name) { first_name + last_name }
```

In theory this gives you some flexibility to manage the method's output. In practice it may mean it's time to abandon RSpec mocks in favor of a dummy object via OpenStruct, or that it's time to rethink the code design.

Mocks with Arguments

You can tune an RSpec double to return different values based on the parameters passed to the method using the with method to filter incoming calls. In its simplest form, shown earlier in the chapter, the with method takes one or more arguments. When the stubbed method is called, RSpec searches for a match between the arguments passed and the declared double and returns the value matching those arguments. Take care; by setting expectations tied to specific input values, you're limiting the RSpec double to only those input values. For instance, the earlier example of stubbing methods calls find(1). If you change the double to expect a different number, the test will fail:

```
it "stubs the class" do
  allow(Project).to receive(:find).with(3).and_return(
      Project.new(:name => "Project Greenlight"))
  project = Project.find(1)
  expect(project.name).to eq("Project Greenlight")
end
```

Here with(3) was added to the double declaration, leading to this:

```
1) Project stubs the class
   Failure/Error: project = Project.find(1)
     <Project(id: integer, name: string, due_date: date, created_at: datetime,
       updated_at: datetime) (class)> received :find with unexpected arguments
       expected: (3)
            got: (1)
       Please stub a default value first if message
           might be received with other args as well.
```

This message is saying that RSpec doesn't know what to do if find is called with the argument 1, but it would know what to do with the argument 3. In other words, you did something RSpec didn't expect, and RSpec doesn't like surprises.

You can have multiple stubs of the same method that use with to expect different arguments and return different values. As implied by the last line of the preceding error message, a stub without a with argument is considered a default and is used if nothing else matches:

```
it "stubs the class" do
  allow(Project).to receive(:find).with(1).and_return(
      Project.new(:name => "Project Greenlight"))
  allow(Project).to receive(:find).with(3).and_return(
      Project.new(:name => "Project Runway"))
  allow(Project).to receive(:find).and_raise(ActiveRecord::RecordNotFound)
  project = Project.find(1)
  expect(project.name).to eq("Project Greenlight")
end
```

Using with does not constrain the eventual return value. You can use either returns or raises after a with call.

Be careful here—using with makes RSpec powerful and flexible, but in general, testing with mock objects works best if they are weak and rigid. The use of a complicated mock object suggests the existence of an overly complex dependency in your code.

Many of these matchers make more sense when you're talking about mock expectations rather than just stubs. When you're actually validating the behavior of the object being mocked, having a tighter filter on the incoming values you expect makes more sense.

RSpec allows you to use many things besides literal values as the arguments to a with call. Here are a few:

- If you expect the method to be called with no arguments, use with(no_args).

- If you don't care what an argument is as long as it's there, use anything, as in with("foo", anything).

- Any Ruby object that implements triple equal (===) can be used and will match anything it's === to. This will most commonly be regular expressions, such as with(/\d{3}/), but could also be classes or Proc objects.

- A hash that includes a particular key can be matched with with(hash_including(key: value)).

- Any RSpec matcher can be used.

Many of these arguments are actually RSpec matchers that are being used to match against potential arguments to a double in the same way they match against expectations. You can see a full list in the RSpec documentation.[2]

Mock Tips

My opinion about the best way to use mock objects changes every few months. I'll try some mocks, they'll work well, I'll start using more mocks, they'll start getting in the way, I'll back off, and then I'll think, "Let's try some mocks." This cycle has been going for years, and I have no reason to think it's going to change anytime soon.

That said, some guidelines always hold true.

The Ownership Rule

Don't mock what you don't own. Use test doubles only to replace methods that are part of your application, and not part of an external framework. (Note that you violated this rule in this chapter when you stubbed ActiveRecord methods like update_attributes.)

> Prescription 22 Don't mock what you don't own.

One reason to mock only methods you control is, well, you control them. One danger in mocking methods is that your mock either doesn't receive or doesn't return a reasonable value from the method being replaced. If the method in question belongs to a third-party framework, the chance that it will change without you knowing increases and thus the test becomes more brittle.

More important, mocking a method you don't own couples your test to the internal details of the third-party framework. By implication, this means the

---

2. https://relishapp.com/rspec/rspec-mocks/v/3-6/docs/setting-constraints/matching-arguments

method being tested is also coupled to those internal details. That is bad, not just if the third-party tool changes, but also if you want to refactor your code; the dependency will make that change more complicated.

The solution, in most cases, is to create a method or class in your application that calls the third-party tool and stubs that method (while also writing tests to ensure that the wrapper does the right thing). You'll see a larger example of this technique in Chapter 14, *Testing External Services*, on page 285. However, in a smaller case you can do this easily as follows:

```
class Project
  def self.create_from_controller(params)
    create(params)
  end
end
```

And then in a test:

```
it "creates a project" do
  allow(Project).to receive(:create_from_controller).and_return(Project.new)
end
```

I admit that, oversimplified like this, the technique seems like overkill. (All object-oriented techniques seem like overkill until you suddenly realize you needed them six months ago.) If you create a method like this wrapper, however, you'll often find that the functionality is shared in multiple places, giving you one point of contact with the third-party tool rather than several. You'll also find that these methods attract what would otherwise be duplicated behavior. Both of these are good things.

When to Mock, When to Stub

If you're using your test doubles to take the place of real objects that are hard or impossible to create in a test environment, it's probably a good idea to use stubs rather than mocks. If you're using the fake value as an input to a different process, then you should test that process directly using the fake value rather than a mock. Adding the mock expectation just gives you another thing that can break, which in this use case is probably not related to what you're testing.

On the other hand, if you're testing the relationship between different systems of your code, you should tend to use mocks to verify the behavior of one part of the code as it calls the other.

Mocks are particularly good at testing across boundaries between subsystems—for example, controller testing to isolate the controller test from the behavior of the model, essentially only testing that the controller makes a specific model call and using the model test to verify model behavior. Among the benefits of using mocks this way is that you're encouraged to make the interface between your controllers and models as simple as possible. However, it does mean that the controller test knows more about your model than it otherwise might, which may make the model code harder to change.

Also be careful of mocking methods that have side effects or that call other methods that might be interesting. The mock bypasses the original method, which means no side effect and no calling the internal method.

Pro tip: saving to the database and outputting to the response stream are both side effects.

Be cautious if you're specifying a value as a result of a mock and then asserting the existence of the very same value. One of the biggest potential problems with any test suite is false positives, and testing results with mocked values is an easy way to generate false positives!

Mocks Are Design Canaries

Test-driven development in general and mock objects in particular are sensitive indicators of your application code's quality. As the code becomes more complex and tightly coupled, the tests become harder and harder to write.

When you're using a true mock to encapsulate a test and isolate it from methods that are not under test, try to limit the number of methods you're mocking in one test. The more mocks, the more vulnerable the test will be to changes in the actual code. Having a lot of mocks may indicate that your test is trying to do too much, or it might point to a poor object-oriented design where one class is asking for too many details of a different class.

What You've Done

You've learned a lot about model testing—about the services Rails provides for testing models, and fixtures and factories as mechanisms for creating consistent test data. With this chapter you've started to transition from testing models to testing the user-facing parts of the application. Mock testing is useful for testing models, but it becomes especially useful when trying to shield the various layers of your application from each other.

In the next section you'll learn about testing the controller and view layers. Mock objects can be an important part of controller testing; creating mock models allows the controller tests to proceed independently of the model test.

CHAPTER 8

Integration Testing with Capybara and Cucumber

You spent the last few chapters focusing on testing the models and business logic of your Rails application. A web application is more than just business logic, though, so for the next few chapters, I'm going to talk about tests that tackle the parts of your application that either respond to user input or output data to the user.

There's a lot of different terminology used to describe the various flavors of input and output tests you can write. First, there are generic terms that are not inherent to Rails, but are terms you might apply to any kind of testing:

- An *integration* test is any test that covers more than one part of the application working together.

- An *end-to-end* test is a specific kind of integration test that covers the entire behavior of the system from, well, end to end.

- An *acceptance* test is written to specify correct behavior from the customer or business perspective. Acceptance tests are often written (or at least planned) before coding even begins.

Within Rails-land, there is a significant functional distinction between integration tests that only use Rails and evaluate the results of a Rails call, and those that also use a JavaScript driver to evaluate JavaScript based on simulated user actions. In this chapter you'll see the non-JavaScript versions; in the next, you'll learn how to add JavaScript client behavior.

A Field Guide to Integration and System Tests

There are a lot of different names for a lot of specific kinds of tests:

- The Rails core testing library defines two similar types of end-to-end tests: *integration tests* and *system tests*. System tests, which were new in Rails 5.1, require the Capybara gem to simulate user interaction with the application and to query application output.[1] Integration tests, which have always been a part of Rails, also simulate user interaction, but use a Rails-specific API that is less complete than Capybara. (To make it more confusing, you can add Capybara for use in integration tests if you want.)

- RSpec defines basically the same kind of tests but gives them different names. RSpec has *system* tests that are wrappers around the Rails core system tests. Historically, most RSpec users wrote *feature* specs, which are end-to-end tests that typically use Capybara. RSpec also has *request* specs, which are basically wrappers around Rails integration tests.

In addition, both RSpec and Rails/Minitest provide tools for specifically testing controllers, views, mailers, background jobs, and helpers. The following table helps sort out the naming.

Test Input	Test Evaluates	Common Name	Minitest Name	RSpec Name
User clicks via Capybara	HTML output	Integration	n/a	System (formerly feature)
User clicks via Capybara with JavaScript	HTML output	Integration	System	System (formerly feature)
URL for routing	HTML output	Integration	Integration	Request
Controller and action	Controller behavior	Controller	Controller	Controller

In RSpec, whether the test uses a JavaScript driver depends not on the kind of test you write, but on the driver you configure when you start the test. My best understanding of expected practice currently is that the Rails core team recommends using Capybara and system tests only if you're also evaluating code that requires JavaScript, and otherwise recommends the non-Capybara integration tests. The RSpec-Rails team, on the other hand, recommends the use of Capybara in system tests whether the test uses JavaScript or not.

---

1.   https://github.com/teamcapybara/capybara

Let's start in RSpec-land. Here I'll talk about the RSpec and Capybara system specs, rather than the RSpec request specs based on Rails integration tests. (Chapter 11, *Testing Rails Display Elements*, on page 217, is where you'll learn about request specs.) RSpec system specs attempt to simulate user interaction. The input to the test is typically a URL to visit, followed by simulated form fills and button clicks. The output from the test is the resulting HTML, against which the test typically searches for specific DOM selectors or text. The tests I'll talk about in this section do not interact with client-side JavaScript; in Chapter 9, *Testing JavaScript: Integration Testing*, on page 181, I'll talk about how to use feature specs to interact with a JavaScript runtime.

Setting Up Capybara

Capybara allows an automated test to simulate a user interaction with a browser. When simulating this interaction, Capybara works in conjunction with a driver, using the simple Capybara API to determine what elements to interact with and using the driver to manage the actual interaction. By default, Capybara uses a native Ruby library that doesn't manage JavaScript interactions, but it can be configured to use a headless browser such as PhantomJS, headless Chrome, or Selenium to allow JavaScript interactions to be simulated.

Capybara and RSpec

Capybara is part of the default Rails Gemfile in Rails 5.1 and later. If you're using an earlier version, add Capybara to your Gemfile's test group:

```
gem "capybara"
```

In either case, there's a useful tool called capybara-screenshot that takes virtual screenshots of any Capybara test failure.[2] Again, add capybara-screenshot in the Gemfile's test group of your Gemfile:

```
gem "capybara-screenshot"
```

Although Capybara is already available, there's a little setup needed to enable capybara-screenshot in RSpec. In a file in the spec.support directory add this:

```
integration/01/spec/support/system.rb
RSpec.configure do |config|
  config.before(:each, type: :system) do
    driven_by :rack_test
  end
end

require "capybara-screenshot/rspec"
```

---

2. https://github.com/mattheworiordan/capybara-screenshot

The first part specifies that system tests should use Rack::Test, which is Capybara's internal Ruby driver, the one without RSpec. This setup is specific to Rails 5.1 and RSpec 3.7 and later. The second part sets you up to have capybara-screenshot available in your specs.

Capybara and Its Own language

At this point you're forced to confront another library syntax decision. Capybara defines its validations mostly as things that look like RSpec matchers. It also defines its own optional integration-test syntax, similar to RSpec but with terms like feature and scenario to drive home the integration-testing point.

All of this adds up to a lot of different ways to express the same test. In the interest of minimizing the amount of time I spend talking about syntax, which is the least interesting thing I could be talking about, I'll stick to the same basic RSpec syntax you've been using in most of the book. Keep in mind that the other forms exist; that way when your coworker shows you her Capybara tests, you know how to read them.

Why are there so many kinds of tests? There are basically three reasons:

- *Functionality.* Because the different kinds of tests cover different parts of the process, they are useful for different kinds of code.

- *Taste.* Some people like writing unit tests for mailers, helpers, and the like, while others prefer to create coverage with end-to-end tests. If you're David Heinemeier Hansson, your taste preferences can lead to significant features of controller tests being deprecated.

- *Genuine tool improvement over time.* The Capybara system tests are easier to write and understand than the original Rails integration tests.

Later in this chapter you'll learn about RSpec's system and feature, and take a look at Cucumber, a different tool for running integration tests.

Using Feature Tests to Build a Feature

When last you left your application, you allowed for the creation of new projects. Let's follow up on that and add a sequence where you can see a page for an existing project and add a task to it. To give this a little bit of back-end logic to play with, let's set up a situation where the tasks are ordered and then move one task above the other task.

Writing a Test

This test has a few parts. Let's take a second to plan the given/when/then:

- Given: You'll need one existing project and at least one existing task on that project so that you can test the ordering. You'll probably want two tasks; that way you can verify that the user interface is correct for the first, last, and middle parts of the list.

- When/then: The user fills out the form for the task and you verify that the new task shows up.

- When/then: The user moves a task up and you verify the order changes.

The fact that you have two distinct when/then pairs suggests this is probably two tests, but for ease of explanation let's keep it as one and see how it looks:

integration/01/spec/system/add_task_spec.rb
```ruby
require "rails_helper"

RSpec.describe "adding a new task" do
  let!(:project) { create(:project, name: "Project Bluebook") }
  let!(:task_1) { create(
    :task, project: project, title: "Search Sky", size: 1) }
  let!(:task_2) { create(
    :task, project: project, title: "Use Telescope", size: 1) }

  it "can add and reorder a task" do
    visit(project_path(project))
    fill_in("Task", with: "Find UFOs")
    select("2", from: "Size")
    click_on("Add Task")
    expect(current_path).to eq(project_path(project))
    within("#task_3") do
      expect(page).to have_selector(".name", text: "Find UFOs")
      expect(page).to have_selector(".size", text: "2")
      expect(page).not_to have_selector("a", text: "Down")
      click_on("Up")
    end
    expect(current_path).to eq(project_path(project))
    within("#task_2") do
      expect(page).to have_selector(".name", text: "Find UFOs")
    end
  end

end
```

The test is kind of long and rambling. It also doesn't completely test the UI, in the sense that it's not validating that all the "Up" and "Down" links that are supposed to be there are actually there—you might do that in a helper or decorator test later on, after you get this one passing. It walks through the interaction, conveniently touching a significant part of the Capybara API.

Let's go through the Capybara API, looking at the Capybara method calls you use in this test and then exploring related methods. Then we'll go through the rest of the process and make the test pass.

The Capybara API: Navigating

Capybara has one method to navigate to arbitrary routes in your system, and it's the first line of your test: visit(project_path(project)). The visit method takes one argument, which is a string URL (in this case, a Rails routing method that returns a string URL). The route generated by the visit method is always an HTTP GET. If you want to simulate a POST or any other kind of HTTP method, the recommended mechanism in Capybara is to navigate to a link or form button on the web page that triggers the desired interaction.

The Capybara API: Interacting

After the test hits the project_path URL, you start to use Capybara methods to interact with the elements on the page. Specifically, you use the fill_in method to place text in a text field, then the select method to choose an option from a select menu, and finally the click_on method to click on a button and submit a form.

Capybara is quite flexible in how it allows you to specify the element you want to work with. You can specify any element by its DOM ID. Form elements can also be specified by their name attribute. Form elements that have attached label tags can be specified by the attached label's text. Elements like HTML anchor tags that have internal text can be specified via that text. An HTML anchor tag whose body is an image can be located by the image's alt text attribute.

In other words, if you have an HTML snippet like this:

```
<form>
  <label for="user_email">Email</label>
  <input name="user[email]" id="user_email" />
</form>
```

You can use Capybara to access that form element with any of the following:

```
fill_in("user_email", with: "noel@noelrappin.com")
fill_in("user[email]", with: "noel@noelrappin.com")
fill_in("Email", with: "noel@noelrappin.com")
```

The first one uses the DOM ID, the second uses the form name, and the third uses the label text.

By default, Capybara matches on a substring of the name or label, not just the entire string, so you could also use "em" as a matcher should you want to. If more than one element matches a locator, Capybara raises an error. If you want an exact match rather than a substring match, pass the option exact: true to any Capybara method that uses a locator.

Which lookup text should you use? It depends on your goals and your context. The label text will usually result in the most readable test. But it's also the most fragile since the user-facing text is most likely to change. In contrast, the DOM ID is probably the most opaque in the test but the least likely to change on a whim.

Here are the Capybara form-interaction methods.[3] First, the ones you'll probably use a lot:

check(locator)

> This asserts that locator finds a check box, and checks it.

choose(locator)

> This is the same as check, but for radio buttons. Other radio buttons in the group are unchecked.

fill_in(locator, with: "TEXT")

> The locator is expected to find a text area or an input text field, and places the value of the with option inside it. Technically the second argument is a generic options hash, but the only option that is unique to this method is with. There are some other options you can pass that are common to all these methods, like the exact option I talked about a moment ago.

select(value, from: locator)

> The method arguments are similar here in that the second argument is technically an options hash, but the only usable option is from. It looks for a select menu that matches the locator passed to the from argument, and sets its value to the first argument. For what it's worth, the fact that fill_in takes its locator argument first and select takes the locator second drives me bananas.

click_on(locator)

> Finds an anchor link or button via the locator and simulates clicking it.

---

3.   http://www.rubydoc.info/github/teamcapybara/capybara/master

Then there are a few methods you'll probably use less often:

attach_file(locator, path)
> This looks for a form-file upload element that matches the locator, and simulates attaching the file at the given path to the form.

click_button(locator)
click_link(locator)
> These are like click_on but work only for a button or a link.

uncheck(locator)
> This unchecks a check box specified by the locator.

unselect(value, from: locator)
> This method unselects the value from the select box being specified by the locator. This one is most useful for multivalue select boxes. For a single-value select box, all you need to do to deselect a value is select the new value.

The Capybara API: Querying

Capybara has a few methods designed to allow you to query the simulated browser page to check for various selector patterns in the page. This is one case where the syntax differs slightly between Minitest and RSpec.

Here the method current_url is used, which returns as a complete string the current URL that the simulated user is viewing. That's useful for testing whether your navigation links take you where they should.

The most common query method in Capybara is written as the matcher have_selector in RSpec, and as assert_selector in Minitest. The two are identical in functionality. By default, Capybara looks for a CSS selector matching the argument to the query method, using the common # shortcut for DOM ID and a dot (.) for DOM class. The assertion passes if the selector is found.

The Capybara query methods, including have_selector, take options that limit whether a selector with the given HTML tag, DOM class, and/or ID matches. These are the most commonly used:

- count. If you expect the selector to appear more than once you can specify exactly how many times, as in count: 3. You can also use minimum and maximum as options, and use a range with between: (1 .. 3)

- text. This takes a string or a regular expression and matches if the text of the selector either contains the text or matches the regular expression.

(There's also exact_text, which just takes a string and requires the string to match the text of the selector exactly).

- visible. By default, Capybara only matches visible elements, but you can change that behavior with visible: :hidden, or visible: :all. (The latter finds all elements regardless of visible state.)

You can augment have_selector in a number of ways. The selector argument to have_selector can be just an element, as in div, or an element plus a class or ID decoration, as in div.hidden. In the latter case, a matching element must have both the HTML tag and the DOM class or ID. As with other DOM selectors, a dot (.) indicates a DOM class and a hash mark (#) indicates a DOM ID. You can also use brackets to indicate arbitrary HTML attributes, as in input[name='email']. The Capybara docs have more details; in particular, see the description of the all method.[4]

If you want to specify that a given selector does not exist on the page, in RSpec you can use either not_to have_selector or to have_no_selector, which are equivalent. In Minitest, though, you must use assert_no_selector.

Our test first uses have_selector to validate that .name and .size elements exist and match any options given. Capybara has some other methods you might use that are less powerful or flexible than have_selector, such as have_text and has_link?.

Our test also uses the within method, which takes a selector argument and a block. Capybara expects the selector passed to within to match a single element on the page. Inside the block argument, any Capybara call is scoped to only find or assert against the contents of that element. So, the part of your test that looks like this:

```
within("#task_2") do
  expect(page).to have_selector(".name", text: "Find UFOs")
end
```

will pass only if there is a .name element inside the #task_2 element. This can also be written as expect(page).to have_selector("#task_2 .name", text: "Cast the designers"), though I find that form a little flaky and hard to read.

Finally, the most useful Capybara method when things go wrong is save_and_open_page, which dumps the contents of the Capybara DOM into a temp file and opens the temp file in a browser (opening in a browser requires a gem called Launchy). You won't have any CSS or images with relative file

---

4.   http://rubydoc.info/github/jnicklas/capybara/master/Capybara/Node/Finders#all-instance_method

names, but it's still usually enough to tell that, say, you're stuck on a login screen because you forgot to set up a logged-in user. As a shortcut, the capybara-screenshot gem automatically places both an HTML file and an image screenshot in the /tmp directory at the point of failure.

What to Test in an RSpec System Test

Before you make this test pass, take a look at what you're trying to do. In a test-driven process, you would write a system spec to start the process, and then move to writing unit tests to drive the underlying logic. A commonly used metaphor for testing is the *testing pyramid* (see the following figure), where your tests have a relatively large number of unit tests that run quickly and test one small segment of the application, backed by significantly fewer integration tests that run more slowly over the application as a whole. The middle part usually refers to tests that are not quite unit tests, but don't quite test end-to-end integration, such as Rails controller tests. In general, you want to also write relatively few of those tests.

The pyramid metaphor is useful as a guide to the relative number of each kind of test, but it does make it sound a little like the integration tests sit passively on top of a foundation of unit tests. It may be more useful to think of feature-level tests as the frame of a house. Without full feature tests, you can't specify how the different parts of your application work together. Without unit tests there are all kinds of potential holes that bugs can sneak through.

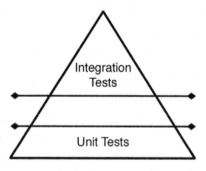

| Prescription 23 | By far the biggest and easiest trap you can fall into when dealing with integration tests is the temptation to use them like unit tests. |

That is to say, don't use feature tests to specify logic that consists largely of internal details of your codebase. One way to tell if your feature test is overly concerned with internal details is to think about what problem in the code would make the test fail. By definition, a feature test can fail in many places, but each test you write should have some specific logic failure that would only be caught by that test.

If that unique point of failure concerns the interaction between two objects (or sometimes, the interaction between two methods of the same object), then an integration test is called for. If the unique point of failure is the internal logic of a single object, then that condition is better covered with a unit test.

In a Rails context, the following are fodder for system tests:

- The interaction between a controller and the model or other objects that provide data

- The interaction between multiple controller actions that comprise a common workflow—for example, presenting a form, filling it out, and then submitting it

- Certain security issues that involve the interaction between a user state and a particular controller action

The following things, generally speaking, are *not* best tested using system tests, or any other kind of integration test. Use unit tests instead for these:

- Special cases of business logic, such as what happens if data is nil or has an unexpected value

- Error cases, unless it genuinely results in a unique user experience

- Internal implementation details of business logic

Two kinds of problems happen when you use system tests to cover things that are better done in unit tests. The first is speed. System tests are slower—not because the tools themselves are slow, but because the tests are winding their way through the Rails stack to get to the method you're interested in. Because the individual tests each cover such a wide range of code, an entire suite of integration tests makes it hard to diagnose where failures are occurring when they occur.

The second is precision. Because the system test is not making any assertions until after the internal logic has executed, it's often hard to piece together what went wrong. Often the way to deal with this is to have a failing feature test trigger the writing of a unit test.

Outside-in Testing

The process you'll use to manage the feature tests is sometimes called *outside-in testing*—you use Capybara to write a test from the outside and use that test to drive your unit tests. In the same way that TDD uses a failing unit test to drive code, outside-in testing uses a failing acceptance test (or a failing line in an acceptance test) to drive the creation of unit tests.

The process is illustrated in the figure that follows—I'm assuming the creation of a new user-facing feature in a Rails application.

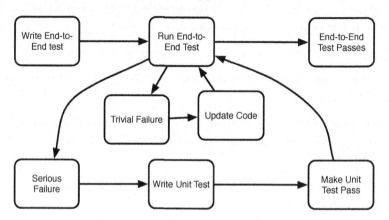

Let's walk through the steps.

1. Write the end-to-end test that shows a user interacting with the new feature. This test should specify data, have one or more user interactions, and validate HTML responses to determine that the interactions behave as expected. This should be the main, error-free, interaction of the feature. Before this process even starts, it's perfectly normal to noodle around with controllers and views trying to figure out exactly how the user interactions look. You may even get a substantive part of the feature done. You need to be willing to rewrite that code once the tests come into play.

2. Run the tests. In a reasonably mature Rails application, the first few steps will often already pass. You'll frequently be adding a new feature to an existing page, so steps where data is prepared, users are logged in, and existing pages are hit might all work.

3. Come to a test failure. The first failures you see in integration testing are often trivial: attempts to click on links that don't exist and form fields that aren't there yet. These can be quickly dispatched, generally without unit tests, on the theory that adding new stuff to a view isn't normally testable logic.

4. Cross the chasm. You'll get to the point where you're validating responses and there's a lot of logic missing. Now you have a focused, well-defined task to accomplish in your code, and it's time to drop to unit tests.

5. Write unit tests. Exactly what unit tests you need to write depends on the situation. You'll probably have model logic to test, and maybe a plain Ruby object managing a transaction. The important thing is that the unit tests may go beyond making the integration test work. They also have some responsibility to cover edge and error cases that integration tests wouldn't cover.

6. When you think the unit tests are done, go back to the integration test. There's a good chance it still fails because you forgot some piece of integration. No problem; that's what the integration test is there for.

7. The integration test passes. Yay!

8. Refactor the code you've written if needed.

9. If there's another significant user case in the feature, write the test for it and start over.

Let's go back to your test and see how this plays out in practice.

Making the Capybara Test Pass

Let's go through the integration-test process. One quick note: you're using factory_bot (see Chapter 6, *Adding Data to Tests*, on page 101) to create the projects and tasks with let!. You could also use fixtures, but for this go-around I've decided the factories are more readable, if slower.

The first failure is that you don't have a show method in the ProjectsController. The show method is easy enough, and probably doesn't need additional testing:

integration/01/app/controllers/projects_controller.rb
```ruby
def show
  @project = Project.find(params[:id])
end
```

You'll also want a template. You know it's going to need a table for the tasks as well as a form to create a new task. Here's one. It's unstyled, but it's got the table and the form to create a new task:

integration/01/app/views/projects/show.html.erb
```erb
<h2>Project <%= @project.name %></h2>

<h3>Existing Tasks:</h3>

<table>
  <thead>
    <tr>Name</tr>
    <tr>Size</tr>
  </thead>
```

```
<tbody>
  <% @project.tasks.each do |task| %>
    <tr>
      <td class="name"><%= task.title %></td>
      <td class="size"><%= task.size %></td>
      <td class="completed"><%= task.completed_at %></td>
    </tr>
  <% end %>
</tbody>
</table>

<h3>New Task</h3>

<%= form_for Task.new(project_id: @project.id) do |f| %>
  <%= f.hidden_field :project_id %>
  <%= f.label :title, "Task" %>
  <%= f.text_field :title %>
  <%= f.label :size %>
  <%= f.select :size, [1, 2, 3, 4, 5] %>
  <%= f.submit "Add Task" %>
<% end %>
```

At this point you fail because the create task doesn't exist on TasksController. That means you need to create new logic.

This feels like it'll be boilerplate enough not to need additional tests. Often, at this point I'll do a mini spike of the controller method to see how much complexity is called for. In this case the controller method is really simple:

```
integration/01/app/controllers/tasks_controller.rb
class TasksController < ApplicationController
  def create
    @task = Task.new(params[:task].permit(:project_id, :title, :size))
    redirect_to(@task.project)
  end
end
```

You don't have any obvious error cases here—Task has no validations. And even if you did have error cases, the remedy would be to go back to the project page anyway. So I'm willing to leave this for now. (In practice, I'd add an error message in the failure case.)

The next error is Capybara::ElementNotFound: Unable to find css "#task_3".

In the original Capybara test you're identifying each row by the order of the task, so the three rows will have DOM IDs task_1, task_2, and task_3. Not only don't you have those IDs in the template, but you don't even have a mechanism for ordering the tasks.

This is a good opportunity for some small-scale design. You want each task to have an order, the project to display the tasks in order, and new tasks to come in at the end of the list.

You can handle the first part, giving tasks an order, with a Rails migration:

```
$ rails generate migration add_order_to_tasks
```

I'm calling the new attribute project_order to avoid confusion with the SQL order statement:

```
integration/02/db/migrate/20170626013611_add_order_to_tasks.rb
class AddOrderToTasks < ActiveRecord::Migration[5.1]
  def change
    change_table :tasks do |t|
      t.integer :project_order
    end
  end
end
```

```
$ rake db:migrate
```

You can make products automatically return tasks in order by going into the Project class definition and changing the declaration of the relationship to this:

```
has_many :tasks, -> { order "project_order ASC" }, dependent: :destroy
```

You don't need a test because it's part of the framework.

For the tests to work, you also need to add the project_order to the let statements in the spec:

```
integration/02/spec/system/add_task_spec.rb
let!(:task_1) { create(
  :task, project: project, title: "Search Sky", size: 1, project_order: 1) }
let!(:task_2) { create(
  :task, project: project, title: "Use Telescope",
         size: 1, project_order: 2) }
```

Giving a new task in an order adds some logic. There are several ways to do this. Here are a few examples:

- You could make the logic an after_save callback on Task, which would be invoked automatically when the task is saved.

- You could make it a method on Project to ask the project for the next order.

- You could create a Task workflow object similar to the CreatesProject object you built earlier that would query the Project to get the new order.

To keep things simple, I'll make a method on Project that will be called when creating the Task. You're now in unit-test mode, so you need to write some unit tests:

integration/02/spec/models/project_spec.rb
```ruby
describe "task order" do
  let(:project) { create(:project, name: "Project") }

  it "makes 1 the order of the first task in an entry project" do
    expect(project.next_task_order).to eq(1)
  end

  it "gives the order of the next task as one more than the highest" do
    project.tasks.create(project_order: 1)
    project.tasks.create(project_order: 3)
    project.tasks.create(project_order: 2)
    expect(project.next_task_order).to eq(4)
  end
end
```

This code passes with the following:

integration/02/app/models/project.rb
```ruby
def next_task_order
  return 1 if tasks.empty?
  (tasks.last.project_order || tasks.size) + 1
end
```

Now you need to integrate it. First, call the new method in the controller. I've slightly reorganized the controller logic so that you have a project to query:

integration/02/app/controllers/tasks_controller.rb
```ruby
class TasksController < ApplicationController
  before_action :load_task, only: %i[up down]

  def create
    @project = Project.find(params[:task][:project_id])
    @project.tasks.create(
      task_params.merge(project_order: @project.next_task_order))
    redirect_to(@project)
  end

  def up
    @task.move_up
    redirect_to(@task.project)
  end

  def down
    @task.move_down
    redirect_to(@task.project)
  end

  private
```

```
def load_task
  @task = Task.find(params[:id])
end

def task_params
  params.require(:task).permit(:project_id, :title, :size)
end
end
```

I still don't think the controller logic warrants another test.

Now, in the app/views/projects/show.html.erb template file, replace the table-row line with the following:

```
<tr id="task_<%= task.project_order %>">
```

That gives you the #task_3 selector, at long last.

And that brings me to the next point of failure, Unable to find link or button with text "Up", meaning that the update logic is not yet in place.

What's the logic you want? And how can you write a test for it?

You want an "Up" link for all tasks but the first one, and a "Down" link for all tasks but the last one. That means you need to be able to tell if a task is first or last. That's testable:

integration/02/spec/models/task_spec.rb
```
describe "order", aggregate_failures: true do
  let(:project) { create(:project, name: "Project") }
  let!(:first) { project.tasks.create!(project_order: 1) }
  let!(:second) { project.tasks.create!(project_order: 2) }
  let!(:third) { project.tasks.create!(project_order: 3) }

  it "can determine that a task is first or last" do
    expect(first).to be_first_in_project
    expect(first).not_to be_last_in_project
    expect(second).not_to be_first_in_project
    expect(second).not_to be_last_in_project
    expect(third).not_to be_first_in_project
    expect(third).to be_last_in_project
  end

  it "knows neighbors" do
    expect(second.previous_task).to eq(first)
    expect(second.next_task).to eq(third)
    expect(first.previous_task).to be_nil
    expect(third.next_task).to be_nil
  end
```

```
it "can move up" do
  second.move_up
  expect(first.reload.project_order).to eq(2)
  expect(second.reload.project_order).to eq(1)
end
it "can move down" do
  second.move_down
  expect(third.reload.project_order).to eq(2)
  expect(second.reload.project_order).to eq(3)
end

it "handles edge case moves up" do
  first.move_up
  expect(first.reload.project_order).to eq(1)
end

it "handles edge case moves down" do
  third.move_down
  expect(third.reload.project_order).to eq(3)
end
end
end
```

That's more assertions than I would normally place in a single test, but they are closely related, so I think it reads best as a single group.

Here's the next step:

integration/02/app/models/task.rb
```
def first_in_project?
  return false unless project
  project.tasks.first == self
end

def last_in_project?
  return false unless project
  project.tasks.last == self
end
```

Since the project has defined the task association to be in order, you can assume that the order returned by project.tasks is what you expect.

Now you need to place that logic in the view template, which you can do by adding some code inside the loop in app/views/projects/show.html.erb. There's a decision point here, which is whether to send that link to the regular update method for TasksController, which already exists and would need to be changed, or to create new up and down controller actions. It's not strictly RESTful, but this isn't strictly a RESTful action. It's a shortcut to a RESTful action, which I'm okay with here because it's constrained.

Let's go with the non-RESTful controller actions for up and down. Define them in the routes file:

integration/02/config/routes.rb
```ruby
Rails.application.routes.draw do
  resources :tasks do
    member do
      patch :up
      patch :down
    end
  end

  resources :projects
end
```

Then attach the routes to the template in app/views/projects/show.html.erb:

```erb
<td>
  <% unless task.first_in_project? %>
    <%= link_to "Up", up_task_path(task.id), method: :patch %>
  <% end %>
  <% unless task.last_in_project? %>
    <%= link_to "Down", down_task_path(task.id), method: :patch %>
  <% end %>
</td>
```

Next you need the ability to swap a task's order with one of its neighbors', which implies the ability to find those neighbors. This would seem to be a model concern, which means you're back writing unit tests.

What do these tests need? The same set of three tasks, presumably, and a move_up and move_down method to test.

Although I wrote and passed these tests one at a time, let's take a look at them together:

integration/02/spec/models/task_spec.rb
```ruby
it "knows neighbors" do
  expect(second.previous_task).to eq(first)
  expect(second.next_task).to eq(third)
  expect(first.previous_task).to be_nil
  expect(third.next_task).to be_nil
end

it "can move up" do
  second.move_up
  expect(first.reload.project_order).to eq(2)
  expect(second.reload.project_order).to eq(1)
end
```

```
it "can move down" do
  second.move_down
  expect(third.reload.project_order).to eq(2)
  expect(second.reload.project_order).to eq(3)
end

it "handles edge case moves up" do
  first.move_up
  expect(first.reload.project_order).to eq(1)
end

it "handles edge case moves down" do
  third.move_down
  expect(third.reload.project_order).to eq(3)
end
```

And here's one set of task methods that passes the tests and has gone through a refactoring step:

```
integration/02/app/models/task.rb
def previous_task
  project.tasks.find_by(project_order: project_order - 1)
end

def next_task
  project.tasks.find_by(project_order: project_order + 1)
end

def swap_order_with(other)
  other.project_order, self.project_order = project_order, other.project_order
  save
  other.save
end

def move_up
  swap_order_with(previous_task) unless first_in_project?
end

def move_down
  swap_order_with(next_task) unless last_in_project?
end
```

And now you're really, really close. All you need to do is wire up the controller:

```
integration/02/app/controllers/tasks_controller.rb
class TasksController < ApplicationController
  before_action :load_task, only: %i[up down]

  def create
    @project = Project.find(params[:task][:project_id])
    @project.tasks.create(
      task_params.merge(project_order: @project.next_task_order))
    redirect_to(@project)
  end
```

```
def up
  @task.move_up
  redirect_to(@task.project)
end

def down
  @task.move_down
  redirect_to(@task.project)
end

private

def load_task
  @task = Task.find(params[:id])
end

def task_params
  params.require(:task).permit(:project_id, :title, :size)
end
end
```

And … now the integration test passes, all the tests are green, and you celebrate.

Retrospective

Let's take a step back and discuss what happened here. You're supposed to be learning about integration tests, and yet you never touched the integration test after you initially wrote it. What good is that? (Full disclosure: in initial writing I did have to go back and clean up the integration test because I had syntax errors and the like. Sometimes I need to fix the assertions after I see what the view looks like.)

The integration test offers a few benefits as you write these tests:

- There's a structure; you know what needs to be done next. This is valuable, although given the nature of a lot of server-side development there does tend to be one large gap where the integration test provides the expected outcome but doesn't give much guidance on how to get there.

- The integration test proves that all of your unit tests work together as a cohesive whole (though you really need to test in a browser when you're done). One danger cited for unit tests is that it's easy to see the trees and not the forest. Having an end-to-end test forces you to describe the forest.

- Although the integration test is slow compared to unit tests, it's often lightning-fast compared to manually setting up the browser integration. If you've ever tested a form with dozens of required fields, you can see the benefit here.

Looking back at the original test, I said it was kind of long and unwieldy. I could go back and split out related lines into their own methods.

Or I could try Cucumber.

Setting Up Cucumber

Cucumber is a tool for writing acceptance tests in plain language.[5] (I almost said in plain English, but that's too limiting—Cucumber speaks a lot of different languages, including LOLcat.) It's designed to allow you to write simple and clear integration and acceptance tests. It can be used to have a nondeveloper client or manager cowrite or sign off on the acceptance tests, though my personal experience with that has been hit-and-miss. Because it adds a level of indirection to acceptance testing, some people feel that Cucumber is more trouble than it's worth.

I think of Cucumber as a tool that does two things. First, it allows me to structure integration tests somewhat cleanly. Second, it allows me the option to describe the system's intended behavior without using the code part of my brain, which I find helpful.

To install Cucumber, you need to add the cucumber-rails gem to the Gemfile:[6]

```
group :development, :test do
  gem 'cucumber-rails', require: false    # The false prevents a warning
end
```

The Database Cleaner gem, which is also recommended for Cucumber, should have already been inserted by Rails in 5.1 or higher. Otherwise, you need to add that as well.

Then bundle install.

Strictly speaking, Database Cleaner isn't required, but it's valuable and gives fixture-like transaction behavior to your nonfixture using tests. The cucumber gem will be installed as a dependency of cucumber-rails. As I write this, I'm talking about version 3.1.0 of Cucumber and version 1.5.0 of cucumber_rails.

To install Cucumber, use the command-line generator:

```
rails generate cucumber:install
```

This creates a config/cucumber.yml file for runtime options, the cucumber command-line script, a rake task, a features directory with subdirectories for step_definitions

---

5.   https://cucumber.io
6.   https://github.com/cucumber/cucumber-rails

and support, and a features/support/env.rb file (the latter is analogous to spec_helper.rb). Also, it modifies the database.yml file to add a cucumber environment that copies the test environment. Cucumber has some additional configuration options; you can type rails generate cucumber:install —help to see them.

Writing Cucumber Features

In Cucumber you write tests as a series of steps using a minimal language called Gherkin. An individual Cucumber test is called a Scenario, and a group of them is called a Feature.

Let's take the Capybara integration test from the last section and convert it to Cucumber. Cucumber feature files go in the features directory and typically end in .feature. Here is features_add_task.feature:

```
integration/03/features/add_task.feature
Feature: Adding a task

  Background:
    Given a project

  Scenario: I can add and change the priority of a new task
    When I visit the project page
    And I complete the new task form
    Then I am back on the project page
    And I see the new task is last in the list
    When I click to move the new task up
    Then I am back on the project page
    And the new task is in the middle of the list
```

This file has three parts. The Feature declaration is at the top. Your Cucumber file needs to have one, but the description there is strictly for the humans; you can put anything there that you want. Gherkin is whitespace-sensitive, so anything that goes beyond that top line needs to be indented.

The next section is the Background, which is optional. It might not be clear from the preceding code, but the Background line is indented subordinate to Feature. In Cucumber, Background is like Minitest's setup and RSpec's before, indicating code that is run to initialize each test. In your case, since you have only one Scenario, it's not necessary to have a Background. But if you did have multiple "Add a task" scenarios, they'd likely all share that one common Background.

After the Background comes the Scenario, which is the actual test. Both Background and Scenario are made up of steps. In Cucumber a step usually consists of Given, When, or Then, followed by a sentence. This corresponds to the same basic structure I've been using informally to discuss tests throughout the book: Given indicates a precondition to the action. When indicates a user action that changes the state of the application. Then specifies the result of the state change. You can also start a line with And or But (or *, if you must) if it's desirable for readability. Using And or But to start a line means that the line belongs to whichever of Given/When/Then is closest above it.

The distinction between Given, When, and Then is for us humans. Cucumber does not require the steps to be in a particular order. As you'll see, each Cucumber step is matched to code to determine its behavior. When it comes time to make that match, the Given/When/Then type of the header is not significant in the match.

This scenario is executable now, using the cucumber command, or you can specify the file with cucumber feature/add_task.feature. The output comes in two parts. The first is a listing of the execution step by step, which starts like this:

```
Background:        # features/add_task.feature:3
  Given a project # features/add_task.feature:4
    Undefined step: "a project" (Cucumber::Undefined)
    features/add_task.feature:4:in `Given a project'

 Scenario: I can add and change priority of a new task
              # features/add_task.feature:6
  When I visit the project page
              # features/add_task.feature:7
    Undefined step: "I visit the project page" (Cucumber::Undefined)
    features/add_task.feature:7:in `When I visit the project page'
```

You can't see this on the page, but all that text other than the Background and Scenario lines will be yellow.

When a scenario is run, Cucumber attempts to run each step by matching it to a step definition and executing that step definition. In this output Cucumber helpfully tells you the line number of each step it tries to execute, and then tells you that the step is undefined. That makes sense because you haven't defined any steps yet.

After it goes through all the steps and reports that you have one scenario with eight steps, of which one scenario and eight steps are undefined, Cucumber adds some extra output to the terminal. It starts like this:

```
You can implement step definitions for undefined steps with these snippets:

Given(/^a project$/) do
  pending # express the regexp above with the code you wish you had
end

When(/^I visit the project page$/) do
  pending # express the regexp above with the code you wish you had
end
```

This output continues for all the undefined steps. Cucumber is doing something really useful here: giving us boilerplate templates for each of the undefined steps that you can paste directly into your editor and then fill out.

Lets do that. I'm taking the whole ball of wax—pasting all eight of those pending blocks into a new file, features/step_definitions/add_task_steps.rb. When I do that and rerun Cucumber ... well, a little bit changes:

```
Background:          # features/add_task.feature:3
  Given a project # features/step_definitions/add_task_steps.rb:1
    TODO (Cucumber::Pending)
    ./features/step_definitions/add_task_steps.rb:2:in `/^a project$/'
    features/add_task.feature:4:in `Given a project'

 Scenario: I can add and change priority of a new task
              # features/add_task.feature:6
  When I visit the project page
              # features/step_definitions/add_task_steps.rb:5
  And I complete the new task form
              # features/step_definitions/add_task_steps.rb:9
  Then I am back on the project page
              # features/step_definitions/add_task_steps.rb:13
  And I see the new task is last in the list
              # features/step_definitions/add_task_steps.rb:17
  When I click to move the new task up
              # features/step_definitions/add_task_steps.rb:21
  Then I am back on the project page
              # features/step_definitions/add_task_steps.rb:13
  And the new task is in the middle of the list
              # features/step_definitions/add_task_steps.rb:25
```

If your terminal supports color, the top lines will be yellow and the lines under Scenario will be light blue. Cucumber is stopping the test at the first pending step and marking each further step as "skipped."

It's time to tell Cucumber what each of those steps should do.

Writing Cucumber Steps

Sadly, it's unrealistic for Cucumber to know what to do just from a step like Given a project. So you must define all the steps so Cucumber can execute them.

When Cucumber gets a step like Given a project, it searches through all the files in the step definition folder looking for one definition that matches. What does matching mean? Let's look at the boilerplate for that step again:

```
Given(/^a project$/) do
  pending
end
```

The first line of the definition is one of those Given/When/Then words (it doesn't matter which one) followed by a regular expression. Cucumber matches a step to a definition when the sentence part of the step, in this case a project, matches the regular expression—such as /^a project$/. You'll see later why Cucumber uses regular expressions instead of just strings. When Cucumber sees the step Given a project, it finds the step definition whose regular expression matches, then runs the code inside the block for the matching step definition. If Cucumber finds more than one matching step definition raises an error.

Inside a step definition you can write any arbitrary Ruby code. Instance variables declared in one step definition will be available to later step definitions in the same test. Be careful with instance variables; it's not always easy to tell what variables might exist from previous steps, or what state they might be in. Cucumber understands Capybara methods and it understands RSpec matchers (assuming RSpec is installed). Arbitrary methods defined in any step-definition file will be available to any step definition.

Your case here is unusual in that you already have this feature managed as a non-Cucumber integration test, so filling the steps is mostly a question of splitting that test into pieces. My copy looks like this:

integration/03/features/step_definitions/add_task_steps.rb
```
Given(/^a project$/) do
  @project = Project.create(name: "Bluebook")
  @project.tasks.create(title: "Hunt the aliens", size: 1, project_order: 1)
  @project.tasks.create(title: "Write a book", size: 1, project_order: 2)
end

When(/^I visit the project page$/) do
  visit project_path(@project)
end

When(/^I complete the new task form$/) do
  fill_in("Task", with: "Find UFOs")
  select("2", from: "Size")
  click_on("Add Task")
end

Then(/^I am back on the project page$/) do
  expect(current_path).to eq(project_path(@project))
end

Then(/^I see the new task is last in the list$/) do
  within("#task_3") do
    expect(page).to have_selector(".name", text: "Find UFOs")
    expect(page).to have_selector(".size", text: "2")
    expect(page).not_to have_selector("a", text: "Down")
  end
end
```

```
When(/^I click to move the new task up$/) do
  within("#task_3") do
    click_on("Up")
  end
end

Then(/^the new task is in the middle of the list$/) do
  within("#task_2") do
    expect(page).to have_selector(".name", text: "Find UFOs")
  end
end
```

There are only a few differences between the Cucumber steps and the original integration test. I've split up "checking that the new task is last" and "clicking to move it up," so each needs its own within block.

Since you've already written the code once, there's no reason to go through the whole process again. The Cucumber process is quite similar to the Capybara-only process: I write a scenario and try to make the steps pass one by one, dropping down to unit tests when I need logic. The biggest difference is that Cucumber makes it easier for me to write the scenario's outline without writing the details of the later steps.

Advanced Cucumber

This section could be titled "Things Cucumber lets you do that are probably bad ideas." Cucumber allows for a lot of flexibility in how steps match with step definitions. By and large, the Cucumber-using community has come to the conclusion that most of these things should be used sparingly, if at all.

Earlier I alluded to the idea that step definitions were regular expressions and not strings. This allows you to have the same step definition apply to multiple strings. More to the point, you can use regular-expression groups to capture those matches. The parts of the string that are in groups are then passed as block variables to the block part of the step definition. This allows you to treat a Cucumber step as a method call with parameters.

In the existing initial step, the project name is hard-coded inside the step definition. If, on the other hand, you wanted to be able to specify the name of the project in the Cucumber feature, you could write the step definition as follows:

```
Given /^a project named "(.*)"$/ do |project_name|
  @project = Project.create!(name: project_name)
end
```

That definition would match steps like this:

```
Given a project named "Rails 5 Test Prescriptions"
Given a project named "Evil Master Plan"
```

In each case the step definition would create a project with the given name.

You can go even further in terms of putting data in the Cucumber feature file. Cucumber allows you to append a table of data to a step. It's a very clever feature, and like a lot of very clever features it should be used judiciously.

You use something like Markdown table syntax to create the table. In the feature file it might look something like this:

```
Given the following users:
    | login| email               | password| password_confirmation|
    | alpha| alpha@example.com| alpha1  | alpha1               |
    | beta | beta@example.com | beta12  | beta12               |
```

The step with the table needs to end with a colon. The table uses pipe characters to delimit entries. They don't have to line up, but usually you'll want them to.

When Cucumber matches a step definition to a step that has a table, the table becomes an argument to the step definition's block—if there are other regular-expression matches, the table is the last argument. The argument is a special Cucumber data type, and there are a few different ways you can deal with it. Most commonly you'll deal with it as an array of hashes, where the keys are the first row of the table and every subsequent row provides a set of values, like so:

```
Given /^the following users$/ do |user_data|
  User.create!(user_data.hashes)
end
```

You can do something similar with a large string literal:

```
Given I have typed the following
  """
  some big amount of text
  """
```

That's an indented line, three quotation marks, some text, and then three more quotation marks at the end. The text inside the triple quotes will be passed as the last argument to the step definition's block.

If you really want to have fun, you can combine scenarios and tables to create a loop called a *scenario outline*, like so:

```
Scenario Outline: Users get created
  Given I go to the login page
  When I type <login> in the login field
```

```
  And I type <password> in the password field
  Then I am logged in
Examples:
  | login| email             | password| password_confirmation|
  | alpha| alpha@example.com | alpha1  | alpha1               |
  | beta | beta@example.com  | beta12  | beta12               |
```

The steps inside the outline are regular Cucumber steps. When the outline runs, it runs once for each data row in the Examples table, with the <login> syntax indicating that a value from that table should be inserted in the row.

All these features give you a tremendous amount of power. I advise you to use it sparingly. It's tempting to use these tools to reduce duplication or make your steps more general. But the flip side is that you're often declaring implementation data explicitly in the Cucumber file rather than implicitly in the step definition.

There are at least three problems with these more advanced Cucumber steps:

- All the flexibility can make for complicated step definitions. Since Cucumber depends on the step definitions doing exactly what they say they're going to do 100% of the time, complex step definitions are bad because they're more likely to contain errors. Debugging step definitions will make you question your life choices. Keeping step definitions simple makes Cucumber easier to manage.
- Putting a lot of codelike things—including data, attribute names, and CSS selectors—in Cucumber feature files makes them hard to read and parse. Since the point of Cucumber is to be natural language–like, writing unreadable steps defeats the purpose.
- Similarly, but more subtly, putting data in the feature file robs the feature file of its ability to declare intent. What is the point of the line Given a user that has been on the site for 2 months? It's hard to tell. Given a user that has been on the site long enough to be trusted is much more clear and explains why the step exists. This is a case where specifics imply greater meaning to your somewhat arbitrary data choices than they deserve.

Is Cucumber Worth It?

That depends on what "it" is. Cucumber is a very helpful acceptance-test framework, provided your expectations of it are reasonable. It's a lousy unit-test framework, and if you try to use it for unit testing you'll hate it and possibly stop eating salads to avoid cucumbers, which is bad for your health.

I use Cucumber for the relatively minimal goals of being able to write my integration tests at the level of user behavior and being able to easily separate my slower integration tests from my faster unit tests. For those things, it works great.

You'll sometimes hear that Cucumber allows for nondeveloper members of your team to participate in the acceptance-testing process because Cucumber is natural language–like. My experiences in that regard are mixed. I've had some success with writing Cucumber scenarios on my own and giving them to managers or clients for approval. Going the other direction, the limiting factor in my experience is not the syntax, but rather experience with how to specify requirements. That's tricky for everybody.

Some tips for better Cukeing:

• Write the scenario in natural language that defines the system's behavior from the user perspective; smooth out details in the step definition.
• Avoid anything in the feature file that looks like code or data—that includes CSS selectors and database attributes.
• Keep step definitions simple.
• Don't worry about duplicating bits of step logic. Prefer multiple simple steps over one big step with complex logic.
• Specify what isn't on the page; that's often as important as specifying what is.
• Worry about implementation details in the unit tests. The suggestions about what is an integration test and what is a unit test also apply here.
• Validate against user-visible pages rather than database internals. (Sometimes this means going to an admin page or similar to validate that a change has taken place.)

What You've Done

In this chapter you used Capybara to drive Rails system tests that cover an entire user interaction, then used Cucumber to show an alternative way to describe requirements for testing.

I'll talk more about these tools in future chapters. In Chapter 9, *Testing JavaScript: Integration Testing*, on page 181, I'll cover how Capybara and Cucumber can be attached to drivers that run the tests against a browser engine that executes JavaScript, allowing for client-side actions to be integration-tested. In Chapter 14, *Testing External Services*, on page 285, I'll talk about integration tests that might need to touch a third-party service. And in Chapter 16, *Running Tests Faster and Running Faster Tests*, on page 319, I'll talk about how to optimize the command-line execution of both tools so as to speed up your feedback loop.

CHAPTER 9

Testing JavaScript: Integration Testing

Nearly every Rails site uses JavaScript for something, and often JavaScript is a critical part of the user experience on sites. However, many sites don't test their JavaScript in any meaningful way.

Part of the reason is that JavaScript can be difficult to test. Interactions and logic are often dependent on user interaction or the specific state of the elements on the page, which can be hard to set up for testing. Often the JavaScript frameworks don't support easy unit testing. And the tools are changing very quickly. The tools I use in this chapter may seem quaint if not downright antiquated by the time you read this.

That said, some general principles for testing JavaScript will continue to be applicable across tools.

I'll talk about JavaScript testing in two parts. In this chapter I'll talk about using integration-testing tools, specifically Capybara, to test JavaScript from outside the client-side code. In the next chapter I'll talk about unit-testing JavaScript using JavaScript tools and the Webpack support that was new in Rails 5.1.

Integration-Testing JavaScript with Capybara

In the last chapter you used Capybara to test buttons in the UI that allowed you to change the order of tasks. As written, clicking up on a task button causes a full server page refresh. This is an interaction that might be more user-friendly if handled client-side with JavaScript.

There are multiple ways to handle this client-side. For our purposes the simplest is to have the up and down buttons manipulate the browser DOM to change the order and send an update request back to the server to register the other change. You need to test two things: that the client interaction actually changes the DOM, and that the changes are sent back to the server accurately.

I want to split the integration test for adding a task into one spec that adds the task, and one test that handles the reordering. This isolates the JavaScript to just the task that handles reordering:

js_integration/01/spec/system/add_task_spec.rb
```ruby
require "rails_helper"

RSpec.describe "adding a new task" do
  let!(:project) { create(:project, name: "Project Bluebook") }
  let!(:task_1) { create(
    :task, project: project, title: "Search Sky", size: 1, project_order: 1) }
  let!(:task_2) { create(
    :task, project: project, title: "Use Telescope", size: 1,
        project_order: 2) }
  let!(:task_3) { create(
    :task, project: project, title: "Take Notes", size: 1,
        project_order: 3) }

  it "can add a task" do
    visit(project_path(project))
    fill_in("Task", with: "Find UFOs")
    select("2", from: "Size")
    click_on("Add Task")
    expect(current_path).to eq(project_path(project))
    within("#task_4") do
      expect(page).to have_selector(".name", text: "Find UFOs")
      expect(page).to have_selector(".size", text: "2")
    end
  end

  it "can re-order a task", :js do
    visit(project_path(project))
    within("#task_3") do
      click_on("Up")
    end
    expect(page).to have_selector(
      "tbody:nth-child(2) .name", text: "Take Notes")
    visit(project_path(project))
    within("#task_2") do
      expect(page).to have_selector(".name", text: "Take Notes")
    end
  end
end
```

I made some relatively minor changes. I added a task to the setup so that you'd have three tasks in the reorder spec. The reorder spec does the reorder, checks to see that it works, then reloads the page and checks to see that the reorder still holds. The old test assumed the entire page was redrawn. The new test moves the same DOM ID around without redrawing the whole page. This means the DOM ID of the row you care about no longer changes, so you need different acceptance criteria. Now you're using the nth-child selector to pick the second .name child of tbody.

I also added a metadata value :js to the reorder task. Right now that metadata tag does nothing. The test passes without the :js tag. (Trust me; I'll come back to that in a moment.)

To make sure the JavaScript client handles the reorder functionality, you need to detach the existing up and down links from sending requests back to the server. In exchange, you'll give those link elements DOM classes and attributes (such as data-task-id) that you'll use in the resulting JavaScript:

```erb
js_integration/01/app/views/projects/show.html.erb
<h2>Project <%= @project.name %></h2>

<h3>Existing Tasks:</h3>

<table>
  <thead>
    <tr>Name</tr>
    <tr>Size</tr>
  </thead>
  <tbody>
    <% @project.tasks.each do |task| %>
      <tr id="task_<%= task.project_order %>" data-task-id=<%= task.id %>>
        <td class="name"><%= task.title %></td>
        <td class="size"><%= task.size %></td>
        <td class="completed"><%= task.completed_at %></td>
        <td>
          <button class="up-button">Up</button>
          <button class="down-button">Down</button>
        </td>
      </tr>
    <% end %>
  </tbody>
</table>

<h3>New Task</h3>

<%= form_for Task.new(project_id: @project.id) do |f| %>
  <%= f.hidden_field :project_id %>
  <%= f.label :title, "Task" %>
  <%= f.text_field :title %>
  <%= f.label :size %>
  <%= f.select :size, [1, 2, 3, 4, 5] %>
  <%= f.submit "Add Task" %>
<% end %>
```

At this point, the reorder test fails, even without the :js metadata tag, because the view is no longer contacting the server to do the reorder and reload the page.

Let's Talk About Drivers

To understand what Capybara is doing and what you need to do to make JavaScript integration testing work, you need to know about *drivers*. The driver is the part of Capybara that actually manages a web page as a series of DOM elements. The Capybara query language interacts with the driver, telling it to click a button or fill a form element, or just querying the driver to return DOM elements that match a selector and some other criteria.

Capybara's default driver is called Rack::Test. It's relatively simple and relatively fast. Rack::Test is written in Ruby and maintains its own DOM element tree. It's also dependent on Rack, which is the web stack that underlies nearly all Ruby web frameworks—not only Rails, but also Sinatra. Rack::Test has been great for our purposes so far, but it has some limitations. The most relevant of those for us is that Rack::Test doesn't have a JavaScript interpreter, and so ignores any JavaScript in the output. Once our code depends on JavaScript to do anything, Rack::Test is no longer useful.

Happily, if you're a web developer, there's about a 100% chance that you have multiple powerful JavaScript runtime interpreters on your computer in the form of web browsers. Capybara allows the use of other drivers that interact with the JavaScript interpreters designed for web browsers. Capybara still manages the query language, but hands over the queries and actions to the driver, which automates the actions using the full web rendering engine, including JavaScript.

Until 2017, I'd have said the three most commonly used JavaScript drivers for Capybara were Selenium, capybara-webkit, and Poltergeist. Selenium is the oldest, Capybara ships with support for it, and it differs from the other two in that it is a toolkit designed to automate a browser that is already installed on your computer and that Capybara can be used to control. That is to say that by default, when you run Selenium tests, you'll see a browser window open and the interactions actually play out in the window. While this has a certain comforting concreteness to it, it's also kind of slow. Poltergiest and capybara-webkit are both tools that extract the WebKit rendering engine used in the Safari browser into a standalone tool that is designed to run "headless," meaning without a window. While capybara-webkit and Poltergeist typically run faster than Selenium, they are both somewhat tricky to install and notoriously a little flaky to run.

The Chrome browser team recently released tools that allow Chrome to be run headless. In fact, as I write this, the maintainer for PhantomJS—which is a key dependency of Poltergeist—is stepping down because of headless Chrome. As of Capybara 2.15, there are default drivers for :selenium-chrome and :selenium-headless-chrome.

To use these drivers, you need a gem and a background application.

The gem is selenium-webdriver, and as of Rails 5.1 it is part of the Rails default gem set. The background application is ChromeDriver, which is basically the transfer protocol between Selenium and Chrome. On Mac OS, you can install it with homebrew using brew install chromedriver. Installation instructions for other platforms can be found online.[1]

We'll use :selenium-headless-chrome. Here's the configuration you can put into your existing Capybara configuration file:

```
js_integration/01/spec/support/system.rb
RSpec.configure do |config|
  config.before(:each, type: :system) do
    driven_by :rack_test
  end

  config.before(:each, type: :system, js: true) do
    driven_by :selenium_chrome_headless
  end
end

require "capybara-screenshot/rspec"
```

All you're doing here is registering :selenium-headless-chrome as a browser configuration that Selenium knows how to deal with, and then specifying that when Capybara needs a JavaScript-friendly driver in a system test, it should use headless Chrome.

Now you need to tell Capybara to use the JavaScript driver. In RSpec, you can set the JavaScript driver for a single test using metadata. The :js metadata that you've already added has Capybara switch to the JavaScript driver for the duration of the spec and then switch back at the end.

> **Prescription 24** Use Capybara's JavaScript integration-testing capabilities sparingly lest you be very, very annoyed. Test as much as possible within each layer, separate from the others.

---

1.   https://sites.google.com/a/chromium.org/chromedriver/getting-started

Using Poltergeist with Cucumber

In Cucumber, to get the JavaScript driver for a specific scenario you simply prefix the scenario with the @javascript tag:

```
@javascript
Scenario: We can change the order of tasks
```

Making the Test Pass

In this section you'll set up the JavaScript and present some passing code without unit testing. In the next chapter you'll set up JavaScript unit-testing tools and see how you might test-drive JavaScript features.

Rails 5.1 makes two important changes to the JavaScript environment:

• jQuery is no longer a default dependency.
• Webpack integration is available via the Webpacker gem.[2] [3]

Webpack is an optional replacement for the Rails asset pipeline and has the same general purpose: take files that might be written in JavaScript, Coffee-Script, TypeScript, Elm, or another language, and build them into JavaScript files that can be passed to the browser. Webpack's advantage is that it's flexible, it's tied into the current JavaScript ecosystem, and it allows for a much wider range of JavaScript and CSS tools to be built into your Rails project. The disadvantage is that Webpack is quite complicated, but the Webpacker extension written by the Rails team provides defaults that will allow you to get pretty far.

Even though jQuery isn't part of the Rails default, it's still probably the quickest way to handle our little feature here, so let's add it back in via Webpack. Rails uses a tool called Yarn to manage JavaScript package dependencies.[4] Yarn is the JavaScript equivalent of Bundler, and even has some of the same developers.

When you generated the Rails application you included Webpacker, but if you haven't yet, you can add it with this:

```
$ bundle exec rails webpacker:install
```

You can add jQuery to your dependencies with the following:

```
$ yarn add jquery
```

---

2. https://webpack.github.io
3. https://github.com/rails/webpacker
4. https://yarnpkg.com

You can see the full list of dependencies in the package.json file, which is the equivalent of Bundler's Gemfile, and in the yarn.lock file, which matches Gemfile.lock. All the code is stored in the node_modules directory, which will become quite large.

There's one other configuration piece. In the file config/webpack/environment.js, you need to register jQuery as owning the global $ and jQuery methods so that other modules that use them will correctly link to them:

```
js_integration/01/config/webpack/environment.js
const { environment } = require("@rails/webpacker")
const webpack = require("webpack")

environment.plugins.append(
  "Provide",
  new webpack.ProvidePlugin({
    $: "jquery",
    jQuery: "jquery",
    jquery: "jquery",
    "window.jQuery": "jquery",
  })
)

module.exports = environment
```

Now you can add your JavaScript code to a file in the javascript/packs directory. The main files here will primarily be manifest files that import from other files. In this case, everything fits nicely in a single file, so you're fine.

The following code uses ES6 syntax:

```
js_integration/01/app/javascript/packs/projects.js
class Task {
  static swapTasks(first, second) {
    second.detach()
    second.insertBefore(first)
  }

  constructor(anchor) {
    this.$anchor = $(anchor)
    this.$rowElement = this.$anchor.parents("tr")
  }

  previous() {
    return $(this.$rowElement.prev())
  }

  next() {
    return $(this.$rowElement.next())
  }
```

```
onUpClick() {
  if (this.previous().length === 0) {
    return
  }
  Task.swapTasks(this.previous(), this.$rowElement)
  this.updateServer("up")
}
onDownClick() {
  if (this.next().length === 0) {
    return
  }
  Task.swapTasks(this.$rowElement, this.next())
  this.updateServer("down")
}
taskId() {
  return this.$rowElement.data("taskId")
}
updateServer(upOrDown) {
  const url = `/tasks/${this.taskId()}/${upOrDown}.json`
  $.ajax({
    url,
    beforeSend: xhr => {
      xhr.setRequestHeader(
        "X-CSRF-Token",
        $('meta[name="csrf-token"]').attr("content")
      )
    },
    data: { _method: "PATCH" },
    type: "POST"
  })
}
}

$(() => {
  $(document).on("click", ".up-button", event => {
    new Task(event.target).onUpClick()
  })

  $(document).on("click", ".down-button", event => {
    new Task(event.target).onDownClick()
  })
})
```

I'll go over the details of this code in the next chapter as you rebuild it.

Finally, you need to add one line to the layout file so that the newly created pack will be included:

```
js_integration/01/app/views/layouts/application.html.erb
<!DOCTYPE html>
<html>
  <head>
    <title>Gatherer</title>
    <%= csrf_meta_tags %>

    <%= stylesheet_link_tag    'application', media: 'all', 'data-turbolinks-track':
        'reload' %>
    <%= javascript_include_tag 'application', 'data-turbolinks-track': 'reload' %>
    <%= javascript_pack_tag "projects" %>
  </head>

  <body>
    <%= yield %>
  </body>
</html>
```

That javascript_pack_tag helper is the new Webpacker equivalent of javascript_
include_tag. It similarly causes the Webpack build from the given file (in this
case projects.js) to be included at the point of the helper.

With all this included, the Capybara JavaScript test now passes. You may
see some output in the test run that says Webpack is compiling the JavaScript
for inclusions.

Webpack in Developer Mode

Like the Rails asset pipeline, Webpack converts the files under its domain
into JavaScript and CSS that the browser can handle. Unlike the Rails asset
pipeline, it uses its own process to monitor the files for changes and to
recompile them. As of Webpacker 3.0 that process, webpack-dev-server, runs
inline with the Rails development server by default. However, you can separate
them if you'd like. Running webpack-dev-server separately allows the compile to
happen when the file changes rather than when you hit the page, which can
feel faster. Also, when run standalone, webpack-dev-server can give you live reload
while editing.

You can use a tool called Foreman to easily run that process alongside your
Rails server.[5]

First, add Foreman to the Gemfile:

```
gem "foreman"
```

Follow that with a bundle install.

---

5.   http://ddollar.github.io/foreman

Then, define the process in a special file named Procfile:

js_integration/01/Procfile

```
rails: bundle exec rails server
webpack: bin/webpack-dev-server
```

In the Procfile, label each of the processes you want to run: a rails server that executes bundle exec rails server and a web pack server that runs bin/webpack-dev-server.

Then you can run using this:

```
foreman start
```

Both processes will run, with their output prefaced by the label, either rails or webpack, so you can see what process the output runs. The default URL for the Rails server changes from localhost:3000 to localhost:5000.

What You've Done

In this chapter we looked at using integration-testing tools, specifically Capybara, to test JavaScript from outside the client-side code. If you're getting the sense that using JavaScript drivers with Capybara is flaky, brittle, and frustrating, the only thing I can say is that you left out *slow*. I recommend using those drivers sparingly. Handle testing client interactions in JavaScript to the extent possible, and use server-side testing to specify what data is sent to the client.

Now let's look at how you can unit-test that JavaScript.

CHAPTER 10

Unit-Testing JavaScript

Unit testing for JavaScript is a big, somewhat contentious subject. For years, JavaScript's testing tools were significantly less powerful than Ruby's, and although I still think the Ruby tools are more flexible, the JavaScript tools are more than powerful enough to be useful.

And yet, many projects don't unit-test JavaScript code much, as there are significant impediments to writing good JavaScript tests:

- The ecosystem is still complicated. There are a lot of different tools, it's hard to differentiate between them, and setup is—as you'll see in a moment—still kind of challenging.

- The major frameworks don't have the same level of testing support that Rails does. To some extent this is getting better.

- A lot of JavaScript code is written to be strongly entangled with the DOM, making it harder to test the logic.

The last point is probably the most important, so let me elaborate on it.

In the discussion of Rails models and controllers, I talked about separating business logic from the database and from the Rails framework to make it easier to test the logic in isolation. I've also made the claim that isolating the business logic is good not just for testing, but also for making the long-term cost of change lower in the codebase.

Similarly, most JavaScript code ultimately is about responding to user action and changing elements in the DOM. And a lot of idiomatic JavaScript code completely intertwines business logic with the DOM in a way that makes the code hard to understand and change. Although I won't be covering the popular JavaScript frameworks here, they tend to do a good job of isolating business logic so as to allow testing, even if not all of them are as tightly integrated with testing framework as Rails.

For example, the JavaScript code you wrote in Chapter 9, *Testing JavaScript: Integration Testing*, on page 181, uses the DOM as the source of truth for the order of the tasks. The code queries the DOM to find the previous and next tasks when the time comes to reorder them. While that might be fine for something as simple as reordering tasks, it's already a little tricky to read if you don't know the expected DOM structure. Adding simple extensions—like hiding the up or down buttons for the first and last tasks—isn't clear. In this chapter you'll take another swing at that code, attempting to drive it from unit testing rather than integration testing.

Setting Up JavaScript Unit Tests

This is going to be a bit involved, I'm afraid. Rails 5.1 uses the Webpacker gem, which allows you to bypass the Rails asset pipeline and use Webpack—an asset-bundling tool that is in common use by JavaScript developers. Webpack allows you to do all the same things the old Rails asset pipeline does: module lookup, compilation, conversion to a single minified file, and the like. But Webpack is more integrated with current JavaScript tools and makes it much easier to integrate with JavaScript code that is distributed using the Node Package Manager (NPM).[1]

That's the good news. The less-good news is that Webpack configuration can be really complicated, especially if you're a Rails developer and are used to convention over configuration. The Rails team has put a lot of effort into Webpacker to control the complexity of Webpack configuration, but you still sometimes need to dig into the details.

Also note that Webpacker is in version 3.2.1 as I write this. It has had two or three major revisions since I started working on this book, each of which substantially changed the configuration files. It's highly likely that there's been another change or two between when I wrote this and when you're reading it.

In this chapter I'll use the Karma test runner,[2] which runs from the command line but executes the tests against browsers and plays reasonably nicely with

---

1. https://www.npmjs.com
2. https://karma-runner.github.io

Webpack. For a testing tool, I'll use Jasmine,[3] mostly because I like the syntax. And for good luck, I'll throw in the TestDouble package.[4]

Rails 5.1 uses the Yarn package manager to support its JavaScript dependencies. You need to get all these tools into your list of modules, meaning you need to load them with Yarn, along with some related modules:

```
$ yarn add jasmine jasmine-core karma karma-chrome-launcher \
  karma-jasmine karma-mocha-reporter karma-sourcemap-loader \
  karma-webpack testdouble testdouble-jasmine --dev
```

That's a mouthful. (These instructions are valid as of January 2018, but the modules may have changed by the time you read this.)

--dev adds the modules to the devDependencies section of the package.json file, meaning the modules are loaded into developer environments and not into production environments.

As for the modules themselves …

- jasmine and jasmine-core are the libraries you'll use to write your tests.

- karma is the command-line program that runs your tests. It searches the project for files that match the test pattern and executes them in a browser environment.

- karma-jasmine is the interface that allows Karma to run Jasmine tests.

- karma-webpack lets the Karma runner use Webpack as a preprocessor. Since you're already using Webpack to transpile ES6 and the like, this allows you to use the JavaScript and configuration files you're already using.

- karma-chrome-launcher is the interface that allows Karma to run tests using the Chrome (or, in our case, headless Chrome) JavaScript engine. There are many, many browser-specific launchers for Karma, and you can even set up Karma to run multiple browsers as your test environment.

- karma-mocha-reporter makes the text output of running Karma more useful. There are also many different kinds of reporters for Karma.

- karma-sourcepack-loader allows Karma to use source maps when reporting output. Since you're writing transpiled ES6 code, this allows Karma to show you the line where the error hits, which is a big deal.

---

3.   https://jasmine.github.io
4.   https://github.com/testdouble/testdouble.js

- testdouble is your mock object package—more on that later in this chapter.

- testdouble-jasmine integrates the TestDouble package with Jasmine.

Karma is easiest to run if you install the karma-cli module, but since that's external to this project, it's best to install it as a global module so that the karma command is just available:

```
$ yarn global add karma-cli
```

Now that all the modules are loaded, some configuration is necessary. Let's start with Karma. All kinds of details that RSpec and Rails handle for you under the banner of "convention over configuration" are actually configuration options in Karma, and the file goes in karma.conf.js. You can get Karma to generate a starting configuration file with the command karma init, but I won't walk through that here; I'll just show the finished product.

Here's the file, edited for space:

js_jasmine/01/karma.conf.js
```javascript
module.exports = function(config) {
  config.set({
    basePath: "",
    frameworks: ["jasmine"],
    files: ["spec/javascripts/**/*_spec.js"],
    preprocessors: {
      "app/javascript/packs/*.js": ["webpack", "sourcemap"],
      "spec/javascripts/**/*_spec.js": ["webpack", "sourcemap"],
    },
    reporters: ["mocha"],
    port: 9876,
    colors: true,
    logLevel: config.LOG_INFO,
    autoWatch: true,
    browsers: ["ChromeHeadless"],
    singleRun: true,
    concurrency: Infinity,
    webpack: require("./config/webpack/test.js"),
    webpackMiddleware: {
      stats: "errors-only"
    }
  })
}
```

There are a number of valid ways to manage Karma. This is just one option. (You can find a full description of the configuration docs online.[5]) Here are the important bits:

---

5. https://karma-runner.github.io/1.0/config/configuration-file.html

- frameworks specifies the test frameworks being used—in this case that means Jasmine.

- files identifies the file pattern Karma will match against when looking for test files. So, in this case, any file in spec/javascripts that ends with _spec.js is a test file.

- preprocessors tells Karma to use Webpack and source maps to process each file.

- reporters tells Karma to run output through the mocha reporter.

- browsers identifies the browser that will run all the tests when Karma is invoked. In this case, you're using headless Chrome.

- singleRun tells Karma to run once when invoked, then stop. Otherwise, it will stay open and autorun when a test file changes. I find autorun kind of irritating these days, so I don't use it.

- webpack denotes your Webpack configuration. You're just loading in the one you've already defined.

First, you need to make some tweaks to the Webpack configuration. The test environment needs to change slightly to look like this:

js_jasmine/01/config/webpack/test.js

```
const environment = require("./environment")
environment.plugins.get("Manifest").opts.writeToFileEmit = process.env.NODE_ENV
        !== "test"
const config = environment.toWebpackConfig()
config.devtool = "inline-source-map"
module.exports = config
```

The change is the env.NODE_ENV !== "test" value for writeToFileEmit. You don't want this manifest file to be written in the test environment, as you don't need it to be served, and it can interact badly with Karma. You're also adding some lines to have Webpack generate source maps.

Finally, I want to add a script section to the project.json file:

js_jasmine/01/package.json

```
{
  "scripts": {
    "test": "NODE_ENV=test karma start"
  },
  "dependencies": {
    "@rails/webpacker": "^3.2.1",
    "jquery": "^3.3.1"
  },
```

```
  "devDependencies": {
    "jasmine": "^2.9.0",
    "jasmine-core": "^2.9.1",
    "karma": "^2.0.0",
    "karma-chrome-launcher": "^2.2.0",
    "karma-jasmine": "^1.1.1",
    "karma-mocha-reporter": "^2.2.5",
    "karma-sourcemap-loader": "^0.3.7",
    "karma-webpack": "^2.0.9",
    "testdouble": "^3.3.3",
    "testdouble-jasmine": "^0.2.1",
    "webpack-dev-server": "^2.11.1"
  }
}
```

That scripts bit at the top will let you run the tests using the command yarn test. The command itself includes NODE_ENV=test to force Webpack to use the test.js version of the configuration.

Okay, everybody still here? It's time to write a sample test.

Writing a Sample Test

This first test is just here to introduce Jasmine and Karma, not to be any kind of useful test. This is Jasmine, using ES6 syntax, mostly the arrows:

```
js_jasmine/01/spec/javascripts/basic_spec.js
describe("JavaScript testing", () => {
  it("works", () => {
    expect(1 + 1).toEqual(2)
  })
})
```

Jasmine's syntax is heavily inspired by RSpec, with JavaScript function objects taking the place of Ruby blocks. Like RSpec test suites, Jasmine test suites start with describe. In Jasmine, describe is a method that takes two arguments: a string and a function. The function defines the behavior of an entire test suite.

Inside the describe function argument, individual specs are defined by calls to the function it, which also takes a string description argument and a function argument. The function argument to it is the actual spec.

Inside the spec, individual expectations are denoted with the expect method. That method takes an argument, which should be the actual value from the test. The return value of expect is an object that Jasmine calls an *expectation*. The expectation can then be called with one of several matchers, such as toEqual. The matchers typically take an argument, which is the predetermined expected value—hence expect(1 + 1).toEqual(2).

You can run this from the command line (output slightly edited for space):

```
$ yarn test
webpack: wait until bundle finished:

webpack: Compiled successfully.
04 08 2017 19:53:40.789:INFO [karma]:
        Karma v2.0.0 server started at http://0.0.0.0:9876/
04 08 2017 19:53:40.792:INFO [launcher]:
        Launching browser ChromeHeadless with unlimited concurrency
04 08 2017 19:53:40.797:INFO [launcher]:
        Starting browser ChromeHeadless
04 08 2017 19:53:41.239:INFO [HeadlessChrome 0.0.0 (Mac OS X 10.13.2)]:
        Connected on socket a3N9XHHP4GaY_KiQAAAA with id 80412174

  JavaScript testing
    ✓ works

Finished in 0.004 secs / 0.003 secs @ 19:53:41 GMT-0500 (CDT)

SUMMARY:
✓ 1 test completed
```

The output tells you that Karma set up a server at http://0.0.0.0:9876/, started a headless Chrome instance pointed at that server, and ran the tests. Notice an RSpec documentation–style listing of the tests (in green on a color terminal) and a summary at the end.

If you want to run Karma in a browser or keep the server running, run the command NODE_ENV=test karma start --no-single-run (or change the singleRun option in the Karma configuration file). If Karma is running, you can point any browser you want at the server address and Karma will run tests in that browser. (Output will go to the console.)

TDD in JavaScript

Now let's try to build the task-rearrangement feature in JavaScript using TDD. You'll use a different approach to the JavaScript than you did in the previous chapter, and you'll be completely rewriting your JavaScript Task class. First, you'll build the logic without regard to how the application will get data into the JavaScript objects and without regard to how the application will interact with the DOM. Approaching the feature this way allows you to focus on the code and not the large external dependencies of the server-side data and the DOM.

You still have the Capybara integration test from Chapter 9, *Testing JavaScript: Integration Testing*, on page 181, and whatever you do here, that test should still work (or at least, should work pending minor changes based on changing DOM structure). So you can think of this process as a slightly different instance of outside-in testing. The Capybara test is still the outside, but instead of using RSpec to write server-side tests, you're using Jasmine to write client-side tests.

I should note that this is a very small feature, and I'm probably overbuilding it based on the current requirements, but it is handy to see a small example. In practice, the idea of using tests to isolate your JavaScript from the server and the DOM becomes more compelling the more logic is needed in the client. In practice, a larger example would likely use a framework like React or Vue that uses data binding to help isolate logic from the DOM.

You'll wind up with a Project and a Test class on the client that are not dissimilar to the ones you already have on the server. This duplication is a common problem in web applications, and there's not a clear solution. One solution is to move all the logic to the client and write a single-page web app backed by a simple server. This may be the right solution in some cases. In my experience, unless the client has a lot of interactivity, the client's single-page app winds up being more complicated than an app that has some logic on the server, some logic on the client, and some duplication. I realize that sounds counterintuitive.

Here's my first batch of Jasmine tests (note that I did write and get these to pass one at a time):

```
js_jasmine/01/spec/javascripts/project_spec.js
import {Project, Task} from "../../app/javascript/packs/projects.js"

describe("Projects", () => {
  let project

  beforeEach(() => {
    project = new Project()
    project.appendTask(new Task("Start Project", 1))
    project.appendTask(new Task("Middle Project", 2))
    project.appendTask(new Task("End Project", 3))
  })

  it("can identify the first element of a project", () => {
    expect(project.firstTask().name).toEqual("Start Project")
    expect(project.firstTask().isFirst()).toBeTruthy()
    expect(project.firstTask().isLast()).toBeFalsy()
    expect(project.firstTask().index).toEqual(0)
  })
```

```
  it("can identify the last element of a project", () => {
    expect(project.lastTask().name).toEqual("End Project")
    expect(project.lastTask().isLast()).toBeTruthy()
    expect(project.lastTask().isFirst()).toBeFalsy()
    expect(project.lastTask().index).toEqual(2)
  })
  it("can move a task up", () => {
    project.tasks[1].moveUp()
    expect(project.firstTask().name).toEqual("Middle Project")
    expect(project.tasks[1].name).toEqual("Start Project")
    expect(project.lastTask().name).toEqual("End Project")
  })
  it("can move a task down", () => {
    project.tasks[1].moveDown()
    expect(project.firstTask().name).toEqual("Start Project")
    expect(project.tasks[1].name).toEqual("End Project")
    expect(project.lastTask().name).toEqual("Middle Project")
  })
  it("handles asking for the top task to move up", () => {
    project.firstTask().moveUp()
    expect(project.firstTask().name).toEqual("Start Project")
    expect(project.tasks[1].name).toEqual("Middle Project")
    expect(project.lastTask().name).toEqual("End Project")
  })
  it("handles asking for the bottom task to move up", () => {
    project.lastTask().moveDown()
    expect(project.firstTask().name).toEqual("Start Project")
    expect(project.tasks[1].name).toEqual("Middle Project")
    expect(project.lastTask().name).toEqual("End Project")
  })
})
```

The test file starts by importing Test and Project from the file where they live. Note that the file name is specified relative to the test file, not relative to the project root. This is using ES6 module syntax; you'll see the export half of this when we look at the passing code.

The rest of the code looks similar to RSpec that was modified to use JavaScript functions rather than Ruby blocks. You start with a describe call that takes a string argument and a function. Inside that function you declare a variable, project. The variable needs to be declared outside the beforeEach and it functions so that it is visible to both of them. You have beforeEach, which takes a function as an argument, and executes that function before each spec runs. You also have it, which takes a name and a function and executes the actual spec. Inside the it you have a similar set of matchers using expect and then a series of matcher functions that are described in *Jasmine Matchers*, on page 201.

Here's the passing code so far:

js_jasmine/01/app/javascript/packs/projects.js

```
export class Project {
  constructor() {
    this.tasks = []
  }

  appendTask(task) {
    this.tasks.push(task)
    task.project = this
    task.index = this.tasks.length - 1
  }

  firstTask() {
    return this.tasks[0]
  }

  lastTask() {
    return this.tasks[this.tasks.length - 1]
  }

  swapTasksAt(index1, index2) {
    const temp = this.tasks[index1]
    this.tasks[index1] = this.tasks[index2]
    this.tasks[index2] = temp
  }
}

export class Task {
  constructor(name, size) {
    this.name = name
    this.size = size
    this.project = null
    this.index = null
  }

  isFirst() {
    if (this.project) {
      return this.project.firstTask() === this
    }
    return false
  }

  isLast() {
    if (this.project) {
      return this.project.lastTask() === this
    }
    return false
  }

  moveUp() {
    if (this.isFirst()) {
      return
    }
```

```
      this.project.swapTasksAt(this.index - 1, this.index)
  }
  moveDown() {
    if (this.isLast()) {
      return
    }
    this.project.swapTasksAt(this.index, this.index + 1)
  }
}
```

Jasmine Matchers

So far you've only seen toEqual as a core Jasmine matcher, but Jasmine defines quite a few. Here are the built-in matchers.

Matcher	Passes if
toBe(actual)	expected === actual (JavaScript triple equal).
toBeCloseTo(actual, precision)	The floating-point value of actual is within precision amount of the expected value.
toBeGreaterThan(actual)	expected > actual.
toBeFalsy()	The expected value is a JavaScript falsy value.
toBeLessThan(actual)	expected < actual.
toBeNull()	The expected value is null.
toBeTruthy()	The expected value is a JavaScript truthy value.
toBeUndefined()	The expected value is undefined; no actual argument needed.
toContain(actual)	expected is an array that contains the actual value.
toEqual(actual)	expected and actual are equal values. Exactly what that means depends on their type. toEqual is based on a (no kidding) 120-line method in Jasmine that uses slightly different criteria for each built-in type and does a deep property comparison of JavaScript objects. Long story short, it tends to do what you'd expect.
toMatch(actual)	expected is a string that matches the actual regular expression.
toThrow()	expected is a function that throws an exception when called.

Any matcher can be negated by chaining not before the matcher, as in expect(1 + 1).not.toEqual(3).

Testing Ajax Calls

Now that you have the internal logic of your task list working, let's focus on how to get data into and out of this code. The previous version of the code read the tasks essentially from the DOM, but in this case you'll make a separate Ajax call to get that information from the server. Let's talk about strategies to test Ajax calls.

Here's the basic structure of an Ajax call—this one uses jQuery, but the basic idea holds no matter how the call gets made:

```
$.ajax({
  url: `projects/${this.id}.js`
  dataType: "json"
}).then((data) => {
  this.name = data.project.name
  // and so on
})
```

The jQuery $.ajax method takes the URL and other information about the call you want to make and returns a JavaScript promise object. (A decent starting point on what promises are can be found online.[6]) Chain the then method to that promise, and the argument to then needs to be a function. That function will be executed once the server call has completed. The promise object lets you manage the asynchronous nature of the server call because the function passed to then is not executed until after the server call has completed.

This $.ajax pattern has a lot of issues for us as testers:

- The external server targeted by the $.ajax call is a dependency outside the realm of your JavaScript unit-test runtime, although it is possible to call it inside the Capybara tests I discussed in the last chapter.

- The asynchronous nature of the call makes it challenging to test for the effects that are supposed to happen after the Ajax call—you just don't know how long to wait for those effects to happen.

Both of these problems are slightly exacerbated by the way the previous code intertwines three things: the Ajax call, the callback, and the structure that relates them. What happens if you write it more like this?

---

6.   https://developers.google.com/web/fundamentals/getting-started/primers/promises

```
function makeAjaxCall(id) {
  return $.ajax({
    url: `projects/${id}.js`
    dataType: "json"
  })
}
function loadFromData(data) {
  const project = new Project()
  project.name = data.project.name
  // and so on
}
function loadProject(id) {
  return makeAjaxCall(id).then((data) => this.loadFromData(data))
}
```

This isn't your actual passing code; that code will be inside a class.

With the structure cleared away behind separate methods with intention-revealing names, two strategies become visible:

- If the callback is defined as a separate function or method, you can test it directly with canned data.

- If the callback is separate, you can stub the Ajax call and make sure it triggers the loader.

- The combination of the two can still be handled by the Capybara integration test.

Here are some Jasmine tests. The first takes data and passes it directly to a method to load the data; the second uses the testdouble.js library to stub the Ajax call:

```
js_jasmine/02/spec/javascripts/project_load_spec.js
import {Project} from "../../app/javascript/packs/project.js"
import {ProjectLoader} from "../../app/javascript/packs/project_loader.js"
import td from "testdouble/dist/testdouble"
import tdJasmine from "testdouble-jasmine"
tdJasmine.use(td)

describe("Project Loader", () => {
  let input

  beforeEach(() => {
    input = {project: {name: "Project Runway",
      tasks: [{title: "Start Project", size: 1},
        {title: "End Project", size: 1}]}}
  })
```

```javascript
  afterEach(() => {
    td.reset()
  })

  it("uses the fake laoder to load a Project", () => {
    const project = new Project(1)
    const FakeLoader = td.constructor(ProjectLoader)
    project.projectLoader = new FakeLoader()
    td.when(FakeLoader.prototype.load()).thenResolve(input)
    project.load().then(() => {
      expect(project.name).toEqual("Project Runway")
      expect(project.firstTask().name).toEqual("Start Project")
      expect(project.lastTask().name).toEqual("End Project")
    })
  })

  it("can generate correct data for a loader", () => {
    const loader = new ProjectLoader(new Project(1))
    expect(loader.ajaxData().dataType).toEqual("json")
    expect(loader.ajaxData().url).toEqual("/projects/1.js")
  })

  it("can create a project and tasks from Data", () => {
    const project = new Project(1)
    project.loadFromData(input)
    expect(project.name).toEqual("Project Runway")
    expect(project.firstTask().name).toEqual("Start Project")
    expect(project.lastTask().name).toEqual("End Project")
  })
})
```

The second and third tests are all things you've seen before: you define some input data in the beforeEach method, call a method on project to load it, and then verify the load.

The first test is more complicated, and before I go over it in detail, let's talk about testdouble.js.

Using testdouble.js

testdouble.js is a test-double library written by Justin Searls and his crew at a company called Test Double. The library is very strict about the kinds of test doubles it helps you create in service of a specific pattern of testing and program design. Searls explains that in the documentation.[7]

For our purposes, the most significant part of the testdouble.js API as compared to RSpec's mock package is that testdouble.js makes it difficult to impossible to stub only one or two methods of an exiting object. That means it's hard to

---

7. https://github.com/testdouble/testdouble.js/blob/master/docs/2-howto-purpose.md#background

create a partial test double. In testdouble.js, the idea is that it is generally safer and clearer to replace an entire object with a test double rather than have an object exist as part test double, part real object. I can't argue with the theory, though if you're used to RSpec's looser test double style, working with testdouble.js requires some adjustment. As you'll see, the design of the resulting code is to some extent determined by drawing a boundary around logic that is easy to stub together. This is by design; the test is being used to determine the logical structure of the code.

Using testdouble.js happens in three steps: declaring the double, defining its behavior with the td.when method, and optionally verifying its usage after the test has run with the td.verify. Please note that this is not a complete guide to testdouble.js; you're invited to check out the very complete documentation online.[8]

Creating Test Doubles

The testdouble.js library has three methods for creating doubles, which are analogous to RSpec's double method. Which one you use largely depends on whether your JavaScript code is primarily structured around functions, objects, or classes.

If you're trying to replace a bare function, you can use the td.function method. If you call it with no arguments, the result is a bare function suitable for passing as a dependency to code under test.

More frequently, you may want to replace an entire object or class instance. To replace an object, use the td.object function. There are two ways to use td.object. If you don't have a real object but you know the interface of the object you want, you can call td.object with an array of strings, which represent properties of the object that are functions. You then get a test-double object where each of those strings is a test double-fake function, like this:

```
const fake = td.object(["name", "weight"])
fake.name
fake.weight
```

But using td.object with an array of strings has a problem that might be familiar from the discussion of RSpec doubles. If the "real" object's attributes change but the td.object arguments don't, you could have a passing test even though the underlying code is broken. A workaround is to pass td.object an existing object instead:

---

8.   https://github.com/testdouble/testdouble.js

```
const real = {
  name: function() {}
  weight: function() {}
  size: "small"
}
fake = td.object(real)
```

When used on a real object, td.object replaces all the functions with test-double functions but doesn't touch any property of the object that is not a function. So, fake.name is a test-double function, but td.size is still "small." The advantage here is that the real definition presumably happens somewhere in your code, and if that definition changes, the test-double object also changes, somewhat analogous to an RSpec verifying double.

In this case, the code uses the classes defined in the ES6 version of JavaScript rather than a plain JavaScript object.[9] For that, testdouble.js provides the td.constructor function. As with td.object, td.constructor has two forms: one that wraps the properties of an existing class and one that can be set free-form. The previous code sample uses the wrapper version, which takes the class object as the argument td.constructor(ProjectLoader). The return value is a stubbed constructor that you can use to instantiate objects whose methods are covered by testdouble.js:

```
const FakeLoader = td.constructor(ProjectLoader)
project.projectLoader = new FakeLoader()
```

Technically the argument to td.constructor is not a class name, but a constructor function (which means you could use td.constructor with pre-ES6 code if you were writing pre-ES6 class-like structures). If that sentence doesn't make sense to you, don't worry; the distinction isn't very important.

You can also pass an array of string function names to td.constructor, in which case you get a constructor that can create objects that respond to those function names. For the pre-ES6 crowd, it's creating an object with fake functions in its prototype object.

No matter which way you build your test-double structure, you'll eventually wind up with a function or method that is controlled by testdouble.js. Next, you need to specify the behavior of those fake functions.

Specifying Test Double Behavior

Once you have a testdouble.js function, you need to specify some behavior for it, analogous to the way RSpec's test doubles use allow and expect with chained methods like to_receive.

---

9.   http://es6-features.org/#ClassDefinition

In testdouble.js, you add behavior with the when method, and the API to it is a little unusual. Here's a basic usage:

```
const fake = td.object["remoteInit"]
td.when(fake.remoteInit(1)).thenReturn(7)
```

There are two parts to this when invocation: the call to when itself, and then the chained method afterward that defines the behavior.

The argument to when is meant to be the entire call to the test double, potentially with arguments specified. It's a demonstration of the call that the test expects to be made by the code under test.

In this case, you expect the test to make the call fake.remoteInit(1) to cause the test double to return the value 7. If you make the call fake.remoteInit(2)—changing the argument—the specified behavior is not triggered and the result of that call is undefined.

This interface to creating test-double behavior has the huge advantage of making the most common action—returning a value when a function is called—very simple. The library does get more complicated from there.

First, if you want to access an instance method of a test double created with td.constructor, the nature of JavaScript objects requires you to invoke that method via the prototype object, as in td.when(FakeLoader.prototype.load()). As in RSpec, you can pass in argument matchers in place of literal arguments if you want the test double to match against a wider array of behavior. (You can see the full list of stubbing behavior online.[10]) Here are some of the most useful ones:

- anything, as in td.when(fake.remoteInit(anything())), which matches, well … anything. You do have to match the number of arguments, so in this case fake.remoteInit(12) matches, but fake.remoteInit(12, 13) does not.

- contains(<something>) matches if the argument to the eventual test double is contained by the argument to contains. The argument can be a string, a regular expression, an array, or an object.

- isA() matches based on type: td.when(fake.remoteInit(isA(Number))). This works for built-in types, ES6 classes, or older-style objects that define constructors.

- not() matches if a particular value doesn't match, as in td.when(fake.remoteInit (not(12))).

---

10. https://github.com/testdouble/testdouble.js/blob/master/docs/5-stubbing-results.md

If you specify multiple potential matches for a value, the last one defined wins. If I define this:

```
td.when(fake.remoteInit(anything())).thenReturn(1)
td.when(fake.remoteInit(isA(Number))).thenReturn(2)
td.when(fake.remoteInit(1)).thenReturn(3)
```

then fake.remoteInit(1) returns 3, fake.remoteInit(2) returns 2 (because 2 is a number but it isn't 1), and fake.remoteInit("Steve") returns 1 (because the only definition that matches is the first one).

You can also trigger different behaviors, typically to allow for different kinds of JavaScript asynchronous behavior. So if the method under test is expected to return a JavaScript promise, you can chain the test double with thenResolve to trigger the positive, with then to branch off the promise, or with thenReject to trigger the negative or catch side.

More generic asynchronous behavior can be captured with thenCallback, which assumes by default that the last argument to the function under test is itself a callback function, and which then invokes the callback function with whatever arguments you pass to thenCallback. You can also simulate an error condition with thenThrow, which expects an Error object.

Here's the when line from your original test:

```
td.when(FakeLoader.prototype.load()).thenResolve(input)
```

Now you can trace all of this. Here you're saying that FakeLoader is a class with an instance method load. If load is called with no arguments, you'd expect it to return a promise and immediately invoke the positive result of that promise.

To see what that does in practice, let's look at the passing code in Project and ProjectLoader:

```
js_jasmine/02/app/javascript/packs/project.js
import {ProjectLoader} from "../../../app/javascript/packs/project_loader.js"
import {Task} from "../../../app/javascript/packs/task.js"
import {ProjectTable} from "../../../app/javascript/packs/project_table.js"

export class Project {
  constructor(id) {
    this.tasks = []
    this.id = id
    this.loader = new ProjectLoader(this)
  }

  load() {
    return this.loader.load().then(data => this.loadFromData(data))
  }
```

```
loadFromData(data) {
  this.name = data.project.name
  data.project.tasks.forEach(taskData => {
    this.appendTask(new Task(
      taskData.title, taskData.size, taskData.project_order))
  })
  return this
}

appendTask(task) {
  this.tasks.push(task)
  task.project = this
}

firstTask() {
  return this.tasks[0]
}

lastTask() {
  return this.tasks[this.tasks.length - 1]
}

swapTasksAt(index1, index2) {
  const temp = this.tasks[index1]
  this.tasks[index1] = this.tasks[index2]
  this.tasks[index2] = temp
  new ProjectTable(this, ".task-table").insert()
}
}
```

js_jasmine/02/app/javascript/packs/project_loader.js
```
export class ProjectLoader {
  constructor(project) {
    this.project = project
  }

  load() {
    return $.ajax(this.ajaxData())
  }

  ajaxData() {
    return {
      url: `/projects/${this.project.id}.js`,
      dataType: "json"
    }
  }
}
```

ProjectLoader is a simple class that takes in a Project and makes an Ajax call, which returns a promise. The test double version of that call automatically resolves the promise. When Project#load calls ProjectLoader#load, it looks at that promise, and when it resolves it passes the data to loadFromData—the code is then(data => this.loadFromData(data)). The test double version resolves the promise and passes control to loadFromData. Since Project#load returns the result of the then call, which is itself a promise, the test waits for that promise to resolve (project.load().then(() => {}) so that you can verify that the results are as expected.

Verifying Test Doubles

Using test doubles is more than just setting stubbed behaviors to replace real behaviors; test doubles are also used to verify behavior by showing that various methods were called as side effects of the code under test. In RSpec, this verification is done with expect and have_received. In testdouble.js, it's done with the td.verify method.

There is a side effect in this code. When you move a task up or down, the Java-Script still makes an Ajax call back to the server to register the change server-side. You don't really care about the result of that call (at least not for the purposes of this test), but you do care that it gets made. So, you can put that validation into the tests by changing the "move up" and "move down" tests.

First some imports at the top of the file:

js_jasmine/03/spec/javascripts/project_spec.js
```
import {Project} from "../../app/javascript/packs/project.js"
import {Task} from "../../app/javascript/packs/task.js"
import {TaskUpdater} from "../../app/javascript/packs/task_updater.js"
import td from "testdouble/dist/testdouble"
import tdJasmine from "testdouble-jasmine"
tdJasmine.use(td)
```

Then the changed tests themselves (the two tests here use slightly different validation syntax, which you'll see more about in a moment):

js_jasmine/03/spec/javascripts/project_spec.js
```
it("can move a task up", () => {
  const FakeUpdater = td.constructor(TaskUpdater)
  project.tasks[1].updater = new FakeUpdater()
  project.tasks[1].moveUp()
  expect(project.firstTask().name).toEqual("Middle Project")
  expect(project.tasks[1].name).toEqual("Start Project")
  expect(project.lastTask().name).toEqual("End Project")
  td.verify(FakeUpdater.prototype.update("up"))
})
it("can move a task down", () => {
  const FakeUpdater = td.constructor(TaskUpdater)
  project.tasks[1].updater = new FakeUpdater()
  project.tasks[1].moveDown()
  expect(project.firstTask().name).toEqual("Start Project")
  expect(project.tasks[1].name).toEqual("End Project")
  expect(project.lastTask().name).toEqual("Middle Project")
  expect().toVerify(FakeUpdater.prototype.update("down"))
})
```

The beginning of these tests is similar to the td.when tests. You first create a test-double object using td.constructor, then inject it into the real object before calling the method under test.

At the end of the first test, you call td.verify, which does your mock-object verification. The argument to td.verify is almost completely parallel to that of td.when—the argument to td.verify is the exact function call you want to have been made on the test-double object. All of the argument matchers I talked about for td.when can also be included in td.verify.

The second test differs only in that the final line uses expect().toVerify rather than td.verify. The two lines are functionally equivalent. The expect().toVerify version is denied by the testdouble-jasmine package specifically to convince Jasmine that there's an expectation being tested. If you only use the first version, Jasmine won't realize that you're asserting something and will not count it when calculating the number of assertions. To be clear, the td.verify will work; it just won't create accurate Jasmine metadata.

That test passes. Here's what Task looks like now:

js_jasmine/03/app/javascript/packs/task.js
```
import {TaskUpdater} from "../../../app/javascript/packs/task_updater.js"

export class Task {
  constructor(name, size, id) {
    this.name = name
    this.size = size
    this.project = null
    this.id = id
    this.updater = new TaskUpdater(this)
  }
  index() {
    return this.project.tasks.indexOf(this)
  }
  isFirst() {
    if (this.project) {
      return this.project.firstTask() === this
    }
    return false
  }
  isLast() {
    if (this.project) {
      return this.project.lastTask() === this
    }
    return false
  }
```

```
moveUp() {
  if (this.isFirst()) {
    return
  }
  this.project.swapTasksAt(this.index() - 1, this.index())
  this.updater.update("up")
}

moveDown() {
  if (this.isLast()) {
    return
  }
  this.project.swapTasksAt(this.index(), this.index() + 1)
  this.updater.update("down")
}
}
```

And here's the code for TestUpdater:

```
js_jasmine/03/app/javascript/packs/task_updater.js
export class TaskUpdater {
  constructor(task) {
    this.task = task
  }

  update(upOrDown) {
    const url = `/tasks/${this.task.id}/${upOrDown}.json`
    $.ajax({
      url,
      beforeSend: xhr => {
        xhr.setRequestHeader(
          "X-CSRF-Token",
          $('meta[name="csrf-token"]').attr("content")
        )
      },
      data: { _method: "PATCH" },
      type: "POST"
    })
  }
}
```

You could unit-test the URL here the way you did before, but it's covered by
the Capybara integration test, so I'm not overly concerned about it.

At this point there's some JavaScript generating HTML in the files app/java-
script/packs/project_table.js and app/javascript/packs/task_row.js, but I won't go into them
in depth. I used jQuery to build up the HTML, which is a bit complicated-
looking. In a real app I'd use a framework or a template tool, but I'm reluctant
to bring in another tool here, especially one that's not particularly relevant to
testing. In any case, the HTML is also covered by the Capybara integration test.

Speaking of those integration tests, now that you've got the JavaScript up and running, let's see how the running JavaScript affects them.

Connecting the JavaScript to the Server Code

Were you to run the RSpec tests now that you've moved all the logic to JavaScript, you'd find that both tests in spec/system/add_task_spec.rb fail. The first test, which did not run in the JavaScript browser, fails because without JavaScript the tasks don't display at all. That's to be expected, and the test can be removed as its logic is now covered elsewhere.

The JavaScript test also fails for a couple of reasons. The simple one is the JavaScript makes a new Ajax call to get the JSON data for the tasks. To make that work, you need to make a small change to the ProjectsController#show method:

js_jasmine/03/app/controllers/projects_controller.rb
```ruby
def show
  @project = Project.find(params[:id])
  respond_to do |format|
    format.html {}
    format.js { render json: @project.as_json(root: true, include: :tasks) }
  end
end
```

Here, the Rails respond_to method is being used to respond to a JavaScript request with the JSON representation of the task, adding project as a root element and adding in the tasks so as to match the expectations of the client side.

However, at this point the test still fails. Here's what the failing test looks like:

js_jasmine/02/spec/system/add_task_spec.rb
```ruby
require "rails_helper"

RSpec.describe "adding a new task" do
  let!(:project) { create(:project, name: "Project Bluebook") }
  let!(:task_1) { create(
    :task, project: project, title: "Search Sky", size: 1, project_order: 1) }
  let!(:task_2) { create(
    :task, project: project, title: "Use Telescope", size: 1,
          project_order: 2) }
  let!(:task_3) { create(
    :task, project: project, title: "Take Notes", size: 1,
          project_order: 3) }

  it "can re-order a task", :js do
    visit(project_path(project))
    find("#task_3")
    within("#task_3") do
      click_on("Up")
    end
```

```
      expect(page).to have_selector(
        "tbody:nth-child(2) .name", text: "Take Notes")
      visit(project_path(project))
      within("#task_2") do
        expect(page).to have_selector(".name", text: "Take Notes")
      end
    end
  end

end
```

The failure point is at the first within("#task_3") call, which does not find an element with the DOM ID task_3.

The problem here is timing. The test performs the visit(project_path(project)) then moves immediately to search for within("#task_3"). In the meantime, the code loads the page and makes an Ajax callback to retrieve the project JSON, and the task_3 selector doesn't exist until that call completes. But the test checks and fails well before that can happen.

There are a few ways to handle this issue. For example, you might explicitly put a delay in the test. However, it's easier to use Capybara's built-in ability to wait. The Capybara method find will wait for an element to appear on the page for a default duration of two seconds. This is perfect since it means you can make the test stand still long enough to make sure the Ajax call catches up.

The resulting test looks like this:

js_jasmine/03/spec/system/add_task_spec.rb
```ruby
require "rails_helper"

RSpec.describe "adding a new task" do
  let!(:project) { create(:project, name: "Project Bluebook") }
  let!(:task_1) { create(
    :task, project: project, title: "Search Sky", size: 1, project_order: 1) }
  let!(:task_2) { create(
    :task, project: project, title: "Use Telescope", size: 1,
          project_order: 2) }
  let!(:task_3) { create(
    :task, project: project, title: "Take Notes", size: 1,
          project_order: 3) }

  it "can re-order a task", :js do
    visit(project_path(project))
    find("#task_3")
    within("#task_3") do
      click_on("Up")
    end
    expect(page).to have_selector(
      "tbody:nth-child(2) .name", text: "Take Notes")
```

```
    visit(project_path(project))
    find("#task_2")
    within("#task_2") do
      expect(page).to have_selector(".name", text: "Take Notes")
    end
  end
end
```

JavaScript testing is a huge topic all by itself, worthy of an entire book, so we've only scratched the surface here, but hopefully this gives you a tool chain and a place to start.

What You've Done

You've covered a lot of ground here. You've seen how to configure Webpacker, Webpack, Jasmine, and Karma to run JavaScript unit tests. Then you saw how you might unit-test some relatively simple JavaScript code and use test doubles to stand in for Ajax servers.

There's a lot to cover still in JavaScript-land. In particular, if you're using a client-side framework, each framework has its own set of testing tools to isolate parts of the code and make testing easier.

Now it's time to go back to Rails and cover some testing tools for other corners of your Rails application.

CHAPTER 11

Testing Rails Display Elements

Rails applications have a specific structure, which starts with the model-view-controller (MVC) pattern. The view layer has the responsibility of presenting data to the user, which in a server-side web application usually means generating HTML. Ideally, the view layer does this with minimal interaction with the model. The controller takes in information about the user request, contacts the appropriate parts of the model layer for data, and passes that information on to the view layer. The following is a simplified diagram of this pattern.

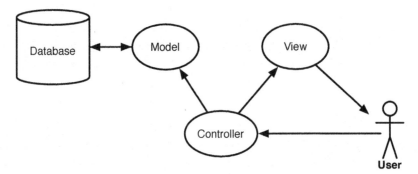

Rails has augmented this pattern with other standard layers for specific purposes. For example, ActiveMailer handles mail, ActiveJob handles background jobs, the router has its own DSL and may have some logic, and helpers straddle the line between display and view.

Each of these layers has tools designed to make them easier to test, though in many cases the best thing to do is put the bulk of the logic in a separate, ordinary Ruby object, test that, and use the Rails structure as minimally as possible. In this chapter I'll talk about the testing tools that Rails and RSpec provide for all of these different layers.

While the Rails framework and third-party testing tools allow you to interact with things like mailers, controller actions, and view templates in your test environment, the issues of isolation and size still exist. A discussion of how to best test these parts of the Rails code often turns into one of the following two discussions:

- What should be tested in integration tests, and what should be tested in unit tests?

- What code belongs in the Rails-specific controller, view, mailer, job, or whatever, and what should be extracted into a different object?

The answers to these questions tend to be related—the more you want to keep code in the Rails constructs, the more likely you are to also want to use integration tests rather than unit tests.

For Rails 5, the Rails core team made a strong statement of preference by deprecating some commonly used features of controller tests in favor of integration or system tests. This is consistent with Rails founder David Heinemeier Hansson's views that extra layers within Rails are unnecessary.

Testing Routes

Let's start the tour with a part of the Rails layer that's not commonly tested in isolation, but where testing can sometimes be valuable. Although the basics of Rails routing are simple, the desire to customize Rails's response to URLs can lead to confusion about exactly what your application is going to do when converting between a URL and a Rails action. Rails provides a way to specify route behavior in a test.

Routing tests are not typically part of my TDD process—usually my integration test implicitly covers the routing. That said, sometimes routing gets complicated and has some logic of its own (especially if you're trying to replicate an existing URL scheme), so it's nice to have this as part of your test suite.

RSpec-Rails puts routing tests in the spec/routing directory. The primary matcher that RSpec-Rails uses for route testing is route_to. Here's a sample test that includes all seven default RESTful routes for the project resource:

```
display/01/spec/routing/project_routing_spec.rb
require "rails_helper"

RSpec.describe "project routing", :aggregate_failures, type: :routing do

  it "routes projects" do
    expect(get: "/projects").to route_to(
      controller: "projects", action: "index")
```

```
  expect(post: "/projects").to route_to(
    controller: "projects", action: "create")
  expect(get: "/projects/new").to route_to(
    controller: "projects", action: "new")
  expect(get: "/projects/1").to route_to(
    controller: "projects", action: "show", id: "1")
  expect(get: "/projects/1/edit").to route_to(
    controller: "projects", action: "edit", id: "1")
  expect(patch: "/projects/1").to route_to(
    controller: "projects", action: "update", id: "1")
  expect(delete: "/projects/1").to route_to(
    controller: "projects", action: "destroy", id: "1")
  end

end
```

All of these are using the same form. The argument to expect is a key/value pair where the key is the HTTP verb and the value is the string form of the route. The argument to route_to is a set of key/value pairs where the keys are the parts of the calculated route (including controller, action, and what have you) and the values are, well, the values.

The route_to matcher tests the routes in both directions. It checks that when you send the path through the routing engine, you get the controller, action, and other variables specified. It also checks that the set of controller, action, and other variables sent through the router results in the path string (which is why you might need to specify query-string elements). It's not clear to me why a route might pass in one direction and not the other.

RSpec also provides a be_routable method, which is designed to be used in the negative to show that a specific path—say, the Rails default—is not recognized:

```
expect(get: "/projects/search/fred").not_to be_routable
```

Testing Helper Methods

Helper modules are the storage attic of Rails applications. They are designed to contain reusable bits of view logic. This might include view-specific representations of data, or conditional logic that governs how content is displayed. Helper modules tend to get filled with all kinds of clutter that doesn't seem to belong anywhere else. Because they are a little tricky to set up for testing, helper methods often aren't tested even when they contain significant amounts of logic. Again, in my own practice I often move this logic into dedicated presenter classes, but you'll see a lot of code in Rails helpers you might want to unit-test.

RSpec helper tests go in spec/helpers. There's not a whole lot of special magic here—just a helper object that you use to call your helper methods.

Let's say you want to change your project view so behind-schedule projects show up differently. You could do that in a helper. My normal practice is to add a CSS class to the output for both the regular and behind-schedule cases, to give the design maximum freedom to display as desired.

Here's a test for that helper:

```
display/01/spec/helpers/projects_helper_spec.rb
Line 1  require "rails_helper"

    -   RSpec.describe ProjectsHelper, type: :helper do
    -     let(:project) { Project.new(name: "Project Runway") }
    5
    -     it "augments with status info when on schedule" do
    -       allow(project).to receive(:on_schedule?).and_return(true)
    -       actual = helper.name_with_status(project)
    -       expect(actual).to have_selector("span.on_schedule", text: "Project Runway")
   10     end
    -   end
```

In this test you're creating a new project using a standard ActiveRecord new method. Rather than define a bunch of tasks that would mean the new project is on schedule, you just stub the on_schedule? method on line 7 to return true. This has the advantage of being faster than creating a bunch of objects and, I think, being more clear as to the exact state of the project being tested. You're using the have_selector matcher, as you did in Chapter 8, *Integration Testing with Capybara and Cucumber*, on page 151, to compare the expected HTML with the generated HTML.

That test will fail, however, because you haven't defined the name_with_status helper. Let's define one:

```
display/01/app/helpers/projects_helper.rb
module ProjectsHelper
  def name_with_status(project)
    content_tag(:span, project.name, class: "on_schedule")
  end
end
```

The test passes. Now let's add a second test for the remaining case. This test will look familiar:

```
display/02/spec/helpers/projects_helper_spec.rb
it "augments with status info when behind schedule" do
  allow(project).to receive(:on_schedule?).and_return(false)
  actual = helper.name_with_status(project)
  expect(actual).to have_selector(
    "span.behind_schedule", text: "Project Runway")
end
```

It passes with the following:

```
display/02/app/helpers/projects_helper.rb
module ProjectsHelper
  def name_with_status(project)
    dom_class = project.on_schedule? ? "on_schedule" : "behind_schedule"
    content_tag(:span, project.name, class: dom_class)
  end
end
```

One gotcha that you need to worry about when testing helpers is using Rails-internal view methods like url_for. Although all core Rails helpers are automatically loaded into the ActionView test environment, one or two have significant dependencies on the real controller object and therefore fail with opaque error messages during helper testing. The most notable of these is url_for. One workaround is to override url_for by defining it in your own test case. (The method signature is def url_for(options = {}).) The return value is up to you; a simple stub response is often good enough.

Sometimes helper methods take a block, which is expected to be ERB text (or the text of whatever template tool you're using to replace ERB). One common use of this kind of helper is access control, in which the logic in the helper determines whether the code in the block is invoked. Blocks also are very helpful as wrapper code for HTML that might surround many different kinds of text—a rounded-rectangle effect, for example.

Here's a simple example of a helper that takes a block:

```
def if_logged_in
  yield if logged_in?
end
```

It would be invoked like so:

```
<% if_logged_in do %>
 <%= link_to "logout", logout_path %>
<% end %>
```

To test the if_logged_in helper, you can take advantage of the fact that the yield statement is the last statement of the helper and, therefore, is the return value, and of the fact that Ruby will let you pass any arbitrary string into the block, giving you tests that look like this:

```
it "does not display if not logged_in" do
  expect(logged_in?).to be_falsy
  expect(if_logged_in { "logged in" }).to be_nil
end
```

```
it "displays if logged in" do
  login_as users(:quentin)
  expect(logged_in?).to be_truthy
  expect(if_logged_in { "logged in" }).to eq("logged in")
end
```

The first test asserts that the block is not invoked, so the helper returns nil. The second asserts that the block is invoked, just returning the value passed into the block.

You have to be a little careful here because these tests are just testing the helper method's return value, not what is sent to the output stream. The output-stream part is a side effect of the process, but it is stored in a variable called output_buffer, which you can access via testing. So you could write the preceding tests as follows:

```
it "does not display if not logged_in" do
  expect(logged_in?).to be_falsy
  if_logged_in { "logged in" }
  expect(output_buffer).to be_nil
end

it "displays if logged in" do
  login_as users(:quentin)
  expect(logged_in?).to be_truthy
  if_logged_in { "logged in" }
  expect(output_buffer).to eq("logged in")
end
```

If for some reason your helper method requires a specific instance variable to be set, cut that out immediately; it's a bad idea. However, if you must use an instance variable in your helper and you want to test it in RSpec, use the assigns method, as in expect(assigns(:project)).to eq(Project.find(1)). That tests that there is an instance variable named @project that has been set to a specific project.

Testing Controllers and Requests

The biggest change in Rails 5 testing when compared to earlier versions is the deprecation of some controller-testing functionality. In this section we'll first look at the RSpec features in Rails 5, then we'll go back and look at how controller testing worked in previous versions of Rails.

For most of this book I've focused on just what Rails 5 has to offer, and not spent time comparing Rails 5 to previous versions. I'm going to make a partial exception here and discuss the deprecated controller features as part of this section, for two reasons:

- Experienced Rails coders new to Rails 5 likely use these features and it's worth talking about what fills the same ecological niche in Rails 5.

- Even if you are a new Rails coder, you are likely to encounter older Rails code that uses controller tests, and you probably want to see what is going on.

RSpec for Rails 5 has two test types that are designed to test a single controller action. They are very similar. *Request specs* are basically wrappers around Rails integration tests, and *controller tests* are basically RSpec wrappers around Rails 5 controller tests. (Rails has always used the name "feature tests" for what RSpec calls "controller tests," which is confusing, because RSpec uses "feature tests" to indicate Capybara tests.) The older controller test behavior, should you need it to pull up a legacy codebase, can be reinstated with the rails-controller-testing gem.[1]

The naming gets confusing, but the basic taxonomy of when to use each test is not that bad. Here are the guidelines for RSpec:

- Use a request spec if you're testing the results of a single request to the Rails server, there's no interaction with the user in the test, and you're checking the behavior of the controller action or a side effect of calling the controller action.

- Use an RSpec system spec with Capybara, as described in Chapter 8, *Integration Testing with Capybara and Cucumber*, on page 151, if you're testing something that requires user interaction, such as simulated clicks or multiple page interactions, and if you're testing against the final result on the page.

- Use a system spec with the :js metadata if the integration test requires JavaScript.

If you're used to older versions of RSpec, be advised that I'm explicitly recommending using request specs in place of controller specs, and using system specs in place of feature specs (for reasons described in Chapter 8, *Integration Testing with Capybara and Cucumber*, on page 151).

Minitest and the standard Rails tools have a slightly different decision pattern, which I cover in Chapter 12, *Minitest*, on page 241.

---

1. https://github.com/rails/rails-controller-testing

Simulating Requests

Ideally, your controllers are relatively simple. The complicated functionality is in a model or other object and is being tested in your unit tests for those objects. One reason this is a best practice is that models are easier to test than requests because they're easier to extract and use independently in a test framework.

> **Prescription 25** A request test should test behavior of a single request. A request test should not fail because of problems in the model.

A request test that overlaps with model behavior is part of the awkward middle ground of testing that the Rails 5 changes are designed to avoid. If the request test is going to the database, then the test is slower than it needs to be. And if a model failure can cascade into the controller tests, then it's harder than it needs to be to isolate the problem.

A request test should have one or more of the following goals:

- Verify that a normal, basic user request triggers expected model or workflow object calls. Test doubles work extremely well for this purpose.

- Verify that a side effect, such as an email or background job, is triggered as part of a user request.

- Verify that an ill-formed or otherwise invalid user request is handled properly, for whatever definition of "properly" fits your app.

- Verify security, such as requiring logins for pages as needed and testing that users who enter a URL for a resource they shouldn't be able to see are blocked or diverted. (I discuss this more in Chapter 13, *Testing for Security*, on page 261.) This is also a good candidate to be offloaded into unit testing with, for example, the Pundit gem.[2]

Your request tests in Rails 5 will usually start with a simulated request. To make this simulation easier, Rails provides a test method to simulate each HTTP verb: delete, get, head, patch, post, and put. Each of these methods works the same way. (Internally, they all dispatch to a common method that does all the work.) A full call to one of these methods has one argument and up to five optional keyword arguments. The argument is a URL string, which can be passed as a string or as a Rails URL helper. The keyword arguments are, alphabetically:

---

2.   https://github.com/elabs/pundit

- as: Specifies the content type you want returned, especially if that content type is :json.

- env: A hash of environment variables. I admit it's not immediately clear to me why you'd want to set those in a request spec.

- headers: A hash of simulated header information you might want passed.

- params: The params hash for controllers, including anything that might be in a query string or a route variable. You can use the params hash to cover items that might otherwise be arguments to the URL.

- xhr: If true, tells the controller to treat the fake request as an Ajax call.

So, a contrived call might look like this:

```
get(projects_url, params: {id: @project.id}, xhr: true, as: :json)
```

If one of the param arguments is an uploaded file—say, from a multipart form—you can simulate that using the Rails helper fixture_file_upload(filename, mime_type), like this:

```
post(:create,
  params: {logo: fixture_file_upload('/test/data/logo.png', 'image/png')}
```

Third-party tools to manage uploads, such as Paperclip and CarrierWave, typically have more specific testing helpers.

If you've done Rails controller tests before, you'll notice that this is an API change. Most notably, you can no longer set the session or the flash via request tests. Rails now considers those to be internal implementation details.

What to Expect in a Request Spec

My main goal in a request spec is to test behavior. I find that test-double validations work well here. If you're interested in testing the final state after the request, in addition to testing the changes to the database, there are a few other substantive things you can test.

After the request has been made, you have access to a response variable. Since request specs wrap Rails integration tests, RSpec does render the view, though if you are testing view behavior, I recommend using system specs, where you have access to the Capybara matchers, and not just the Rails integration spec matchers as described in Chapter 12, *Minitest*, on page 241.

After the request has been made, you have access to three special hash variables that you can test—cookies, flash, and session—all of which test the values the Rails process stored in those buckets.

RSpec provides the response.status value and there is, at least in theory, a have_http_matcher, which allows you to compare against logical values like :success and :error.

Let's talk about these three types of assertions in more detail.

You can use have_http_status to verify the HTTP response code sent back to the browser from Rails. Normally you'd use this assertion to ensure that your controller correctly distinguishes between success and redirect or error cases.

The value passed to have_http_status is usually one of four special symbols:

Symbol	HTTP Code Equivalent
:success	200–299
:redirect	300–399
:missing	404
:error	500–599

If you need to test for a more specific response, you can pass either the exact HTTP code number or one of the associated symbols defined by Rack.[3] Note that RSpec uses the codes defined by SYMBOL_TO_STATUS_CODE. The most common case I've had for specific HTTP codes is the need to distinguish between 301 permanent redirects (:moved-permanently) and other redirects.

When you expect the controller to redirect, you can use the redirect_to matcher to assert the exact nature of the redirect. The argument to redirect_to is pretty much anything Rails can convert to a URL, although the method's behavior is slightly different based on what the argument actually is. The code for redirect_to explicitly includes have_http_status(:redirect), so you don't need to duplicate that assertion.

If the argument to redirect_to is the name of a URL because it's a string or a method for a Rails named route, or because it's an object that has a Rails RESTful route, then the assertion passes if and only if the redirecting URL exactly matches the asserted URL. For testing purposes, Rails will assume that the application's local hostname is http://www.example.com. If that's too exact a test for your taste, you can pass a hash to redirect_to, which specifies the :controller, :action, and any parameters. If the argument is a hash, then assert_redirected_to checks only the exact key/value pairs in the hash; other parts of the URL are not checked.

---

3. https://github.com/rack/rack/blob/master/lib/rack/utils.rb

Request and controller tests do not—repeat, *do not*—follow the redirect. Any data-validation tests you write apply only to the method before the redirect occurs. If you need your test to follow the redirection for some reason, you're cordially invited to try a system test; see Chapter 8, *Integration Testing with Capybara and Cucumber*, on page 151.

Older Rails Controller Tests

In Rails 5, two features of controller testing—one commonly used, one less so—were deprecated. This deprecation has the effect of limiting the scope of controller testing. In the eyes of the Rails core, this scope should be picked up by integration testing, though I'd suggest that some of it should be picked up by moving code out of the controller and unit-testing it. The following is a quick guide to what Rails 4 controller tests looked like, as you'll probably see a bunch of them.

Controller Test Requests

Rails 4 provided the same set of methods we've covered for creating a request—get, post and their friends—but the method parameters were different:

```
get :show, {id: @task.id}, {user_id: "3",
    current_project: @project.id.to_s}, {notice: "flash test"}
```

Here, the method name, get, is the HTTP verb being simulated—sort of. While the controller test will set the HTTP verb if for some reason you query the Rails request object, it does not check the Rails routing table to see if that action is reachable using that HTTP verb. As a result, you can't test routing via a controller test. (Refer back to *Testing Routes*, on page 218, to see how Rails provides a mechanism for testing routes.)

The first argument, in this case :show, is the controller action being called. The second argument, {id: @task.id}, is a hash that becomes the params hash in the controller action. In the controller action called from this test, you would expect params[:id] to equal @task.id. The Rails form name-parsing trick is not used here—if you want to simulate a form upload, you use a multilevel hash directly, as in user: {name: "Noel", email: "noel@noelrappin.com"}, which implies params[:user][:name] == "Noel" in the controller.

Any value passed in this hash argument is converted to a string—specifically, to_param is called on it. So you can do something like id: 3, confident that it will be "3" in the controller. This, by the way, is a welcome change in recent versions of Rails; older versions did not do this conversion, which led to heads occasionally pounding against walls.

The third and fourth arguments to these controller methods are optional and rarely used. The third argument sets key/value pairs for the session object, which is useful in testing multistep processes that use the session for continuity. The fourth argument represents the Rails flash object, which is useful ... well, never, but if for some reason the incoming flash is important for your logic, there it is.

You may occasionally want to do something fancier to the simulated request. In a controller test you have access to the request object as @request, and access to the controller object as @controller. (As you'll see in *Evaluating Controller Results*, on page 228, you also have the @response object.) You can get at the HTTP headers using the hash @request.headers.

There is one more controller action method: xml_http_request (also aliased to xhr). This simulates a classic Ajax call to the controller and has a slightly different signature:

```
it "makes an ajax call" do
  xhr :post, :create, :task => {:id => "3"}
end
```

The method name is xhr, the first argument is the HTTP verb associated with the xhr call, and the remaining arguments are the arguments to all the other controller-calling methods in the same order: action, params, session, and flash. The xhr call sets the appropriate headers such that the Rails controller will appropriately be able to consider the request an Ajax request (meaning .js format blocks will be triggered), then simulates the call based on its arguments.

Evaluating Controller Results

Rails 4 controller tests have a few other features that were deprecated in Rails 5. In Rails 4 you could use the render_template matcher to assert which template rendered a method. I didn't use this much.

Rails 4 also exposed an assigns hash that had all the instance values that the controller passes to the view. This is deprecated now, but it was at one time a very common way to test Rails controllers. RSpec controller tests do not render the view by default, and you should use request or system specs if you would like that behavior.

Testing Mailers

Testing Rails mailers involves two separate bits of functionality: specifying whether the email gets sent as a result of some action, and specifying the contents of that email. Specifying whether the email gets sent often starts as part of a request or system test, while specifying the content has a lot in common with view testing. The somewhat indirect nature of the Rails ActionMailer makes testing email less obvious than it might be, but it's not hard. We'll also look at a third-party library that makes email testing easier.

Let's say, for example purposes, that you want to send an email in your project-management system when a task is marked as complete. You don't have a user model yet (I'll talk about users in this system when we get to Chapter 13, *Testing for Security*, on page 261), so let's assume for the moment that all the emails go to some kind of common audit or monitoring address. (Insert nsa.gov joke of your choosing.)

At this point you have one of those weird, unique-to-book-examples problems. Specifically, you haven't written very much of the task-tracker site—just a project index and a new-project page. You don't have a list of tasks on a single project, let alone a way to mark a task as complete.

Let's wildly hand-wave our way out of that, writing a request test for just the mail being sent when a task is complete. This will probably imply the existence of pages or functionality you haven't really written yet, but let's all agree to pretend it's already there.

With that hand-waving out of the way, let's write the test, starting with thinking about what you need:

- Given: You'll need one task that starts off incomplete.

- When: The action of this test is a controller action. In a RESTful Rails interface, that action would be TasksController#update. Let's go with that. The controller action has a completed: true parameter.

- Then: The task updates and an email is sent.

There's a simple case to start with, where completed is not set and no email is sent. Writing that test first will let you write the structure of the method.

> **Prescription 26** When testing a Boolean condition, make sure to write a test for both halves of the condition.

These tests cover the "send email" and "don't send email" cases:

```
display/04/spec/requests/task_requests_spec.rb
Line 1  require "rails_helper"

        RSpec.describe "task requests" do

    5     before(:example) do
            ActionMailer::Base.deliveries.clear
          end

          let(:task) { create(:task, title: "Learn how to test mailers", size: 3) }
   10
          it "does not send an email if a task is not completed" do
            patch(task_path(id: task.id), params: {task: {completed: false}})
            expect(ActionMailer::Base.deliveries.size).to eq(0)
          end
   15
          it "sends email when task is completed" do
            patch(task_path(id: task.id), params: {task: {completed: true}})
            expect(ActionMailer::Base.deliveries.size).to eq(1)
            email = ActionMailer::Base.deliveries.first
   20       expect(email.subject).to eq("A task has been completed")
            expect(email.to).to eq(["monitor@tasks.com"])
            expect(email.body.to_s).to match(/Learn how to test mailers/)
          end

   25  end
```

Most of this is a standard request test, but two lines are specific to the code you're testing. On line 6 you're using the before(:example) block to clear the ActionMailer::Base.deliveries object. Doing so ensures that the data structure holding the mailings is emptied. Otherwise, emails from other tests will linger and make your test results invalid.

You also need to ensure that in the config/environments/test.rb file you have the line config.action_mailer.delivery_method = :test. This configuration should be done by default, and ensures that mail delivery in tests saves the outgoing email messages to a data object whose behavior you can examine. In the test, on line 13, you can look at the mailer object, ActionMailer::Base.deliveries, and confirm that no emails have been sent.

This test passes with this boilerplate controller method (plus a blank template in app/views/tasks/edit.html.erb):

```
display/03/app/controllers/tasks_controller.rb
def update
  @task = Task.find(params[:id])
  if @task.update_attributes(task_params)
    redirect_to @task, notice: "project was successfully updated"
```

```
    else
      render action :edit
    end
end
```

And here's the test with the complete task that specifies email behavior:

display/04/spec/requests/task_requests_spec.rb
```
it "sends email when task is completed" do
  patch(task_path(id: task.id), params: {task: {completed: true}})
  expect(ActionMailer::Base.deliveries.size).to eq(1)
  email = ActionMailer::Base.deliveries.first
  expect(email.subject).to eq("A task has been completed")
  expect(email.to).to eq(["monitor@tasks.com"])
  expect(email.body.to_s).to match(/Learn how to test mailers/)
end
```

Again you're simulating the request to the update method, this time with a pseudo-attribute, completed, which you can assume indicates a check box of some kind. Note that you're not testing the actual behavior of completing the test here; that would normally be a model or workflow concern.

Instead, you're testing the mailer. You can verify that one email has been sent by checking the count of ActionMailer::Base.deliveries and then looking at the email object, ActionMailer::Base.deliveries.first,[4] and querying it for its subject and the list of addresses it's going to. You can also check that the body contains the task's title. (Generally the accessors have the names you would expect.)

The passing controller logic uses the completed param to trigger whether the task is updated and the mailer is sent—usually I'd create a workflow object here, but I'll spare you looking at a separate file and keep the code in the controller:

display/04/app/controllers/tasks_controller.rb
```
def update
  @task = Task.find(params[:id])
  completed = params[:task][:completed] == "true" && !@task.complete?
  params[:task][:completed_at] = Time.current if completed
  if @task.update_attributes(task_params)
    TaskMailer.task_completed_email(@task).deliver if completed
    redirect_to @task, notice: "project was successfully updated"
  else
    render action :edit
  end
end
```

4.　http://guides.rubyonrails.org/action_mailer_basics.html

Now all you need is the mailer. You can build a mailer from the command line using a Rails generator:

```
$ rails generate mailer TaskMailer
      create  app/mailers/task_mailer.rb
      invoke  erb
      create    app/views/task_mailer
      invoke  rspec
      create    spec/mailers/task_mailer_spec.rb
      create    spec/mailers/previews/task_mailer_preview.rb
```

Note that RSpec creates its own mailer files (I'll come back to those in a moment). I won't cover the preview file here, as that's not strictly an automated-testing thing. (You can find details online.[5])

The mailer itself is straightforward; you need to take the task object and set some mail variables:

display/04/app/mailers/task_mailer.rb
```
class TaskMailer < ApplicationMailer
  default from: "from@example.com"

  def task_completed_email(task)
    @task = task
    mail(to: "monitor@tasks.com", subject: "A task has been completed")
  end
end
```

And you need a template. Let's keep this simple:

display/04/app/views/task_mailer/task_completed_email.text.erb
```
The task <%= @task.title %> was completed at <%= @task.completed_at.to_s %>

Thanks,

The Management
```

The tests pass.

You can also unit-test the mailer. This example tests the same functionality:

display/04/spec/mailers/task_mailer_spec.rb
```
require "rails_helper"

RSpec.describe TaskMailer, type: :mailer do

  describe "task_completed_email" do
    let(:task) { create(:task, title: "Learn how to test mailers", size: 3) }
    let(:mail) { TaskMailer.task_completed_email(task) }

    it "renders the email" do
      expect(mail.subject).to eq("A task has been completed")
```

---

5.   http://guides.rubyonrails.org/action_mailer_basics.html#previewing-emails

```
      expect(mail.to).to eq(["monitor@tasks.com"])
      expect(mail.body.encoded).to match(/Learn how to test mailers/)
    end
  end
end
```

In this case you're not actually sending the email through the Rails mailer; you're just generating an email object and testing its values.

Outside of core Rails, the email-spec library provides a number of useful helpers.[6] For the most part they are ways of performing the tests you've already examined, but with a slightly cleaner syntax. The library also provides the ability to follow a link in an email back to the its source, which is helpful for acceptance-testing of user interactions that include email.

Testing Views and View Markup

You've tested a helper for project status, but when you go to the browser the new status DOM elements don't show up. This is because you haven't placed your new helper in the view template itself. Naturally, you would like your dazzling two-line helper to be incorporated into the view. From a TDD perspective, you have a few options:

- Write no further tests; just insert the helper into the view template. Technically you're not adding logic, so you can kind of squeak by with this one. I don't mean to be glib here—having no extra test may be the right choice when the test is expensive, trivial in the larger scheme of things, and easy to visually inspect.

- Write an integration test using Capybara, as you saw in Chapter 3, *Test-Driven Rails*, on page 41, and in Chapter 8, *Integration Testing with Capybara and Cucumber*, on page 151. If you've been using outside-in development, you may already have an integration test in place.

- Write a Rails view test. This has the advantage of being somewhat faster than the integration test, and you may be able to piggyback it on existing controller tests.

RSpec allows you to specify view tests independent of controllers. (Though you can get views to run from controller tests, it's not the default and it's not recommended.) The RSpec convention is to place view tests in the spec/views folder, with one spec file to a view file, so the view in app/views/projects/index.html.erb is specified in spec/views/projects/index.html.erb_spec.rb.

---

6.   http://github.com/bmabey/email-spec

I rarely write these tests. I find the file structure hard to maintain, and what logic I do have in views is often tested between objects like presenters and integration tests. In general, I find full TDD on views difficult—I often have to see a scratch implementation of a view before I know exactly what to test. That said, they are surprisingly easy to write because they have no dependency on any other part of the code, and if you think of the ERB template as sort of being a function, they are basically unit tests for views. So let's try one.

Let's take a second to plan this test. What does it need to do?

- Given: You need just two projects, one that is on schedule and one that's not. That allows you to verify both halves of the helper. The projects you create need to be visible to the controller method, meaning you either need to put the data in the database or do some clever mocking. (Fixtures could be used too, but I don't want to create fixtures because I don't want this project data to be global.) Let's start with the database; it's simpler for the moment.

- When: You just need to hit the index action of the controller.

- Then: Your on-schedule project has the on-schedule DOM class and your behind-schedule class has the behind-schedule one.

In code, that becomes the following:

```
display/05/spec/views/projects/index.html.erb_spec.rb
require "rails_helper"

describe "projects/index" do

  let(:completed_task) { Task.create!(completed_at: 1.day.ago, size: 1) }
  let(:on_schedule) { Project.create!(
    due_date: 1.year.from_now, name: "On Schedule", tasks: [completed_task]) }
  let(:incomplete_task) { Task.create!(size: 1) }
  let(:behind_schedule) { Project.create!(
    due_date: 1.day.from_now, name: "Behind Schedule",
    tasks: [incomplete_task]) }

  it "renders the index page with correct dom elements" do
    @projects = [on_schedule, behind_schedule]
    render
    expect(rendered).to have_selector(
      "#project_#{on_schedule.id} .on_schedule")
    expect(rendered).to have_selector(
      "#project_#{behind_schedule.id} .behind_schedule")
  end

end
```

I cheated here in one respect—the have_selector matcher is not part of core RSpec; it's actually part of Capybara, but you've already loaded Capybara, so that's fine. But have_selector is way better than the core way of querying DOM trees, so it's worth including here.

What does this view test do?

First you create your given: the data. Use let to create the on-schedule project and task. The objects need to be in the database so that the Rails associations all work. But there are other choices here that might make the test faster, including creating projects and stubbing the on_schedule? method or using FactoryBot.build_stubbed to create real objects without having to save them in the database.

In the spec itself, you set the @projects variable. You're testing the view in isolation, so you don't have a controller to set this up for you; you need to create the instance variables that will be given to the view.

Our "when" section is one line, render, which tells RSpec to render the view. Which view? The one specified by the outermost describe block. In this case, that's projects/index—Rails will connect that to the index.html.erb file in the file base. Alternatively, you can explicitly pass the view as an argument, render template: "projects/index". If the view is a partial, you need to specify that: render partial: "projects/data_row". An optional locals argument with key/value pairs specifies local variables to the partial. As with the regular Rails render method, you can use a shortcut of the form render "projects/data_row, project: @project".

All Rails helpers are loaded. If you want to stub one of their values, the helper methods are accessible via a view object, as in view.stub(:current_user).and_return(User.new). You can also use stub_template to stub a partial that you don't want to render; stub_template takes a key/value pair where the key is the exact file name of the partial and the value is the string you want returned in place of rendering the partial.

In the "then" portion of the spec, the rendered text is available via the method rendered. You can then use any RSpec matcher to set expectations on that value. In this test you're using have_selector, but you can also use match to do a simple regular-expression match.

In this case you're testing for the existence of a selector pattern with a DOM ID #project_#{on_schedule.id} that has a subordinate object containing the DOM class.on_schedule, and a similar selector pattern with the DOM ID #project_#{behind_schedule.id} containing an item with the DOM class .behind_schedule. You're passing the result of the rendered view to the matcher.

The selector syntax that have_selector uses is very similar to jQuery and other DOM selection tools. As in jQuery, the use of two separate selectors means you'd expect to match an instance of the first selector, which contains an instance of the second. For example, you're looking for an HTML element with the DOM ID of the form project_12, where 12 is the on_schedule project's ID. You also need that outer HTML element to contain an inner HTML element with a DOM class on_schedule.

The pattern project_12 is exactly what the Rails dom_id helper uses, and you previously put that in the tr element of each project in the index listing. So you're looking for an on_schedule class inside that view.

This test will fail with an error message that looks something like this, showing that the test is looking for a pattern that is not found:

```
Failure/Error:
    expect(rendered).to have_selector(
        "#project_#{on_schedule.id} .on_schedule")

    expected to find visible css "#project_1 .on_schedule" but there
    were no matches
```

A minor change in your index template gets the test to pass—change the project-name cell to use the name_with_status helper:

```
display/04/app/views/projects/index.html.erb
<h1>All Projects</h1>
<table>
  <thead>
    <tr>
      <td>Project Name</td>
      <td>Total Project Size</td>
    </tr>
  </thead>
  <tbody>
    <% @projects.each do |project| %>
      <tr class="project-row" id="<%= dom_id(project) %>">
        <td class="name"><%= name_with_status(project) %></td>
        <td class="total-size"><%= project.size %></td>
      </tr>
    <% end %>
  </tbody>
</table>
```

Now the tr field with the appropriate DOM ID has a span element from the helper that contains the expected DOM class.

Prescription 27 When testing for view elements, try to test for DOM classes that you control rather than text or element names that might be subject to design changes.

Using Presenters

Testing helpers is handy, but if you have a lot of logic in your helpers, I recommend moving the logic into presenter objects. This is especially true if you have a series of helpers that take the same argument.

There's nothing complicated about using presenters in Rails; I often roll my own using Ruby's SimpleDelegator class. If you want a little more structure, you can use the draper gem.[7]

You can convert the project helper to a project presenter. This version of the code uses SimpleDelegator and includes a method for converting a list of projects into a list of presenters. In a break from convention, I'll show you the code first:

```
display/05/app/presenters/project_presenter.rb
Line 1  class ProjectPresenter < SimpleDelegator
   -      def self.from_project_list(*projects)
   -        projects.flatten.map { |project| ProjectPresenter.new(project) }
   -      end
   5
   -      def initialize(project)
   -        super
   -      end
   -
  10      def name_with_status
   -        dom_class = on_schedule? ? "on_schedule" : "behind_schedule"
   -        "<span class='#{dom_class}'>#{name}</span>"
   -      end
   -    end
```

The main action here starts on line 6, with the initializer. All you need to do is call super, and SimpleDelegator will take care of the rest: if SimpleDelegator gets a message it doesn't understand, it automatically delegates it to the object passed to the constructor. In practice this delegation means you can treat the presenter as though it were an instance of the original object, plus the presenter includes any new methods you choose to add to the presenter itself.

The name_with_status method in the presenter is simpler than the pre-existing helper method in one way and more complex in another. Since calls to

---

7.   https://github.com/drapergem/draper

methods like on_schedule? or name are now automatically delegated, there's no need to explicitly have the project as the message receiver, so you can use on_schedule? rather than project.on_schedule?. However, since you're no longer inside a Rails helper you no longer have access to the content_tag method you used to build the HTML output. Instead, build the output as a string. (There are other options, such as explicitly including the module that content_tag is a part of, but building the string is simplest in this case.)

Finally, at the top of the class, you have a method that takes in a list of Project instances and converts them to presenters. The *projects argument in conjunction with projects.flatten allows the method to be called with either an explicit array, ProjectPresenter.from_project_list([p1, p2]), or an implicit arbitrary list of projects, ProjectPresenter.from_project_list(p1, p2). If you were using presenters more frequently, this kind of method would be easy to abstract to something generic rather than needing to be rewritten for each presenter class.

The test for the presenter is a little simpler than the tests you've seen so far:

`display/05/spec/presenters/project_presenter_spec.rb`
```ruby
require "rails_helper"

describe ProjectPresenter do
  let(:project) { instance_double(Project, name: "Project Runway") }
  let(:presenter) { ProjectPresenter.new(project) }

  it "handles name with on time status" do
    allow(project).to receive(:on_schedule?).and_return(true)
    expect(presenter.name_with_status).to eq(
      "<span class='on_schedule'>Project Runway</span>")
  end

  it "handles name with behind schedule status" do
    allow(project).to receive(:on_schedule?).and_return(false)
    expect(presenter.name_with_status).to eq(
      "<span class='behind_schedule'>Project Runway</span>")
  end
end
```

Do you see what you've done here? Since your presenter class has no dependencies on Rails, you can write a test class that also has no dependency on Rails. Rather than have the project be an actual project, you've replaced it with a double that responds to the only messages of project that you care about for this test.

However, you've given up a couple of things. You don't have have_selector, which belongs to controller and view groups (though it'd be possible to add it back in if you really wanted it).

But you've gained something big.

Since this test has no dependencies on Rails, you don't need the Rails environment—with a little bit more work you could replace require rails_helper at the top of the file with require spec_helper. That means you could execute the test without running Rails—which is great because it's potentially much faster not to load Rails than to load it.

Hold that thought; I'll come back to it in Chapter 16, *Running Tests Faster and Running Faster Tests*, on page 319.

Testing Jobs and Cables

Rails provides minimal support for testing ActiveJob background jobs and ActiveCable web sockets.

In RSpec a spec of type: :job or one placed in the spec/jobs directory exposes a couple of matchers. Before you run job specs, you need to specify that the jobs queue is using the test setting and not running off to Sidekiq or whatever. You do that with ActiveJob::Base.queue_adapter = :test, which you can use in a before block.

The basic matcher is have_been_enqueued, and the argument to it is the class of the job being enqueued, as in

```
it "should enqueue a mailer job" do
  AddsTaskWorkflow.new.run
  expect(TaskAddedMailJob).to have_been_enqueued
end
```

You can chain a lot of things to have_been_enqueued for more specific tests. You can check how many times the job has been enqueued with have_been_enqueued.exactly(:once), have_been_enqueued.at_most(:once), or have_been_enqueued.at_least (:once). There are special symbols for :once, :twice, and :thrice, or you can just use numbers. There are also special methods for those three cases, as in have_been_enqueued.once.

If you want to specify the arguments to the job, you can chain the with method. The arguments are exactly as you'd send them to a test double. You can also indicate a specific time for the job to be executed with the at method, and a specific queue as the target with the on_queue method.

There's no custom support for unit-testing ActionCable. Basecamp tests ActionCable with system tests. The gem Action Cable Testing provides support,[8] and may get incorporated into a future version of Rails.

---

8. https://github.com/palkan/action-cable-testing

What You've Done

In this chapter you walked through many of the different layers and tools in Rails, and saw how RSpec provides the ability to test those layers in isolation. You learned about views, controllers, mailers, routing, and background jobs. Focused view tests are possible in Rails but overlap heavily with helper tests, logic placed in presenter objects, and integration testing. Mailers and background jobs can also be tested in isolation. Although each of these layers has testing tools built for them, you may choose to test them via isolation tests or by placing most of the logic in non-Rails Ruby objects and testing those as their own unit.

Testing specific parts of the Rails framework is often tricky. Unlike model testing (which tends to be isolated to the particular model) or integration testing (which covers the entire stack), other layers have boundaries that are more blurred and objects that are harder to isolate for test purposes. Controlling those boundaries is the difference between tests that run quickly and fail only when the logic being tested is incorrect, and tests that are slower and dependent on logic outside the test.

Ideally, request tests are written so that they have minimal interaction with the model. There are costs to be balanced. A request action that has minimal contact with the model and can therefore have that interaction stubbed will often run faster and have fewer points of failure. On the other hand, the stubbing and additional classes that may be needed to mediate a controller-and-model interaction may feel overly complex, especially for boilerplate actions.

I'm aggressive about moving controller logic that interacts with the model to some kind of action object that doesn't have Rails dependencies. The controller logic and controller testing then tends to be limited to correctly dispatching successful and failed actions. That said, many Rails developers, notably including David Heinemeier Hansson, find adding an extra layer of objects to be overkill and think that worry about slow tests is misplaced. I recommend you try both ways and see which one best suits you.

Next up, you'll see the tools the Rails core team uses for testing, and how Minitest and its associated libraries let you test Rails.

CHAPTER 12

Minitest

Some people like the classics.

Some people don't like RSpec's syntax or its metaprogramming.

Some people use Minitest.

Minitest is the standard testing framework in the Ruby 2.0 Standard Library. It is also the default test framework for Rails. Compared to RSpec, Minitest is smaller, simpler, and less flexible. Minitest is also the testing suite used by the Rails team to test Rails itself. Minitest proponents say that a test suite is a terrible place to be dependent on metaprogramming and magic, and Minitest is easier to understand. RSpec proponents say that Minitest is not "expressive" and that Minitest tests are harder to understand.

It is *much more important* that you write tests than that you use a specific test framework. The overwhelming majority of the differences between RSpec and Minitest come down to style and taste, not functionality. To prove it, I offer the fact that an earlier version of this very book was centered on Minitest, and I changed it to a version centered on RSpec with basically no change to the underlying features or advice.

> Prescription 28   The decision to write tests is much more important than the testing tool you choose to write them.

Minitest's design is based on a structure that was created by Kent Beck for the SUnit framework in Smalltalk and popularized by Beck and Erich Gamma in JUnit for Java. In Ruby this design was originally implemented in the Test::Unit framework, which Minitest supplanted. Minitest is considered cleaner and easier to extend than RSpec. It uses traditional testing terms like "test" and "assert" and defines individual tests as Ruby methods (although you'll be using a Rails add-on that lets you define tests as blocks).

In this chapter you'll learn the Minitest way of doing basically everything you've done to test Rails in RSpec.

Getting Started with Minitest

Installing Minitest itself is easy: do nothing.

Minitest is part of core Ruby, and the Rails extensions I cover here are part of the core Rails bundle.

However, a couple of add-on libraries you've come across so far in this book require specific installations for Minitest. Minitest's included test-double package, Minitest::Mock, is small and lacks some useful features. I'll demonstrate test doubles using Mocha, which is the package the Rails team uses.[1]

To install Mocha, place the following in the Gemfile in the development test group:

```
gem "mocha", require: false
```

Minitest uses the test/test_helper.rb file to store setup. You'll need to load Mocha in that file:

minitest/01/test/test_helper.rb
```
require File.expand_path("../../config/environment", __FILE__)
require "rails/test_help"
require "mocha/mini_test"

module ActiveSupport
  class TestCase
    # Setup all fixtures in test/fixtures/*.yml for all tests in alphabetical
    # order.
    fixtures :all

    # Add more helper methods to be used by all tests here...
  end
end
```

And you're off to the races.

Minitest Basics

Your project's test directory contains Minitest equivalents of many of the RSpec tests you've written thus far.

Here's an example—specifically, the tests for the Task model:

---

1.   http://gofreerange.com/mocha/docs

```
minitest/01/test/models/task_test.rb
Line 1  require "test_helper"

  -   class TaskTest < ActiveSupport::TestCase
  -     test "a completed task is complete" do
  5       task = Task.new
  -       refute(task.complete?)
  -       task.mark_completed
  -       assert(task.complete?)
  -     end
  10

  -     test "an uncompleted task does not count toward velocity" do
  -       task = Task.new(size: 3)
  -       refute(task.part_of_velocity?)
  -       assert_equal(0, task.points_toward_velocity)
  15      end

  -
  -     test "a task completed long ago does not count toward velocity" do
  -       task = Task.new(size: 3)
  -       task.mark_completed(6.months.ago)
  20      refute(task.part_of_velocity?)
  -       assert_equal(0, task.points_toward_velocity)
  -     end

  -
  -     test "a task completed recently counts toward velocity" do
  25      task = Task.new(size: 3)
  -       task.mark_completed(1.day.ago)
  -       assert(task.part_of_velocity?)
  -       assert_equal(3, task.points_toward_velocity)
  -     end
  30  end
```

This looks broadly similar to the RSpec you've been looking at, but the syntax has some clear differences. Let's take a look at the main ones.

On line 1 the file test_helper is required; it contains Rails and application-related setup common to all Minitest files. It's the file to which you just added Mocha.

In Minitest you can't put a test method just anywhere or name it just anything; tests need to be methods of a subclass of the class Minitest::Test. (The class ActiveSupport::TestCase that the test uses is, in fact, a subclass of Minitest::Test.) In standard Minitest, a test method is any method whose name starts with test_, as in test_this_thing_with_a_long_name. However, this test uses a Rails ActiveSupport extension that allows you to just say test "some string", followed by a block. Rails uses metaprogramming to convert test "some string" into a method called test_some_string, which invokes the block and is, by virtue of the name, executed by Minitest during a test run. I find the test_long_name syntax to be significantly less readable, so let's use the shortcut here.

Quick note for RSpec fans: unlike in RSpec, the name-munging in Minitest means that two tests in the same class cannot have the same string description—they'd resolve to the same Minitest name. Second quick note: there is a minitest-spec extension that gives Minitest a more RSpec-like syntax, but that version has been specifically turned down for usage in core Rails, and I won't be discussing it here.

Inside the test method you need to do two things. First, create a Task instance. Then, on lines 6 and 8, make your first assertions. Use refute to claim that task.complete? will be false on a new instance, and then after marking the task as complete, assert that the method call task.complete? will result in a true value. The assert method is the most basic of Minitest's assertions. It takes one argument, and the assertion passes if the argument is true (for Ruby values of true), and fails if the argument is false. The refute method is the exact opposite; it passes if the sole argument is false, and fails otherwise.

Minitest defines about a dozen assertion methods and their opposites. (See the documentation for a full list.[2]) The following table lists the six assertions you'll probably use most frequently.

Assertion	Passes if
assert(test)	test is true
assert_block block	The associated block returns true
assert_equal(expected, actual)	expected == actual
assert_includes(collection, object)	collection.include?(object)
assert_match(expected, actual)	expected =~ actual
assert_nil(expected)	expected == nil
assert_raises(exception) block	The associated block raises the exception

All Minitest assertions share two useful features. First, they all take an optional additional argument that is a string message. Here's an example:

```
assert_equal("Noel", author.name, "Incorrect author name")
```

If the assertion fails, the message is output to the console. I don't normally use message arguments, because the messages create more overhead and clutter the tests. But if you're in a situation where documentation is particularly important, messages can be useful to describe a test's intent.

Second, every assert method has an opposing refute method: refute_equal, refute_match, and so on. The refute methods pass where the assert methods would

---

2.   http://docs.seattlerb.org/minitest/Minitest/Assertions.html

fail, so refute_equal passes if the two arguments are not equal. These are occasionally useful, but go light on them; most people find negative logic harder to reason about.

Rails ActiveSupport provides a subclass called ActiveSupport::TestCase that provides a handful of shortcuts and goodies:

- The ability to load data from fixtures before tests

- The declarative test "test name" do syntax described earlier

- The assertions assert_difference and assert_no_difference

- Support for asserting the existence of Rails deprecations, unlikely to be helpful unless you're working on Rails itself

- Logging support to put the test class and test name in the Rails test.log before each test

- Support for multiple setup and teardown blocks, defined with the method name, similar to RSpec before and after blocks

Running Minitest

Rails provides some standard tasks for running all or part of the test suite.

The one to use most of the time, which is not the Rails default, is rails test (often bin/rails test, depending on how your bundle is set up); it grabs any files ending with _test.rb in the test directory or any of its subdirectories (except for system tests) and executes them through Minitest. For running a single file or directory, Minitest and Rails use the syntax rails test test/models/task_test.rb. For now let's assume you're using rails test. In Chapter 16, *Running Tests Faster and Running Faster Tests*, on page 319, I'll cover better ways to focus test execution.

When you run racks test, the Rake task identifies any files matching the pattern test/**/*_test.rb and passes them all to Minitest. (The related task rails test:db first resets the database using db:test:prepare.) Once Minitest gets the list of matching files, it does the following for each file:

- The Ruby interpreter loads the file. In a Rails context, the line require test_helper is important, as the test_helper file includes global and Rails-specific setup.

- Inside any subclass of Minitest::Test, Minitest identifies test methods in the file—either because the method name starts with test or because you're using the ActiveSupport test method directly.

That gives Minitest a list of test methods to run. For each of those methods it does the following:

- Loads or resets all fixture data, as discussed in *Fixtures*, on page 103.

- Runs all setup blocks. Setup blocks are defined as def setup or, in Rails, setup do.

- Runs the test method. The method execution ends when a runtime error or a failed assertion is encountered. Otherwise it passes. Yay!

- Runs all teardown blocks. Teardown blocks are declared similarly to setup blocks, but their use is much less common.

- Rolls back or deletes the fixtures as described in the first bullet point. The result of each test is passed back to the test runner for display in the console or IDE window running the test.

The following figure shows the flow.

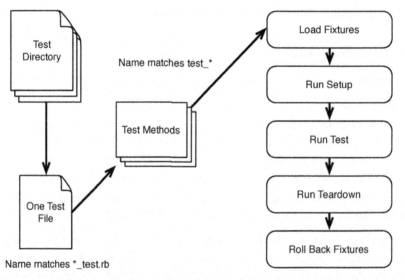

You can control fixture loading with a few parameters, which are set in the test/test_helper.rb file. The most important is the fixtures :all method call, which ensures that all your fixture files are loaded in all your tests. This line being written in the file is a little bit of framework archeology. The original default in Rails was to load fixtures for only the class under test. You can still specify particular fixtures to be loaded by passing the model names as symbols to the fixtures method, though I'm not sure there's a good reason for doing so these days.

Minitest Setup

One of the clearest differences between the RSpec way and the Minitest way is how you set up different data for different tests. In RSpec, the describe method is used to enclose an arbitrary number of tests for the purpose of giving each group of tests a different setup. For example, your Project specs in spec/models/project_spec.rb has three different groups, one without a task, one with a task, and one with a bunch of tasks.

In Minitest, each class has one setup method. (Technically, you can define multiple setup do blocks, but all of them are executed for all tests—you can't use Minitest setup to have different setups for different tests.) While you could solve this problem by putting each setup in a different class, I think it's somewhat more common to have explicit methods called from the beginning of the test to handle setup.

Here's one way to handle multiple setup blocks in a Minitest version of your Project tests:

```
minitest/01/test/models/project_test.rb
require "test_helper"

class ProjectTest < ActiveSupport::TestCase
  setup do
    @project = FactoryBot.create(:project)
  end

  def add_one_task
    @task = FactoryBot.create(:task, project: @project)
  end

  def add_many_tasks
    newly_done = FactoryBot.build(:task, :newly_complete)
    old_done = FactoryBot.build(:task, :long_complete, :small)
    small_not_done = FactoryBot.build(:task, :small)
    large_not_done = FactoryBot.build(:task, :large)
    @project.tasks = [newly_done, old_done, small_not_done, large_not_done]
    @project.save!
  end

  test "a project with no tasks is done" do
    assert(@project.done?)
  end

  test "a project with no tests is estimated" do
    assert_equal(0, @project.completed_velocity)
    assert_equal(0, @project.current_rate)
    assert(@project.projected_days_remaining.nan?)
    refute(@project.on_schedule?)
  end
```

```
test "a project with an incomplete task is not done" do
  add_one_task
  refute(@project.done?)
end

test "a project with complete tasks is done" do
  add_one_task
  @task.mark_completed
  @task.save
  assert(@project.done?)
end

test "can calculate sizes" do
  add_many_tasks
  assert_equal(10, @project.size)
  assert_equal(6, @project.incomplete_tasks.map(&:size).sum)
  assert_equal(3, @project.completed_velocity)
  assert_equal(1.0 / 7, @project.current_rate)
  assert_equal(42, @project.projected_days_remaining)
end
end
```

This is the same set of tests, with a couple of minor changes—most notably, the Minitest version saves test data to the database so that it can use full Rails ActiveRecord associations.

Instead of three different describe blocks, the Minitest version has three different setup methods—the basic setup that creates a project, and the add_one_task and add_many_tasks methods. The two methods are called at the beginning of whatever tests need them. The Minitest version has the advantage of being quite explicit about what setup happens in what test. RSpec is often criticized for being opaque here, especially if the describe blocks are nested. The cost is a little bit more typing and a little bit less structure. In the Minitest version there's no grouping of tests, so it can be harder to determine which tests are related.

To clear up one other difference between this Minitest example and the RSpec example, this Minitest example uses factory_bot's create build strategy rather than build_stubbed. This is kind of incidental to Minitest—you could write a Minitest version that used build_stubbed; it's just that the limitations of build_stubbed not being able to touch the database conflicted with the setup structure for creating the associations, so I decided it was clearer to create the database items. I did combine all the sizing assertions into one test to minimize the amount of setup.

Mocha

The Mocha library is the one Rails uses for its own testing, so it seems the natural choice for a test-double library to use with Minitest. Full Mocha docs are available online.[3]

Installing Mocha

Mocha needs to be installed after Minitest, which requires a slight indirection to ensure your Rails app does the right thing.

First, in the Gemfile's :test group, add the Mocha gem:

```
gem "mocha"
```

Then, inside the test/test_helper.rb file, you manually require Mocha at any point in the file after the rails/test_help library is loaded:

```
require "mocha/mini_test"
```

At that point you should be good to go. Please see Chapter 7, *Using Test Doubles as Mocks and Stubs*, on page 129, for a full discussion of test doubles. Here I'll cover only Mocha syntax.

In Mocha you can call stub to create a full double that is just a set of stubbed methods; stub is available throughout your test cases.

```
test "here's a sample stub" do
  stubby = stub(name: "Paul", weight: 100)
  assert_equal("Paul", stubby.name)
end
```

Mocha has verification syntax for full doubles. In Mocha you use responds_like and responds_like_instance_of to trigger verification that the object matches a given object's API. You might do so like this:

```
stubby = stub(size: 3)
stubby.responds_like(Task.new)
```

Or this:

```
stubby = stub(size: 3)
stubby.respond_like_instance_of(Task)
```

In either case, if you called stubby with a method that is not defined for the Task class—say, stubby.due_date—Mocha will raise a NoMethodError. Internally this uses the Ruby respond_to? method, so if you're using dynamically generated

---

3. http://gofreerange.com/mocha/docs

methods via define_method, method_missing, or something more esoteric, you need to ensure that your respond_to? method works in sync.

For partial test doubles, Mocha provides the method stubs, which is mixed in to any Ruby object:

```
minitest/01/test/models/project_with_stubs_test.rb
Line 1  test "let's stub an object" do
     2    project = Project.new(name: "Project Greenlight")
     3    project.stubs(:name)
     4    assert_nil(project.name)
     5  end
```

This test passes. Line 3 sets up the stub, which intercepts the project.name call in line 4 to return nil, and never even gets to the project name.

Mocha allows you to specify a return value for the stubbed method:

```
minitest/01/test/models/project_with_stubs_test.rb
test "let's stub an object again" do
  project = Project.new(name: "Project Greenlight")
  project.stubs(:name).returns("Fred")
  assert_equal("Fred", project.name)
end
```

The stubs method returns a Mocha Expectation object, which is effectively a proxy to the real object, but responds to a number of methods that let you annotate the stub. The returns method is one of those annotation messages that associates the return value with the method. Mocha also provides the shortcut project.stubs(name: "Fred"), allowing you to specify messages and return values as key/value pairs.

As with RSpec, you can stub classes as well as instances:

```
minitest/01/test/models/project_with_stubs_test.rb
test "let's stub a class" do
  Project.stubs(:find).returns(Project.new(name: "Project Greenlight"))
  project = Project.find(1)
  assert_equal("Project Greenlight", project.name)
end
```

And you can stub all instances of a class with the method any_instance, as in this example:

```
Project.any_instance.stubs(:save).returns(false)
```

```
stubby.stubs(:user_count).raises(Exception, "oops")
```

As with stubs, Mocha provides a way to create whole mocks that exist just as mocks, as well as a way to create partial mocks that add expectations to an existing object. The method for whole-mock creation is mock:

```
test "a sample mock" do
  mocky = mock(name: "Paul", weight: 100)
  assert_equal("Paul", mocky.name)
end
```

The method for adding a mock expectation to a message on an existing object is expects. (I know, you'd think they'd have used mocks. But they didn't.)

minitest/01/test/models/project_with_stubs_test.rb
```
test "let's mock an object" do
  mock_project = Project.new(name: "Project Greenlight")
  mock_project.expects(:name).returns("Fred")
  assert_equal("Fred", mock_project.name)
end
```

Mocha has its own set of methods that can be chained to the mock declaration to add specifics:

```
proj = Project.new
proj.expects(:name).once
proj.expects(:name).twice
proj.expects(:name).at_least_once
proj.expects(:name).at_most_once
proj.expects(:name).at_least(3)
proj.expects(:name).at_most(3)
proj.expects(:name).times(5)
proj.expects(:name).times(4..6)
proj.expects(:name).never
```

If you have multiple return values specified, the stubbed method returns them one at a time:

minitest/01/test/models/project_with_stubs_test.rb
```
test "stub with multiple returns" do
  stubby = Project.new
  stubby.stubs(:user_count).returns(1, 2)
  assert_equal(1, stubby.user_count)
  assert_equal(2, stubby.user_count)
  assert_equal(2, stubby.user_count)
end
```

As with RSpec, the last value is repeated over and over again.

You can get the same effect with a little more syntactic sugar by using the then method. You can chain together as many of these as you want:

```
stubby.stubs(:user_count).returns(1).then.returns(2)
```

Mocha also has the with method to specify arguments to a mock or a stub, as in Project.expects(:find).with(1). There are also some more advanced but occasionally useful things you can do with with. First off, with can take a block as an argument, in which case the value passed to the method is passed on to the block. If the block returns true, then the expectation is considered matched:

```
proj = Project.new()
proj.expects(:status).with { |value| value % 2 == 0 }
    .returns("Active")
proj.expects(:status).with { |value| value % 3 == 0 }
    .returns("Asleep")
```

If more than one block returns true, the last one declared wins. If none of the blocks return true, you get the same unexpected invocation error as in the preceding code.

The argument to with can also be one of a series of parameter matchers. Probably the most useful one is instance_of, which you can use to simulate behavior given different types of input:

```
proj = Project.new()
proj.expects(:tasks_before).with(instance_of(Date)).returns(3)
proj.expects(:tasks_before).with(instance_of(String)).raises(Exception)
```

The instance_of matcher or any other Mocha matcher can be negated with the Not method. (Yes, it's capitalized, presumably to avoid weird parse collisions with the keyword not.)

```
proj = Project.new()
proj.expects(:tasks_before).with(Not(instance_of(Date))).returns(3)
```

The only other such specialized matcher I've ever found remotely valuable in practice is has_entry, which works against a hash:

```
proj.expects(:options).with(has_entry(verbose: true))
```

The stub in this snippet will match any hash argument that contains a verbose: true entry, no matter what the other contents of the hash might be. Using the has_entry matcher is occasionally valuable against, say, an ActiveRecord or controller method that expects a hash where you care about only one of the methods.

There's about a dozen more of these matchers, many of which are, shall I say, somewhat lacking in real-world value. Rather than cluttering your head with a bunch of stuff you'll never use, I invite you to check out the Mocha docs online for a full listing if you're interested.[4]

---

4. http://gofreerange.com/mocha/docs

System Tests and Others

In addition to ActiveSupport::TestCase, Rails provides some other subclasses of Minitest::TestCase that provide custom functionality. In most of these cases, the RSpec functionality you've already seen is built on top of these classes:

- ActionDispatch::SystemTestCase is the parent class for system tests, which you saw in Chapter 8, *Integration Testing with Capybara and Cucumber*, on page 151.

- ActionDispatch::IntegrationTest is wrapped by RSpec request specs, as seen in Chapter 11, *Testing Rails Display Elements*, on page 217.

- ActionView::TestCase, ActionMailer::TestCase, and ActiveJob::TestCase all provide specific support similar to the RSpec support discussed in Chapter 11, *Testing Rails Display Elements*, on page 217.

Let's look at the system and integration tests because they are the ones the Rails core uses most frequently.

Minitest System Tests

In Minitest, the Rails core team recommendation is to use system tests and Capybara only when invoking a JavaScript runtime; in other cases, the team recommends using integration tests.

You have one JavaScript test in your suite. Here's what it looks like in Minitest. You need to specify that you're using headless Chrome as your driver (the Rails default is Selenium with a visible browser):

minitest/02/test/application_system_test_case.rb
```
require "test_helper"

class ApplicationSystemTestCase < ActionDispatch::SystemTestCase
  driven_by :selenium_chrome_headless
end
```

The driven_by method takes the same options you listed in Chapter 8, *Integration Testing with Capybara and Cucumber*, on page 151.

Here's the test itself:

minitest/02/test/system/tasks_test.rb
```
require "application_system_test_case"

class TasksTest < ApplicationSystemTestCase
  test "reordering a task" do
    project = FactoryBot.create(:project, name: "Project Bluebook")
    FactoryBot.create(
      :task, project: project, title: "Search Sky", size: 1, project_order: 1)
```

```
    FactoryBot.create(
      :task, project: project, title: "Use Telescope", size: 1,
             project_order: 2)
    FactoryBot.create(
      :task, project: project, title: "Take Notes", size: 1,
             project_order: 3)
    visit(project_path(project))
    find("#task_3")
    within("#task_3") do
      click_on("Up")
    end
    assert_selector(
      "tbody:nth-child(2) .name", text: "Take Notes")
    visit(project_path(project))
    find("#task_2")
    within("#task_2") do
      assert_selector(".name", text: "Take Notes")
    end
  end
end
```

It's very similar to the RSpec version, with two exceptions:

- Minitest doesn't have let, so I've pulled the object creation into the test.
- Rather than use matchers, Minitest uses assert_selector, which takes the same arguments.

Since the rest of the test uses Capybara, it uses the same calls as the RSpec version we've been using in the rest of the book.

Rails does not run system tests as part of a general rails test command, on the theory that system tests are slow and you might want to run them separately. The command to run the system tests is rails test:system, which will successfully run these tests.

Minitest Integration Tests

Rails uses integration tests for end-to-end tests when the runtime is not using JavaScript. These are a little different from the system tests in that they don't use Capybara, and therefore typically pass parameters directly to the test.

You have end-to-end tests that you used to create projects. Here's how those look as integration tests:

minitest/02/test/integration/add_project_test.rb
```
require "test_helper"

class AddProjectTest < ActionDispatch::IntegrationTest
  test "allows a user to create a project with tasks" do
    post(projects_path, params: {project:
```

```
        {name: "Project Runway", tasks: "Choose Fabric:3\nMake it Work:5"}})
    @project = Project.find_by(name: "Project Runway")
    follow_redirect!
    assert_select("#project_#{@project.id} .name", "Project Runway")
    assert_select("#project_#{@project.id} .total-size", text: "8")
  end

  test "does not allow a user to create a project without a name" do
    post(projects_path, params: {project:
      {tasks: "Choose Fabric:3\nMake it Work:5"}})
    assert_select(".new_project")
  end

  test "behaves correctly with a database failure" do
    workflow = stub(success?: false, create: false, project: Project.new)
    CreatesProject.stubs(:new)
      .with(name: "Project Runway",
            task_string: "Choose Fabric:3\nMake it Work:5")
      .returns(workflow)
    post(projects_path, params: {project:
      {name: "Project Runway", tasks: "Choose Fabric:3\nMake it Work:5"}})
    @project = Project.find_by(name: "Project Runway")
    assert_select(".new_project")
  end
end
```

There are a few differences between these tests and the system tests you wrote before.

Rather than simulating filling out the form with Capybara, you're sending arguments through the Rails routing table directly using the post helper. This is the same method taking the same arguments as RSpec request specs, as discussed in Chapter 11, *Testing Rails Display Elements*, on page 217.

In the first test, the successful action of the controller is a redirect. Rails integration tests don't follow redirects by default, so use follow_redirect! to force the test to continue so that you can check the output.

Rails integration tests use assert_select to check output, which is similar to the Capybara have_selector matcher you've already seen, but is a separate implementation with its own syntax quirks. By default assert_select works against the test's response body.

The selector syntax that assert_select uses is very similar to jQuery and other DOM selection tools, though assert_select uses its own HTML parser. As in jQuery, the use of two separate selectors means you'd expect to match an instance of the first selector, which contains an instance of the second. For example, you're looking for an HTML element with the DOM ID of the form project_12, where 12 is the ID of the newly created project. That outer HTML element also needs to contain an inner HTML element with a DOM class name.

You can augment assert_select in a number of ways. The selector argument to assert_select can be just an element, as in div, or an element plus a class or ID decoration, as in div.hidden. In the latter case, a matching element must have both the HTML tag and the DOM class or ID. As with other DOM selectors, a dot (.) indicates a DOM class and a hash mark (#) indicates a DOM ID. You can also use brackets to indicate arbitrary HTML attributes, as in input[name='email']. All this code has been pulled out into a gem called Rails::Dom::Testing.[5]

You can make a more specific match by including a second argument.

Value Type	Assertion Passes If
True	At least one element matches the selector
False	No elements match the selector
Integer	Exactly the integer number of elements match the selector
Range	The number of elements that match the selector is in the range
Regular expression	The text of a matching element matches the Regex
String	The text of a matching element equals the string

You can also use keyword arguments, meaning that assert_select("li", "Noel") is equivalent to assert_select("li", text: "Noel"). The keyword versions allow you to use multiple assertions in one assert_select call.

Keyword	Assertion Passes If
:count	The number of matching elements equals the argument
:html	A matching element contains the HTML content
:text	A matching element contains the text content
:maximum	The number of matching elements is less than or equal to the argument
:minimum	The number of matching elements is greater than or equal to the argument

---

5.   https://github.com/rails/rails-dom-testing

Minitest Helper Tests

Rails provides the ActionView::TestCase class, which is a subclass of ActiveSupport::TestCase designed to load enough of the Rails controller structure to enable helpers to be called and tested. Let's look at the Minitest version of the name_with_status helper tests:

```
minitest/02/test/helpers/project_helper_test.rb
require "test_helper"
class ProjectsHelperTest < ActionView::TestCase
  test "project name with status info" do
    project = Project.new(name: "Project Runway")
    project.stubs(:on_schedule?).returns(true)
    actual = name_with_status(project)
    expected = "<span class='on_schedule'>Project Runway</span>"
    assert_dom_equal(expected, actual)
  end

  test "project name with status info behind schedule" do
    project = Project.new(name: "Project Runway")
    project.stubs(:on_schedule?).returns(false)
    actual = name_with_status(project)
    expected = "<span class='behind_schedule'>Project Runway</span>"
    assert_dom_equal(expected, actual)
  end

  test "project name using assert_select" do
    project = Project.new(name: "Project Runway")
    project.stubs(:on_schedule?).returns(false)
    assert_select_string(name_with_status(project), "span.behind_schedule")
  end
end
```

The assert_dom_equal method doesn't have an RSpec equivalent. You use assert_dom_equal to compare the string you expect to the string you get from the helper. The assert_dom_equal assertion checks that two strings both resolve to equivalent DOM structures; it tests that attributes have identical values but don't necessarily need to be in the same order. It's nice to have because it spares you having to do some fiddling with HTML strings in your test.

There's another assert_select trick I wanted to mention—the ability to pass a block to assert_select and then have assert_select work on an arbitrary HTML element rather than the entire page output.

If you pass a block to assert_select, then asset_select invokes the block with a single argument containing an array of all HTML elements that match your selector. You can then do whatever you want with that array. One choice is to iterate over the array and run further assertions, perhaps using assert_select.

This is a different way to test for nested elements. The original assert_select from the controller test, which was "#project_#{@project.id} .name", could instead be written as follows:

```
assert_select("#project_#{@project.id}") do |matches|
  matches.each do |element|
    assert_select(element, ".name")
  end
end
```

This may be more explicit in some cases or may allow for more complex logic for the internal selector.

The inner assert_select in that snippet is doing something you haven't seen. The first argument, element, is one of the matching HTML node objects. When assert_select is passed an HTML node, it searches that HTML for the matching selector rather than the default behavior, which is to use the current HTTP response object.

That first argument is handy for the block syntax, but you can also take advantage of it to use assert_select against arbitrary strings that happen to be valid HTML with a parent root element. All you need is a helper method, which you'd place in your test_helper.rb file:

minitest/02/test/test_helper.rb
```
require File.expand_path("../../config/environment", __FILE__)
require "rails/test_help"
require "mocha/mini_test"

module ActiveSupport
  class TestCase
    # Setup all fixtures in test/fixtures/*.yml for all tests in alphabetical
    # order.
    fixtures :all

    # Add more helper methods to be used by all tests here...
  end
end

def assert_select_string(string, *selectors, &block)
  doc_root = Nokogiri::HTML::Document.parse(string).root
  assert_select(doc_root, *selectors, &block)
end
```

You're using Rails HTML parsing classes, which aren't normally part of a balanced Rails breakfast but allow you to parse a string into an HTML document and take the root element. That root element can then be used as the basis for an assert_select search. You'd then use this method in your helper test.

Minitest and Routing

The primary method that Rails/Minitest uses for route testing is assert_routing. Here are the Minitest versions of the same standard routes:

minitest/02/test/controllers/projects_controller_test.rb
```
require "test_helper"

class ProjectsControllerTest < ActionController::TestCase
  test "routing" do
    assert_routing "/projects", controller: "projects", action: "index"
    assert_routing({path: "/projects", method: "post"},
      controller: "projects", action: "create")
    assert_routing "/projects/new", controller: "projects", action: "new"
    assert_routing "/projects/1", controller: "projects",
                                  action: "show", id: "1"
    assert_routing "/projects/1/edit", controller: "projects",
                                       action: "edit", id: "1"
    assert_routing({path: "/projects/1", method: "patch"},
      controller: "projects", action: "update", id: "1")
    assert_routing({path: "/projects/1", method: "delete"},
      controller: "projects", action: "destroy", id: "1")
  end
end
```

The first argument to assert_routing represents the path. As you can see from the preceding examples, this argument is either a string representing the URL, or a hash with a :path key representing the URL and a :method key representing the HTTP method being invoked. If no method is specified, the default is GET.

The second argument is a hash representing any of the elements of the route after it is processed by the Rails router, meaning you would expect this argument to specify a :controller, an :action, and any other symbols defined by the route. This second argument does not contain any elements that are expected to be part of the query string as opposed to the base URL.

The third argument is defined as defaults. As far as I can tell, it's essentially merged into the second argument. (The documentation says this parameter is unused, though it's clearly referenced in the source code.) It seems to be safe to leave it as an empty hash if you need the fourth argument. That fourth argument is where you specify key/value pairs for any part of the route you expect to be in the query string.

The assert_routing method validates the routing in both directions. You can also run the routing tests in one direction using assert_generates to go from a string to a hash, and assert_recognizes to go from a hash to a string.

What You've Done

Minitest has a couple of advantages over RSpec. It's less complex and is often faster in practice. In this chapter you've seen how to use Minitest to write unit, system, and integration tests. In many cases, the RSpec functionality is based on the Rails test extensions to Minitest.

In the rest of this book I'll describe how every new library is set up for both RSpec and Minitest. Although the examples will primarily be RSpec, the sample-code download has analogous Minitest examples for most of them in the test directory of each successive version of the application.

CHAPTER 13

Testing for Security

Web security is a scary topic. All of your applications depend on cryptography and code that is beyond your immediate control. Despite that, certain parts of web security *are* in your control—all the logins and access checks and injection errors that happen on your site as a result of programming choices you make.

When it comes to security and testing, there's good news and bad news. The good news is that all kinds of access and injection bugs are amenable to automated developer testing. Sometimes unit testing will do the trick; other times end-to-end testing is the correct tool, but the effects of a security problem are often easily reproducible in a test environment. The bad news is that you need to actively determine where access and injection bugs might lurk in your code. This chapter focuses on user logins, roles, and using tests to make sure basic user authentication holds in your application.

> **Prescription 29** Security issues are often just bugs. Most of the practices you follow to keep your code bug-free will also help prevent and diagnose security issues.

User Authentication and Authorization

You've gotten quite far in your example without adding a user model to it, which we'll rectify now.

We need to get users and passwords into the system without spending too much time in the setup weeds—so you can focus your attention on the security issues that having users causes. To do that, use the Devise gem for basic user authentication and focus on how to use Devise as part of your security and testing goals.[1] (Part of me wants to derive user authentication from first principles, and someday when I publish a book from "The Purist Press" I'll do that.)

Devise is a big, multifaceted gem, and I'll only be scratching the surface of what it can do. It handles all kinds of login needs, including confirmation emails, password changes, "remember me" cookies, and much more. First up, you need to put it in the Gemfile:

```
gem "devise"
```

As of this writing, the current version of Devise is 4.4.1.

After you install the gem with bundle install, you need to take two generation steps. The first is the general installation of the Devise setup:

```
$ rails generate devise:install
      create  config/initializers/devise.rb
      create  config/locales/devise.en.yml
```

This gives you a devise.rb initializer containing a lot of setup options that you aren't going to worry about at the moment, and a locale file containing all the static text Devise uses. You won't worry about that file, either.

At the end of the generation process, Devise gives you a useful list of a few tasks you need to do by hand to allow Devise to integrate with the application. The relevant tasks are as follows:

- In config/environments/development.rb, set some default mailer options by adding the suggested default line, config.action_mailer.default_url_options = { host: 'localhost:3000' }. In a real application you'd need that in your other environments as well, with the host pointing to the host URL.

- Give your config.routes.rb a root route—for example, by adding root to: "projects#index", which is the closest thing you have to a root route.

- Devise uses the Rails flash to distribute messages of success and failure. Add the following to app/views/layouts/application.html.erb any place in the file that seems relevant:

```
<p class="notice"><%= notice %></p>
<p class="alert"><%= alert %></p>
```

That's it. If you wanted to copy all of the Devise view code for the dialogs and stuff, you could also run rails generate devise:views from the command line. We'll skip that for now.

---

1.   http://devise.plataformatec.com.br

Now you need to generate a User model compatible with Devise:

```
% rails generate devise User
```

This creates a User model, a migration, a spec or test file, and a factory_bot factory if factory_bot is installed. It also adds a line to the routes.rb file that handles all the login and logout routes.

Your User model has nothing but some Devise commands:

security/01/app/models/user.rb
```
class User < ApplicationRecord
  # Include default devise modules. Others available are:
  # :confirmable, :lockable, :timeoutable and :omniauthable
  devise :database_authenticatable, :registerable,
    :recoverable, :rememberable, :trackable, :validatable
end
```

Each of those symbols passed to the devise method enables another of Devise's features and assumes a certain set of database columns, the list of which you can see in the generated migration file.

To get these new columns in the database, you need to run the migrations:

```
% rake db:migrate
```

Finally, Devise has some test helpers that you need to include in your controller tests to enable login behavior in tests. Let's add a support file:

security/01/spec/support/devise.rb
```
RSpec.configure do |config|
  config.include Devise::Test::ControllerHelpers, type: :controller
  config.include Devise::Test::ControllerHelpers, type: :view
  config.include Devise::Test::IntegrationHelpers, type: :system
  config.include Devise::Test::IntegrationHelpers, type: :request
end
```

Minitest fans should go into the test_helper.rb file and add the following:

security/01/test/test_helper.rb
```
module ActionController
  class TestCase
    include Devise::Test::ControllerHelpers
  end
end

module ActionDispatch
  class IntegrationTest
    include Devise::Test::IntegrationHelpers
  end
end
```

This line adds the same test helpers. (Minitest fans should note that from here out the code directory for this book will often have Minitest versions of tests in the text, even though I won't specifically call out all of them.)

Adding Users and Roles

Now that you have Devise installed, let's see how you can use testing to expose security issues.

The most basic security issue is user login. Since your application involves projects that would presumably be limited to a specific, private set of users, it makes sense that you would need to be logged in to access the application. This is testable logic—a logged-in user can access a page, whereas any random person who happens across the page cannot.

Here's an integration test for the project index page:

security/01/spec/system/user_and_role_spec.rb
```
Line 1  require "rails_helper"

        RSpec.describe "with users and roles" do

   5      def log_in_as(user)
            visit new_user_session_path
            fill_in("user_email", with: user.email)
            fill_in("user_password", with: user.password)
            click_button("Log in")
  10      end

          let(:user) { User.create(email: "test@example.com", password: "password") }

          it "allows a logged-in user to view the project index page" do
  15        log_in_as(user)
            visit(projects_path)
            expect(current_path).to eq(projects_path)
          end

  20      it "does not allow a user to see the project page if not logged in" do
            visit(projects_path)
            expect(current_path).to eq(user_session_path)
          end

  25  end
```

This test uses Capybara, and you've seen most of the component parts before. However, this test has the first of several answers to the question, "How do I simulate a user login in an automated test?" In the helper method log_in_as on line 5, you simulate a user login by actually going through the steps of a user login. The method uses Capybara and the standard Devise login route and login form to simulate heading to the login page. Devise calls this the new_user_session_path, and fills in the user's email and password and clicks a button, for which the default Devise caption is "Log in." This method will be boilerplate across projects, depending on the name of the model that controls login and how much you customize the login page.

Directly simulating a login has the benefits of exercising the real login page and making sure Devise is correctly integrated with your application. However, it's an extra page load, so it's kind of slow. You'll see a shortcut in the next example. In practice, you should use the real login page at least once in your test suite.

In your test, you create a user and pass it to the log_in_as method. You then visit the project index page, projects_path, and verify that the program got there.

And the test passes as is, which should be a little suspicious.

In your case it means you've done only half the test. You've done the "this is okay" part, but you haven't done the "blocking miscreants" part.

> **Prescription 30** Always do security testing in pairs: the blocked logic and the okay logic.

The test for blocking unauthorized access is to simulate unauthorized access—to hit the page without logging in, which you can see in the second test.

You're asserting that a user who goes to the project page and is not logged in is redirected to the login page, which is standard Devise behavior.

The test fails. To make it pass, add Devise's authenticate behavior to the parent controller, which will make the entire application login-protected:

`security/01/app/controllers/application_controller.rb`
```ruby
class ApplicationController < ActionController::Base
  protect_from_forgery with: :exception

  before_action :authenticate_user!
end
```

The line added is before_action :authenticate_user!. The before_action part means it will run before any action in the application, and the authenticate_user! part is the Devise check to see if the current session has a logged-in user.

The good news is that both of the new security tests now pass.

Here's the bad news (slightly edited output here):

```
$ rspec                       ruby-2.4.1 security_01 0322db3 ×
Running via Spring preloader in process 51973
FF  HTML screenshot: <filename>
F   HTML screenshot: <filename>
F   HTML screenshot: <filename>
F   HTML screenshot:
<filename>

.....................................................
```

A lot of other tests fail.

When a change in your code breaks multiple tests, that's often a good time to revisit your testing strategy. It's common for new data or security constraints to break tests that are unaware of new requirements. But multiple tests breaking can be a sign that your tests are too entangled with the internals of classes that are not directly under test.

> **Prescription 31** When a single change in your code breaks multiple tests, consider the idea that your testing strategy is flawed.

The specific test failures are all due to code attempting to hit the site without having a login. It might mean that some of the testing you're doing at the controller level would be better done at a unit-test level against an action object. In your case, it also means you have some spurious tests floating around from Chapter 7, *Using Test Doubles as Mocks and Stubs*, on page 129.

You need to simulate a logged-in user for each failing test. There are three different failing test areas: the request specs and the two other system specs you have for adding projects and adding tasks.

You need to create a fake user that can fake logging in. There are a couple of options. You could use fixtures to create a sample user or you could use factory_bot. For the tests you've previously written, you don't need to know anything about the user; you just need to log in. Here's a simple factory_bot user factory:

security/01/spec/factories/users.rb
```ruby
FactoryBot.define do
  factory :user do
    sequence(:email) { |n| "user_#{n}@example.com" }
    password("password")
  end
end
```

In this case you're taking advantage of factory_bot's ability to use attributes that are attributes of the class but aren't directly database columns. Devise uses the password attribute to take the plain-text password, which it encrypts and saves in a database column called encrypted_password.

Devise provides helper methods to simulate a login. Actually, Devise provides two sets of helper methods, both of which use the same method name but are implemented differently. Both kinds are included in the support file shown earlier: Devise::Test::ControllerHelpers for controller tests where you have direct access to the session object, and Devise::Test::IntegrationHelpers for integration, request, and system tests.

You use the sign_in method to sign in a particular user. This user is signed in to the test session and appears as the currently logged-in user for the duration of the test, or until you use the Devise helper method sign_out:

```
security/01/spec/system/add_project_spec.rb
before(:example) do
  sign_in(create(:user))
end
```

Alternatively, you could stub the controller method current_user, which most of the rest of the code uses to determine if there is an active logged-in user.

Creating Users in Fixtures

The user factory depends on factory_bot being able to access attributes that aren't database columns. If you're creating users via fixtures, you don't have that ability, so you need to generate an encrypted password directly. You can do that by setting the encrypted_password attribute directly, as in encrypted_password: <%= Devise::Encryptor.digest(Administrator, 'password!') %>. The code inside the ERB execute markers is there to ensure that the password is being sent to the database encrypted in exactly the way Devise expects so you can match the user on login.

For the integration tests, the sign_in sign-in shortcut has the same name but is implemented differently, using a helper method provided by Warden, which is the tool Devise uses for the authentication functionality. (This method is called login_as, which I mention because you may see it in old code.) Warden works at the Rack layer. Without spending a page or two explaining Rack,[2] suffice to say you can use Warden to fake a logged-in user from outside the Rails stack, suitable for using within your integration tests.

With that addition to the system tests, your suite passes again. (Minitest equivalents are available in the security/01/gatherer/test directory of the code download.) You have nothing to gain right now from trying to move any of

---

2.   https://rack.github.io

these tests to avoid the additional setup, but I will note that the action tests for creating a project in test/actions/creates_project_test.rb didn't have to be changed.

Restricting Access

Having required a login for your application, you've solved part of the potential security problem. The next problem involves limiting a user's access to projects the user is associated with.

Let's start with an integration test. The test needs as its *given* a project and at least two users—one who has access and one who does not. The *when* action is an attempt to view the project show page, and the *then* specification is the successful or unsuccessful page view. There are a couple of other security aspects you might test, such as whether the index list of projects is filtered by what projects the user is part of, whether a user can edit or create a project, and so on. But this set of tests will give the basic idea:

```
security/02/spec/system/user_and_role_spec.rb
describe "roles" do

  let(:user) { create(:user) }
  let(:project) { create(:project, name: "Project Gutenberg") }

  it "allows a user who is part of a project to see that project" do
    project.roles.create(user: user)
    login_as(user)
    visit(project_path(project))
    expect(current_path).to eq(project_path(project))
  end

  it "doesn't allow a user who is not part of a project to see the project" do
    login_as(user)
    visit(project_path(project))
    expect(current_path).not_to eq(project_path(project))
  end

end
```

The tests both create a project, log in as a user, and visit the project page. In the first test you also add the user to the project. In the second test you assert that the user goes anywhere but the actual project page. Both tests fail at the moment.

In writing these tests, you have a new concept to represent in the code: the combination of a user and a project. This requires you to make a design decision. As you write the test, you're making a claim about how you want the application data to be structured. Often just planning the test will expose the need for new data or new structures, and something as simple as this migration might be done before writing the test. That's fine as long as the larger idea of using the test process to drive the design of the code still holds.

You've added the concept of roles to handle the list of users attached to a project. The test suggests that project has a relationship to roles—in fact, the first point of failure for the test will be that call to project.roles.

You could create a whole round of integration testing to drive the addition of a user interface for adding users to projects and allow the data model to be driven as part of that process. Or you could hand-wave the UI, add a basic data model, and focus on the security aspect.

In a full project the add-user-to-project story would get full treatment. For our purposes, you can start with just a migration and a new model. We'll assume somebody else did the add-user-to-project story.

Let's create the migration:

```
$ rails generate model role user:references project:references role_name:string
$ rake db:migrate
```

That gives you the following migration:

```
security/02/db/migrate/20170904004010_create_roles.rb
class CreateRoles < ActiveRecord::Migration[5.1]
  def change
    create_table :roles do |t|
      t.references :user, foreign_key: true
      t.references :project, foreign_key: true
      t.string :role_name

      t.timestamps
    end
  end
end
```

This goes a tiny bit beyond the test by adding a role_name.

You'll also need to add the associations—first to Project:

```
security/02/app/models/project.rb
has_many :roles, dependent: :destroy
has_many :users, through: :roles
```

and then to User:

```
security/02/app/models/user.rb
has_many :roles, dependent: :destroy
has_many :projects, through: :roles
```

At this point, the test has the expected failure, which is that you want to block access to a user who's not part of the project, but the code doesn't have that block yet.

Time to move to unit tests to drive that logic. But where do the tests go? You have more design decisions to make.

There are two distinct responsibilities in blocking a user. There's the actual logic to determine whether a user can see a project, and there's the logic to redirect the user if the access checker fails. Let's test those responsibilities separately.

Let's deal with the access control first. That method is probably either Project#can_be_viewed_by?(user) or User#can_view?(project). The active-voice version in User seems more clear. Another option is the Pundit gem,[3] which puts the access-control policy in its own separate object, but I'm reluctant to bring in another non-test-related gem here. If the access code gets more complex, though, I'd move it to prevent the User class from getting too big.

Right now you're testing just the access logic, which means that all you need for each test is one user and one project:

```
security/02/spec/models/user_spec.rb
require "rails_helper"

RSpec.describe User, type: :model do
  let(:project) { create(:project) }
  let(:user) { create(:user) }

  it "cannot view a project it is not a part of" do
    expect(user.can_view?(project)).to be_falsy
  end

  it "can view a project it is a part of" do
    Role.create(user: user, project: project)
    expect(user.can_view?(project)).to be_truthy
  end
end
```

The two cases here are similar to the integration tests: either the user is a member of the project and can see it, or the user isn't a member of the project and can't see it.

The second test has one subtle point about how Rails handles associations. In the first test, where the user is not a member of the project, you technically don't need to save the user, project, and role to the database to run the test. In the second test you do. (I'm saving them to the database to keep the test cases similar, but you could get away with not saving them in the first test in order to have a faster test).

---

3. https://github.com/elabs/pundit

You need to save them all to the database because of how Rails handles associations—specifically has_many through: associations such as the relationship between projects and users in this example. If the associations were just ordinary has_many associations, Rails would be able to manage the two-way relationship in memory without touching the database (at least Rails 4 can; older versions don't do that). However, when there is a join relationship denoted by has_many: through, Rails internals will always need to have saved objects with IDs to resolve the relationship. Although you can work around this problem (and I'll discuss some workarounds when I talk about fast tests in Chapter 16, *Running Tests Faster and Running Faster Tests*, on page 319), for the moment the workarounds are more complicated and distracting than the straightforward creation of the data.

A user can view a project in which he or she has a role. This method in User will make the tests pass:

```
security/02/app/models/user.rb
def can_view?(project)
  project.in?(projects)
end
```

Although the unit test passes, the integration test still fails because you haven't added the access check into the controller. That brings in the second kind of logic you need to add: does the controller successfully block the page if the user doesn't have access? In some cases I might write a unit test for this behavior; for example, a workflow or service object might help determine whether the code redirects and to where, but in this case I think I'll let the existing integration tests cover the logic.

To make this test pass, you need to incorporate the check of can_view? into the controller. You can make this work in a couple of ways—here's one:

```
security/02/app/controllers/projects_controller.rb
def show
  @project = Project.find(params[:id])
  unless current_user.can_view?(@project)
    redirect_to new_user_session_path
    return
  end
  respond_to do |format|
    format.html {}
    format.js { render json: @project.as_json(root: true, include: :tasks) }
  end
end
```

This controller method redirects to the login screen and returns if the user is blocked; otherwise it continues normally.

With this code in place, the controller test and the integration test pass.

You're all green.

Except you're not.

The add_task_spec.rb test, which displays a project show page, now redirects. You created a user but didn't add the user to the project. You need to make a slight change to the setup—you must create a Role associating the user and the project in order for the code to let you view the project page:

```
security/02/spec/system/add_task_spec.rb
let(:project) { create(:project, name: "Project Bluebook") }
let!(:task_1) { create(
  :task, project: project, title: "Search Sky", size: 1, project_order: 1) }
let!(:task_2) { create(
  :task, project: project, title: "Use Telescope", size: 1,
        project_order: 2) }
let!(:task_3) { create(
  :task, project: project, title: "Take Notes", size: 1, project_order: 3) }
let(:user) { create(:user) }

before(:example) do
  Role.create(user: user, project: project)
  sign_in(user)
end
```

Now you're green.

More Access-Control Testing

The advantage of splitting responsibility and testing into separate controller and model concerns becomes even more clear when you add another requirement. Let's allow for the possibility of administrative users who can see any project, as well as public projects that can be seen by any user.

You'll want to represent these properties in the database—in this case, you're doing the design work based on planning your test. You'll generate a migration using the command rake generate migration add_public_fields, which gives a skeleton file. Add the following and then run rake db:migrate:

```
$ rails generate migration add_public_fields
```

```
security/03/db/migrate/20170904151009_add_public_fields.rb
class AddPublicFields < ActiveRecord::Migration[5.1]
  def change
    change_table :projects do |t|
      t.boolean :public, default: false
    end
```

```
      change_table :users do |t|
        t.boolean :admin, default: false
      end
    end
  end
end
```

Let's think about where this needs to be tested. The behavior of the User#can_view? method needs to change. Crucially, though, the controller code won't change; it will still just call can_view?. The logic is still *if users can view, let them; redirect otherwise.* So you don't need to write new integration tests. You can write this logic as unit tests:

security/03/spec/models/user_spec.rb
```
describe "public roles" do
  it "allows an admin to view a project" do
    user.admin = true
    expect(user.can_view?(project)).to be_truthy
  end

  it "allows an user to view a public project" do
    project.public = true
    expect(user.can_view?(project)).to be_truthy
  end
end
```

These tests set up the pass-through condition for administrators and public projects—the negative condition is already covered by the "user cannot view an unrelated project" test.

And the test passes with an additional line in the method:

security/03/app/models/user.rb
```
def can_view?(project)
  return true if admin || project.public?
  project.in?(projects)
end
```

Now we're at a refactoring step, but we seem pretty clean at the moment.

There's an open question in the testing strategy: whether you should have started the process of adding admin users and public projects with an end-to-end integration test.

The answer to the question depends on the goal of your tests.

From a TDD integration-test perspective, you don't need an integration test because the integration logic didn't change. The code changes you made were localized to a single class, so the behavior of any code that uses that class is unchanged. Although you could write an integration test that would expose this behavior, this test would be slower than the unit tests you just wrote, and it would be harder to diagnose failures.

That said, you may be in a situation where there's value in writing the test strictly as an acceptance test, to verify behavior as part of a set of requirements rather than to drive development.

> **Prescription 32** Write your test to be as close as possible to the code logic that's being tested.

Using Roles

Now that you have the concept of users and roles in the system, you need to look at other places where users need access to a project. Two interesting places spring to mind:

- The project index list, where access should be limited to only the projects that the user can see

- The new tasks form, which should be limited to only the projects a user can see

Let's look at the index page. Two places need code here. A User instance needs some way to return the list of projects the user can see, and the controller index action needs to call that method. That argues for an integration test, though only weakly. Sometimes I'll skip an integration test if the logic is very close to Rails default integration and would easily be caught manually. Another option would be a request test that used test doubles to confirm that a specific method is called on User or Project:

```
security/04/spec/system/user_and_role_spec.rb
describe "index page" do
  let!(:my_project) { create(:project, name: "My Project") }
  let!(:not_my_project) { create(:project, name: "Not My Project") }

  it "allows users to see only projects that are visible" do
    my_project.roles.create(user: user)
    login_as(user)
    visit(projects_path)
    expect(page).to have_selector("#project_#{my_project.id}")
    expect(page).not_to have_selector("#project_#{not_my_project.id}")
  end

end
```

This test creates two projects, adding one to the user (the user is defined in a let statement earlier in the file). On visiting the index page, you expect to see the project you've added and not to see the project you haven't. You don't need to cover all the possibilities of admins and public projects, for the same reason as before. From the controller's perspective it's all the same call, and you just need to test that call is made.

This test fails on the last line because you haven't actually implemented the restrictions yet. You do have to be careful with not_to have_selector—it's easy for a typo to look like a passing test.

On the user side, this functionality must deal with admin users and public projects. The logic is parallel to the can_view? logic.

Here are the unit tests for the User behavior of being able to access a list of projects. Again, I wrote them and passed them one at a time:

```
security/04/spec/models/user_spec.rb
describe "visible projects" do
  let!(:project_1) { create(:project, name: "Project 1") }
  let!(:project_2) { create(:project, name: "Project 2") }

  it "allows a user to see their projects" do
    user.projects << project_1
    expect(user.visible_projects).to eq([project_1])
  end

  it "allows an admin to see all projects" do
    user.admin = true
    expect(user.visible_projects).to match_array(Project.all)
  end

  it "allows a user to see public projects" do
    user.projects << project_1
    project_2.update(public: true)
    expect(user.visible_projects).to match_array([project_1, project_2])
  end

  it "has no duplicates in project list" do
    user.projects << project_1
    project_1.update(public: true)
    expect(user.visible_projects).to match_array([project_1])
  end
end
```

A few notes on these unit tests: The user is created by a let earlier in the file. The projects need to be created using let! rather than let. This is a common problem when you're testing ActiveRecord database access for objects that you don't otherwise refer to. If you don't refer to them before trying to find them, then let's lazy initialization doesn't create them, so you need to force creation with let!.

The expectations use match_array because you haven't specified an ordering, and match_array will work no matter what order the arrays are in. The admin test checks against Project.all to protect against other projects being added by fixtures or tests that might run earlier in the file.

The last test is the direct result of realizing that the code as I left it following the test before might duplicate an entry if a project were both public and had the user as a member—though in fact, Rails 5 makes it easy to handle this.

Here's the "fast to green" passing code:

security/04/app/models/user.rb
```
def visible_projects
  return Project.all if admin?
  Project.where(id: project_ids).or(Project.where(public: true))
end
```

This method returns a scope rather than an array, so it can be chained with other ActiveRecord code.

First off, in your refactor, move the Project logic to its own class method:

security/05/app/models/project.rb
```
def self.all_public
  where(public: true)
end
```

This makes the visible_projects method look like this:

security/05/app/models/user.rb
```
def visible_projects
  return Project.all if admin?
  Project.where(id: project_ids).or(Project.all_public)
end
```

The User code has a larger problem. It now has two methods, can_view? and visible_projects, that duplicate the logic of whether a user can view a project. One possible solution is to rewrite can_view? in terms of visible_projects:

security/05/app/models/user.rb
```
def can_view?(project)
  project.in?(visible_projects)
end
```

If you do that, you have some test failures—one test that didn't update a project's status to the database now needs to. Actually, you have a test refactoring here—two sets of tests covering the same logic. Let's combine them to make it even more clear that the two methods are in parallel:

```
security/05/spec/models/user_spec.rb
require "rails_helper"

describe User do

  RSpec::Matchers.define :be_able_to_see do |*projects|
    match do |user|
      expect(user.visible_projects).to eq(projects)
      projects.all? { |p| expect(user.can_view?(p)).to be_truthy }
      (all_projects - projects).all? do |p|
        expect(user.can_view?(p)).to be_falsy
      end
    end
  end

  describe "visibility" do
    let(:user) { create(
      :user, email: "user@example.com", password: "password") }
    let(:project_1) { create(:project, name: "Project 1") }
    let(:project_2) { create(:project, name: "Project 2") }
    let(:all_projects) { [project_1, project_2] }

    it "a user can see their projects" do
      user.projects << project_1
      expect(user).to be_able_to_see(project_1)
    end

    it "an admin can see all projects" do
      user.admin = true
      expect(user).to be_able_to_see(project_1, project_2)
    end

    it "a user can see public projects" do
      user.projects << project_1
      project_2.update_attributes(public: true)
      expect(user).to be_able_to_see(project_1, project_2)
    end

    it "no dupes in project list" do
      user.projects << project_1
      project_1.update_attributes(public: true)
      expect(user).to be_able_to_see(project_1)
    end

  end

end
```

You've created a custom matcher, be_able_to_see, which takes in a list of projects and validates the can_view? and visible_projects in parallel, thereby asserting that the two methods stay in sync. It also validates that projects that aren't specified are not visible—you get around the fixture data by explicitly specifying the universe of all_projects. (In Minitest I'd use a custom assertion; you can see an example in the sample code at code/security/05/gatherer/test/models/user_test.rb.)

At this point, your original integration test is still failing because you haven't integrated the controller with the new model function. The controller method still calls Project.all, but you can fix that:

security/05/app/controllers/projects_controller.rb
```
def index
  @projects = current_user.visible_projects
end
```

Now the new integration test passes, but you have an interesting regression failure:

```
adding a project allows a user to create a project with tasks
    Failure/Error:
      expect(page).to have_selector(
          "#project_#{@project.id} .name", text: "Project Runway")

      expected to find visible css "#project_1 .name" with text
      "Project Runway" but there were no matches
    # ./spec/system/add_project_spec.rb:18:in `block (2 levels) in
    <top (required)>'
```

The test in question is an integration test that creates a new project using CreatesProject and then goes to view the page. The test is failing because the user isn't added as a member of the new project and therefore can't see the project page.

Fixing this involves changing the CreatesProject action to take a user (or users) and add that user to the project when the project is created. Since CreatesProject is a workflow, you can isolate the test and just make sure that a passed user is applied to the project—or in this case, set the API to take an array of users:

security/05/spec/workflows/creates_project_spec.rb
```
it "adds users to the project" do
  user = create(:user)
  creator = CreatesProject.new(name: "Project Runway", users: [user])
  creator.build
  expect(creator.project.users).to eq([user])
end
```

Then add the new keyword argument to the action and use the value when creating the new project:

security/05/app/workflows/creates_project.rb
```
class CreatesProject
  attr_accessor :name, :project, :task_string, :users

  def initialize(name: "", task_string: "", users: [])
    @name = name
    @task_string = task_string || ""
```

```
    @success = true
    @users = users
  end

  def success?
    @success
  end

  def build
    self.project = Project.new(name: name)
    project.tasks = convert_string_to_tasks
    project.users = users
    project
  end

  def create
    build
    result = project.save
    @success = result
  end

  def convert_string_to_tasks
    task_string.split("\n").map.with_index do |one_task, index|
      title, size_string = one_task.split(":")
      Task.new(title: title,
               size: size_as_integer(size_string), project_order: index + 1)
    end
  end

  def size_as_integer(size_string)
    return 1 if size_string.blank?
    [size_string.to_i, 1].max
  end
end
```

Next, update the controller method to pass the user to the action:

security/05/app/controllers/projects_controller.rb
```
def create
  @workflow = CreatesProject.new(
    name: params[:project][:name],
    task_string: params[:project][:tasks],
    users: [current_user])
  @workflow.create
  if @workflow.success?
    redirect_to projects_path
  else
    @project = @workflow.project
    render :new
  end
end
```

That breaks the test double you use in the controller test to bypass the action—which I admit is more fumbling in the codebase than I thought was necessary when I started this example:

```
security/05/spec/controllers/projects_controller_spec.rb
require "rails_helper"

RSpec.describe ProjectsController, type: :controller do
  let(:user) { create(:user) }

  before(:example) do
    sign_in(user)
  end

  describe "create" do
    it "calls the workflow with parameters" do
      workflow = instance_spy(CreatesProject, success?: true)
      allow(CreatesProject).to receive(:new).and_return(workflow)
      post :create,
        params: {project: {name: "Runway", tasks: "start something:2"}}
      expect(CreatesProject).to have_received(:new)
        .with(name: "Runway", task_string: "start something:2", users: [user])
    end

  end

end
```

A similar change to the test double needs to be made to the add_project_spec workflow, which also uses a test double for one test.

After all that, you have basic user and role authentication in the system. Now you need to protect against a couple of attacks that require the user to not use the application's UI directly.

> **Prescription 33** Adding user authentication can be very disruptive to existing tests. Try to get the basic infrastructure in place early.

Protection Against Form Modification

There is at least one blind spot in the user and role protection. The project show page has a form that submits a new task. That form is submitted to the TasksController, which doesn't handle any user-access control. The use case here is a malicious user not going through the web UI but rather creating his own HTTP request and pointing it at the server.

There are two important issues here, at least from my perspective as Rails Testing Author Guy. First is the habit of noticing when you're using a resource that's being accessed as a result of a user request as opposed to being stored server-side. This is even true when the resource is protected indirectly, as in this case, where you're accessing a Task that belongs to the Project, which is where the access control is attached. Second, you need to discuss how to test such a case.

You have two similar cases to deal with—task creation from the project form via TaskController#create and any of the update and move task methods in the controller.

Let's plan the create test. For the *given* you need a user, a project that the user belongs to, and a project the user doesn't belong to. The *when* is the creation of the task; the *then* is whether the task is created.

The design question is where to put the access check, and by extension where to write the test. You're at a slight disadvantage; since the potentially malicious request is coming from outside the UI, Capybara isn't going to be effective in crafting an integration test. You also didn't really write the full add-task feature before; you just kind of assumed its existence.

In other words, you can't easily write an integration test for this because the situation is outside the regular UI—if users don't have the ability to create a task, they also don't have the ability to see the project page. So, I somewhat reluctantly turn to a request spec. If the functionality were much more complex, I'd probably add Pundit and unit-test the Pundit object:

security/05/spec/requests/task_requests.rb
```ruby
require "rails_helper"

RSpec.describe "task controller requests" do
  let(:project) { create(:project, name: "Project Bluebook") }
  let(:user) { create(:user) }

  describe "creation" do
    before(:example) do
      login_as(user)
    end

    it "can add a task to a project the user can see", :js do
      Role.create(user: user, project: project)
      post(tasks_path, params: {task: {name: "New Task", size: "3"}})
      expect(request).to redirect_to(project_path(project))
    end

    it "can not add a task to a project the user can see", :js do
      post(tasks_path, params: {task: {name: "New Task", size: "3"}})
      expect(request).to redirect_to(new_user_session_path)
    end

  end
end
```

To make the test pass, you need to add a bit of logic to the controller action:

```
security/05/app/controllers/tasks_controller.rb
def create
  @project = Project.find(params[:task][:project_id])
  unless current_user.can_view?(@project)
    redirect_to new_user_session_path
    return
  end
  @project.tasks.create(
    task_params.merge(project_order: @project.next_task_order))
  redirect_to(@project)
end
```

The new part is the unless statement, which checks to see if the current_user can see the project in question. You can trust the current_user value because it is not dependent on any data coming from the user; it's managed by the Rails session.

There are a lot of possibilities from here. You could extract the current controller method to a CreatesTask action item, which would make it easier to separate the access logic from the rest of the code. You could also add similar protection to the update, up, and down methods, which involves the design question of modeling access control from the task's perspective.

Mass Assignment Testing

Mass assignment is a common Rails security issue, caused by Rails's ability to save an arbitrary hash of attribute names and values to an instance by sending an entire hash as a parameter, as in new(params[:user]), create(params[:user]), or update_attributes(params[:user]). The security issue happens when somebody hacks a request and adds unexpected attributes to the incoming parameters, typically an attribute that you wouldn't want an arbitrary user to be able to change, such as User#admin or Project#public. (GitHub was famously hacked via this vector by a user who added himself as a committer to the Rails repo.)

Rails 4 added the concept of *strong parameters* to allow you to identify parts of the parameter hash from an incoming request as required or permissible. To be used in a mass assignment, the attributes need to be identified using the require or permit methods of the Rails parameter object. Attributes that aren't whitelisted aren't passed on to the ActiveRecord object, and they are helpfully listed in the Rails log as a warning and to make debugging these issues easier.

The Gatherer application currently uses strong parameters in one location, TasksController#update, where there is a method that defines them:

```
security/05/app/controllers/tasks_controller.rb
def task_params
  params.require(:task).permit(:project_id, :title, :size)
end
```

We manage the strong-parameters issue in other ways. The ProjectsController#create method explicitly lists the items that are being passed to CreatesProject:

```
security/05/app/controllers/projects_controller.rb
def create
  @workflow = CreatesProject.new(
    name: params[:project][:name],
    task_string: params[:project][:tasks],
    users: [current_user])
  @workflow.create
  if @workflow.success?
    redirect_to projects_path
  else
    @project = @workflow.project
    render :new
  end
end
```

As with other features the framework provides, the important part from the testing framework is the behavior—preventing the user from setting a particular attribute—rather than the implementation.

> **Prescription 34** Test for mass assignment any time you have an attribute that needs to be secure and a controller method that touches that class based on user input.

Normally in code I do one of two things: use strong parameters or pass an explicit list of parameters to a workflow object.

Testing strong parameters often has the same problem as the previous security issue: integration tests don't work because the potential problem is not accessible via the UI, so Capybara can't be used to trigger a test failure. Request specs can again be useful here, since you can send arbitrary hashes as the parameters.

Sometimes you'll pass the params object directly to the workflow and need to do the strong-parameter check there, in which case you have a problem when testing because the params object isn't a hash. You need to create the underlying Rails object directly:

```
CreatesProject.new(ActionController::Parameters.new(name: "Project"))
```

Rails provides the class ActionController::Parameters, which wraps the hash and allows for the permit and require behavior needed to support strong parameters.

Other Security Resources

There's a limit to what you can test with security using TDD. It's a good idea to use a static analysis tool to look for security issues. Two options are Brakeman,[4] which you would run yourself, and CodeClimate, which automatically runs Brakeman on each commit.[5] Brakeman looks for a variety of security issues and provides some tips on working around them.

> **Prescription 35** Use an automatic security scanner to check for common security issues.

The Open Web Application Security Project has all kinds of useful information on security risks.[6] Of particular interest is WebGoat, a deliberately insecure application designed to allow you to hack and test solutions. The Rails version is called RailsGoat.[7]

What You've Done

In this chapter you applied testing techniques to security. You added a user model to the application and saw how to simulate a user login for test purposes. You then used that simulated login to test access control through the system.

You also used tests to isolate responsibilities and verify that certain users had access to only certain application resources. Then you applied tests to mass assignment and form modification, which required you to go outside normal integration tests. In the next chapter, you'll go beyond the application and interact with external services.

---

4.   http://brakemanscanner.org
5.   http://www.codeclimate.com
6.   https://www.owasp.org
7.   https://github.com/OWASP/railsgoat

CHAPTER 14

Testing External Services

The one thing your project-management tool really needs is a bit of graphical spark. Specifically, you've been asked to have users' Twitter avatars show up on the site attached to tasks they have completed. (Handily, Twitter has a Ruby gem that's not too hard to set up.) Since this is *Rails 5 Test Prescriptions* and not *Rails 5 Connecting to Twitter Prescriptions*, you'd like to be able to test your interaction with the Twitter API.

Unfortunately, interacting with a third-party web service introduces a lot of complexity to your testing. Connecting to a web service is slow—even slower than the database connections you've already tried to avoid. Plus, connecting to a web service requires an Internet connection, and you'd like your test suite to be able to run on a train, on a boat, or during a network outage. Some external services are public—you don't want to post an update to Twitter every time you run tests, let alone post a credit-card payment to PayPal. Some services have rate limits, some cost money to access, some actually deal with money, and some require API keys and authentication.

The point is, you'd really, really like to be able to write and execute tests without hitting the service more than strictly necessary.

The strategies we've developed so far for test isolation and for using mocks to limit the scope of tests will help you successfully test an external service. You'll be able to test it on a train and test it on a boat and test it in the rain and test it on a goat.

External Testing Strategy

Your external-service testing story has two main characters:

- The *client*, the part of your application code that uses the external API, either because it needs data accessible via the API or because it's sending data to the API to be used by somebody else. In either case, you're dealing with a request and a response, even if the response is just a status code.

- The *server*, which for our purposes here is outside your application and reachable via some kind of network request (though many of the strategies in this chapter also apply even if the service isn't separated by the network).

I also introduce two characters to the story for design and testing purposes:

- A *fake server*, which intercepts HTTP requests during a test and returns a canned response object. You'll be using the VCR gem to manage your fake server (more about VCR shortly).

- An *adapter*, which is an object that sits between the client and the server to mediate access between them.

The diagram that follows shows the relationship between these objects and the tests you'll write using them.

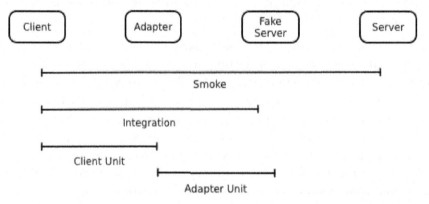

There are several test types for you to use, each of which uses different combinations of these objects:

- A *smoke test*, which goes from the client all the way to the real server. In other words, it's a full end-to-end test of the entire interaction. You don't want to do this often, because it's slow, but it's useful to be able to guard against changes in the server API.

- An *integration test*, which goes from the client to the fake server. This tests the entire end-to-end functionality of your application but uses a stubbed response from the server. This will be our go-to strategy for integration-testing the external server.

- A *client unit test*, which starts on the client and ends in the adapter. The adapter's responses are stubbed, meaning that the adapter isn't even making fake server calls. This allows you to unit-test the client completely separate from the server API.

- An *adapter unit test*, which starts in the adapter and ends in the fake server. These tests are the final piece of the chain and allow you to validate the behavior of the adapter separate from any client or the actual server.

Prescription 36	Mediating interaction to an external server through an adapter that is part of your code makes the interaction both easier to test and easier to use.

The Service Integration Test

You'll use the Twitter gem to interface with Twitter.[1] You're also going to need the VCR and Webmock gems in the test environment.[2][3] Add them to the Gemfile:

```
gem 'twitter'
gem 'vcr', group: :test
gem 'webmock', group: :test
```

You'll also have to reinstall the bundle with bundle install.

You need a Twitter API key and a secret key, which you can get from the Twitter Application Management page.[4] In Rails 5, those get placed in the secrets.yml file, which typically is not stored in your code repository, though I've put it in the sample code for ease of setup:

external/01/config/secrets.yml
```
shared:
  api_key: 123

development:
  secret_key_base: 1fe3edb870eff077105cff3ed19f0bdf15a5f999ef09ba1043a4916

test:
  secret_key_base: 8baba343e347eadbfcbfa77afb3ba0b13b403fa2dcfb643edf18e44
  twitter_api_key: "FuiCOb9knp5USp6Si1rlAscHa"
  twitter_api_secret: "WYcZZdrPBteO4UCbjqFDfm8SakmeVILgO3tJ7SFADwqLjnPNsJ"

production:
  secret_key_base: <%= ENV["SECRET_KEY_BASE"] %>
```

---

1. https://github.com/sferik/twitter
2. https://github.com/vcr/vcr
3. https://github.com/bblimke/webmock
4. https://apps.twitter.com

You'll use those keys when you connect to the Twitter API. By the way, those keys will have long since been changed by the time you read this. The existing tests might work because they'll have been stubbed via VCR. But you also might want to go to the Twitter Application Management page and generate your own application and set of keys.[5]

You want to attach the current user to a task when the task is completed and then show the user's Twitter avatar next to that task on the project page. As has been my fashion so far, I'm going to hand-wave over some UI functionality that doesn't relate to our focus. In this case we're going to pretend that the pair down the hall has already covered the ability to connect a user to a task, and you're just going to add the data migration. This migration includes the connection between a user and a task and adds the user's Twitter handle, which you need to access the person's avatar via the Twitter API:

```
external/01/db/migrate/20170904225321_add_user_to_task.rb
class AddUserToTask < ActiveRecord::Migration[5.1]
  def change
    change_table :tasks do |t|
      t.references :user
    end

    change_table :users do |t|
      t.string :twitter_handle
    end
  end
end
```

Don't forget to run the migration:

```
$ rake db:migrate
```

No, really—don't forget. As I was writing this chapter I added the migration and then started running tests without ever running the migration—which doesn't work.

Next, add the association in app/models/task.rb:

```
belongs_to :user, require: false
```

The user isn't required because a task might legitimately be unassigned.

And add this for completeness's sake in app/models/user.rb:

```
has_many :tasks, dependent :nullify
```

---

5.   https://apps.twitter.com

With that bit of setup out of the way, you can write an integration test. In this case, you'll integrate your code with Twitter:

```
external/01/spec/system/shows_twitter_avatar_spec.rb
require "rails_helper"

RSpec.describe "task display" do

  let(:project) { create(:project, name: "Project Bluebook") }
  let(:user) { create(:user, twitter_handle: "noelrap") }
  let!(:task) { create(:task, project: project, user: user,
                             completed_at: 1.hour.ago, project_order: 1) }

  before(:example) do
    project.roles.create(user: user)
    sign_in(user)
  end

  it "shows a gravatar", :vcr do
    visit project_path(project)
    url = "http://pbs.twimg.com/profile_images/40008602/head_shot_bigger.jpg"
    within("#task_1") do
      expect(page).to have_selector(".completed", text: user.email)
      expect(page).to have_selector("img[src='#{url}']")
    end
  end

end
```

With one exception, this test is a simplified version of the integration test you wrote in Chapter 8, *Integration Testing with Capybara and Cucumber*, on page 151. The *given* here is the project, user, and task along with a simulated login. The *when* is visiting the show page for the project, and *then* you validate that the user associated with the task is displayed by both the user's email and Twitter avatar. I've seeded this test with a known Twitter avatar—mine—by setting the user's Twitter handle and then setting the expected image source to my known Twitter-profile URL.

You've probably noticed that the test has an unusual piece of metadata: :vcr. Since I've mentioned VCR a couple of times in this chapter you may have further assumed that, in this context, VCR has more to do with external service testing than it does with that Blockbuster store that closed 10 years ago.

Introducing VCR

VCR is one of my favorite testing tools. The concept is simple. When VCR is enabled, it intercepts any third-party HTTP request. By default, the first time the request is made, VCR allows the request to proceed normally. However, VCR saves the response and associated metadata to a YAML file, which VCR calls a *cassette*. When the test is run again, VCR intercepts the request. Rather than actually making the request as a network call, VCR converts the cassette back into a response object and returns that response object. By default, if you then make an HTTP request that the VCR cassette doesn't know about, the test will fail.

VCR has many great features. Because the data that VCR stores is based on a real request, it's real data, meaning your tests are not running on some slapdash mock object you put together. This makes the tests have greater fidelity to the runtime environment, which makes them more trustworthy. Often, VCR is just a "set it and forget it" tool. Sometimes when you change a test, you need to manually force VCR to re-record data, though. You can even set VCR to automatically regenerate the cassette on an arbitrary time frame to protect against changes in the API. One potential downside is that having easy and fast stubbed data can lead to writing integration tests against the API when unit tests might be more appropriate.

Prescription 37	Use the VCR gem to allow your integration tests to run against server response data.

VCR is very configurable, allowing you to specify URLs or patterns that should be allowed to pass through without VCR caring (a common one being localhost). You can also do some pattern matching as to what constitutes the same URL for VCR purposes—many APIs have some kind of timestamp parameter that you'd want VCR to overlook for the purposes of returning stubbed output.

VCR and RSpec

You can use RSpec metadata to specify that any RSpec it or describe block uses a VCR cassette. The configuration goes into another RSpec support file:

external/01/spec/support/vcr.rb
```
VCR.configure do |c|
  c.cassette_library_dir = "spec/cassettes"
  c.hook_into :webmock
  c.configure_rspec_metadata!
  c.ignore_localhost = true
end
```

Here, four options are specified: first, the directory where VCR is going to place its cassette files (which can be anything you want, but something like spec/cassettes is customary).

The second option involves the HTTP stub library. VCR handles the creation and use of the cassette files, but it subcontracts the actual stubbing of HTTP calls to another library. You can specify which HTTP library is used; here I'm using webmock, but that's an implementation detail and this is the last time I'm going to talk about webmock.

The third option, c.configure_rspec_metadata!, configures the RSpec metadata. This allows you to specify VCR as a metadata option in the spec, as you just saw. When you declare the test, if you declare :vcr as metadata, the cassette is automatically named using the names of the describe block as the directory name and the name of the it block as a file name. If you want to pass options to the VCR call, change the metadata declaration from :vcr to vcr: {options}.

The fourth, and last, option causes VCR to ignore requests back to localhost, which can be a problem specifically because Capybara JavaScript drivers will ping the server on localhost, and you want to just let that through.

Within a spec with VCR declared, VCR will behave in one of two ways.

It may think that the cassette needs to be recorded. Most commonly this occurs because the cassette doesn't exist yet, but there are ways to tell VCR to overwrite an existing cassette. If VCR is trying to record a cassette, it'll allow all HTTP requests to happen but save all the requests and responses in a single file—which it'll store in the directory specified in the config, and with the file name specified by the spec name or by an option passed to the metadata.

If VCR doesn't believe the cassette needs to be recorded, it'll act in play mode. In play mode any HTTP request that matches a request in the cassette file will be intercepted, and its response will be crafted by the data on the cassette. Any HTTP request that doesn't match a request in the cassette file will trigger an error and a test failure. You can also optionally make VCR fail if a request in the cassette file isn't matched during the test; in this case VCR is behaving like a mock expectation. You can specify this behavior by including the option allow_unused_http_interactions: false to the spec metadata. If multiple requests in the cassette file match, VCR will use them one at a time in sequence as long as there are further requests to the same URL during the test.

Alternatively, you can use the method call VCR.use_cassette inside RSpec specs just as you would in Minitest, which I'll explain next.

VCR and Minitest

To make VCR work in your Minitest environment, you need to add some configuration to the test_helper.rb file:

external/01/test/test_helper.rb
```ruby
VCR.configure do |c|
  c.cassette_library_dir = "test/vcr"
  c.hook_into :webmock
  c.ignore_localhost = true
end
```

To use a cassette in Minitest, surround some code with the method VCR.use_cassette, which takes a string argument and a block. The argument is the name of the cassette file, so it needs to be unique, and the block is the body of the test that is being recorded by that cassette. You can pass options to the use_cassette method—I'll get to those in a bit.

external/01/test/integration/shows_twitter_avatar_test.rb
```ruby
require "test_helper"

class TaskShowsTwitterAvatar < Capybara::Rails::TestCase
  include Warden::Test::Helpers

  setup do
    projects(:bluebook).roles.create(user: users(:user))
    users(:user).update_attributes(twitter_handle: "noelrap")
    tasks(:one).update_attributes(user_id: users(:user).id,
                                  completed_at: 1.hour.ago)
    login_as users(:user)
  end

  test "I see a gravatar" do
    VCR.use_cassette("loading_twitter") do
      visit project_path(projects(:bluebook))
      url = "http://pbs.twimg.com/profile_images/40008602/head_shot_bigger.jpg"
      within("#task_1") do
        assert_selector(".completed", text: users(:user).email)
        assert_selector("img[src='#{url}']")
      end
    end
  end
end
```

Inside the block, VCR behaves exactly as it would in an RSpec spec that was defined with the :vcr metadata.

VCR and Cucumber

To use VCR with Cucumber, first place the same configuration code in a file somewhere in the Cucumber features/support directory. Once that's done, you have two options: you can put VCR.use_cassette calls inside step definitions or you can use Cucumber tags.

To use tags, you need to define them by writing additional configuration code, presumably in the same file where you put the basic configuration. The tag configuration will look like this:

```
VCR.cucumber_tags do |t|
  t.tag '@vcr', use_scenario_name: true
  t.tags '@twitter', '@facebook'
end
```

Any options you would pass to use_cassette can be passed as key/value pairs after the tag name. If you want to define multiple tags at once, you can use the tags method.

The tags can then be used like normal Cucumber tags:

```
@vcr
Scenario: Get the user's Twitter avatar
  Given a logged-in user
  When that user has completed a task
  And I view the project page
  Then I should see the user's Twitter avatar
```

When a VCR-related tag is used for a Cucumber scenario, VCR is activated for the duration of the scenario. The resulting cassette file is named after the tag unless the use_scenario_name: option is true, in which case VCR generates a name based on the feature and scenario names, similar to how it generates a name when using RSpec metadata.

Client Unit Tests

VCR is set up; now let's make the Twitter integration work. As it stands, the test fails because the user data is not in the view at all. The test suggests that the user email and the Twitter avatar should be in the view, so let's add them to the view file.

You have a design decision to make about how the application should interact with Twitter. There are many options, ranging from calling the gem and service directly from the view to placing the interaction within the User class.

My design here tends toward more objects and structure on the grounds that we're using this avatar to stand in for a more complex third-party integration. The set of classes might feel like overkill, but I want to demonstrate what this is like with all the moving parts.

With that throat-clearing out of the way, let's write some tests. It seems like getting the Twitter avatar-image URL is a User responsibility.

When last you saw the view code for projects, you were busy writing Java-Script. In the interest of keeping this example simple, I'm going to move the code back into the ERB. Having to manage the image back down to the JavaScript is just going to be a distraction here.

The relevant view code looks like this in app/views/projects/show.html.erb. (I've added a reference to the task.user.avatar_url.) I've also removed the task-table class from the div surrounding the table, which will prevent the JavaScript from being activated here:

```
<td class="completed">
  <% if task.complete? %>
    <%= task.user.email %>
    <%= task.completed_at.to_s %>
    <img src="<%= task.user.avatar_url %>" />
  <% end %>
</td>
```

If I were being stricter, I'd argue that the avatar_url is only a view-level respon-sibility—which would imply a decorator, the same way I talked about for the ProjectsController#index action. Let's hold that thought for a possible refactoring.

The test now fails because user.avatar_url doesn't exist. Let's write tests for it.

These are client unit tests, which assume the existence of an adapter. In this testing plan, the adapter is frequently stubbed in the client unit test. You can use this test as a place to design the adapter's interface with the rest of the application. In this case, the logic from the user object's perspective is simple. The user's email is passed to the adapter and is expected to call a method on the adapter that returns the avatar URL.

The test looks like this:

```
external/01/spec/models/user_spec.rb
describe "avatars" do
  let(:user) { create(:user) }
  let(:fake_adapter) { instance_double(AvatarAdapter) }

  it "can get a twitter avatar URL" do
    allow(AvatarAdapter).to receive(:new).with(user).and_return(fake_adapter)
    allow(fake_adapter).to receive(:image_url).and_return("fake_url")
    expect(user.avatar_url).to eq("fake_url")
    expect(fake_adapter).to have_received(:image_url)
    expect(AvatarAdapter).to have_received(:new)
  end
end
```

This test does not depend in any way on the actual HTTP request; instead it defines the API of the adapter. The test creates a User instance and then creates a fake adapter using RSpec's instance_double method to ensure that any method you stub actually exists in the AvatarAdapter class. Then, spies are used to set the expectation that the avatar will receive the image_url method.

> **Prescription 38** Use the adapter to test client behavior without being dependent on the server API.

The "when" part of this test is the last line: the call to the user.avatar_url method. At this point, you've set up the following expectations for what happens next:

- The AvatarAdapter class will be sent the new method with the user instance as an argument.

- The resulting instance of AvatarAdapter will be sent the image_url method.

To make this test pass, you need a method in User:

```
external/01/app/models/user.rb
def avatar_url
  adapter = AvatarAdapter.new(self)
  adapter.image_url
end
```

And you need a new AvatarAdapter class:

```
external/01/app/models/avatar_adapter.rb
class AvatarAdapter
  def initialize(user); end

  def image_url; end
end
```

Right now the AvatarAdapter class is just a skeleton, which is all you need to make the unit tests pass.

Now it's time to get that adapter done.

Why an Adapter?

Using an adapter class to mediate interaction with the external service is a good idea even when, like Twitter, the external service already has a Ruby gem. The adapter encapsulates logic that is specific to the interaction between your application and the service.

An adapter is useful if your code has any or all of the following qualities:

- The external service will be accessed from multiple points in your code.

- The interaction with the external service has logic of its own, such as authentication or type changing or common sets of options.

- There's a mismatch between the language or metaphor of the API and the domain terms and structures of your code.

The Twitter example doesn't have the first quality, at least not yet. You do have the second feature: the adapter needs to manage a Twitter client object that nothing else in the application needs to care about or be aware of. It also manages an argument to the Twitter API: the :bigger argument, which specifies the size of the image you want to download.

Whether there is a mismatch between the API and the code is a matter of interpretation, but I think there is. At the very least, the Twitter client exposes a lot of data that the application doesn't care about, so limiting access to the full set of Twitter data seems like a good idea.

My experience with adapters like the one we've written is that they tend to attract functionality as you use them, with the side effect that it's much easier for a full range of complexity to be available at each use. For example, if you allow the adapter to take an argument to image_url to represent the size, then that ability is automatically available whenever the adapter is used. Attracting functionality is especially valuable for security and error handling, which are easy to leave off when you're creating each connection separately.

Adapter Tests

The adapter tests work between the adapter and the server, using VCR as a medium:

external/02/spec/models/avatar_adapter_spec.rb
```
require "rails_helper"

describe AvatarAdapter do

  it "accurately receives image url", :vcr do
    user = instance_double(User, twitter_handle: "noelrap")
    adapter = AvatarAdapter.new(user)
    url = "http://pbs.twimg.com/profile_images/40008602/head_shot_bigger.jpg"
    expect(adapter.image_url).to eq(url)
  end

end
```

This test has no dependency on the client, which is shown passing in a double rather than an actual User instance. Using a VCR cassette, you create a new adapter and assert that the adapter provides the expected URL when queried. The test also doesn't have a particular dependency on the Twitter gem, beyond the specific URL value being from Twitter's asset storage. This is a test of the adapter's behavior, not of the implementation.

The passing code requires a bit of Twitter connection setup:

```
external/02/app/models/avatar_adapter.rb
class AvatarAdapter
  attr_accessor :user

  def initialize(user)
    @user = user
  end

  def client
    @client ||= begin
      Twitter::REST::Client.new(
        consumer_key: Rails.application.secrets.twitter_api_key,
        consumer_secret: Rails.application.secrets.twitter_api_secret)
    end
  end

  def image_url
    client.user(user.twitter_handle).profile_image_uri(:bigger).to_s
  end
end
```

The Twitter gem requires a client to be created using the API keys you put in the secrets.yml file. The adapter lazily creates that client as needed.

Once the client is created, it calls the user method on the client with the Twitter handle and then grabs the profile_image_uri property. The gem uses the :bigger argument to determine the size of the resulting image, and you need to call to_s, because the actual property is an internal class of the Twitter gem and all you want is the URL. All of these are features of the interaction with the Twitter API that the rest of the application doesn't need to care about because the adapter is managing that information.

At this point, the adapter test passes. Even better, all the parts of the interaction have now been written and connected, so the integration test passes as well.

If you go to the spec/vcr directory, you now see two cassette files, one for each test. They are both about 150 lines long, so I'm not putting them in the book. The first few lines look like this:

```
---
---
http_interactions:
- request:
    method: post
    uri: https://api.twitter.com/oauth2/token
    body:
      encoding: UTF-8
      string: grant_type=client_credentials
    headers:
      Accept:
      - "*/*"
      User-Agent:
      - TwitterRubyGem/6.1.0
      Authorization:
      - Basic <big string>
      Content-Type:
      - application/x-www-form-urlencoded; charset=UTF-8
      Accept-Encoding:
      - gzip;q=1.0,deflate;q=0.6,identity;q=0.3
  response:
    status:
      code: 200
      message: OK
```

Each cassette file chronicles two HTTP requests to the Twitter API: one for authentication of the API key and one to get the user data. If you delete the files and try again, you'll hopefully notice that the first test run is slow because the HTTP requests are being made. Once the VCR cassette is in place, the test speeds up. (On my machine, the VCR specs went from to 1.6 to about 0.2 seconds.)

Testing for Error Cases

The application design allows multiple ways to simulate errors for testing purposes:

- You can make an API call to the actual service that results in an error and then capture the result using VCR. You can use this approach in an integration or adapter test.

- You can stub a method that's internal to the adapter. For example, you can stub the client method to return a double that simulates an API error. You'd use this in an adapter test.

- You can stub the adapter to return an unexpected value in a client test.

Which approach you choose depends on the details of the library you're working with. Often, stubbing the external service makes sense for the same reason that stubbing ActiveRecord methods does—crafting a call that will reliably return an error is not always possible. If you can, try to stub methods of your adapter rather than methods of the third-party gem; it's generally a good idea to stub only code you control.

Keeping tests consistent with the location of the logic being tested is still a good policy. Use adapter tests to ensure that the adapter behaves gracefully when it gets weird responses from the server. (Normally, server or gem exceptions shouldn't leak out of the adapter.) Use unit tests to make sure that the clients are able to handle whatever the adapter does in response to unexpected input.

> **Prescription 39** Test the error code based on which object in the system needs to respond to the error.

Smoke Tests and VCR Options

So far you've used VCR to record an interaction once and preserve it for all time. VCR provides other options. These options are passed as key/value arguments to VCR.use_cassette(re_record_interval: 7.days) or, if you're using RSpec metadata, as the value part of the metadata, as in vcr: {re_record_interval: 7.days}.

That re_record_interval I just used as an example allows you to use the same VCR test as both an integration and a smoke test. The re_record_interval is an amount of time. If the requests on the associated cassette are older than the interval, then VCR will attempt to reconnect to the HTTP server and re-record the cassette. If the server is unavailable, VCR will just use the existing cassette.

This allows you to protect your application against API changes in the server. If the server API changes, eventually your VCR cassette will pick up the change and your test will fail. This can be a useful feature. It can also be a little on the opaque side when a test randomly fails, but it's better to have an opaque failure in testing than to have one in production.

VCR lets you set different record modes with the :record option. The default, which you've been using so far, is :once, which records new interactions if they don't exist but raises an error for new interactions if the cassette already exists.

The table on page 300 lists all the VCR recording options.

Option	Description
:all	Always connects to HTTP and re-records. Useful for forcing cassette updates.
:new_episodes	Replays a request that is already on the cassette. New requests are made via HTTP and added to the cassette.
:none	Only replays existing cassettes; never makes an actual request.
:once	Replays existing cassettes; records new requests if the cassette doesn't exist. Raises an error on new requests if it does.

If you want to specify the recording options for all cassettes at once, you can do so in the configuration with the default_cassette_options method:

```
VCR.configure do |c|
  # existing configuration
  c.default_cassette_options = { record: :all }
end
```

By occasionally adding the previous line to the configuration for one test run, you get one run of smoke tests as all the VCR cassettes go back to their servers for data.

Let's look at a couple of other important configuration options.

Sometimes you want VCR to not deal with specific requests. The c.ignore_localhost = true property handles one common case, where you don't want VCR to touch requests back to the actual application being tested, such as Ajax requests or callbacks for authentication information. The method c.ignore_hosts takes an optional list of hostnames to ignore, and the method ignore_request {|req| CODE} ignores any request for which the associated block returns true.

By default, VCR looks for an exact match on the URI being requested when attempting to match a cassette request to a new HTTP request from the code, including query strings and HTTP methods. However, some services never have the exact same URI twice. For example, the Amazon API calls contain a timestamp. In other cases, additional headers may be relevant to how the request is processed. VCR provides the match_requests_on configuration option to manage the matching between cassette and request.

You use match_requests_on as an option to a VCR call or as a default. The argument is an array of elements that you want to use in the match. Valid values are :method, :uri, :host, :path, :query, :body, :headers, and :body_as_json. You can also use the method uri_without_params as a substitute for uri where there are parameters in the query string that are not important for the match.

For example, the following configuration was used to match all the dynamic elements in an application that used the Amazon API:

```
VCR.configure do |c|
  c.cassette_library_dir = 'test/vcr'
  c.hook_into :webmock
  c.ignore_localhost = true
  c.default_cassette_options = {
    :match_requests_on => [:method,
      VCR.request_matchers.uri_without_params(
        "Timestamp", "Signature", "AWSAccessKeyId", "AssociateTag")]
  }
end
```

The `match_requests_on` option is used to match on the combination of HTTP method and URI but with several parameters to the URI ignored.

The `filter_sensitive_data` option lets you keep passwords and the like from appearing in your VCR cassette. It allows you to use a block to grab the sensitive text from the HTTP response and replace it with a custom dummy string.

VCR has other options for more elaborate use. You can see the full list in the documentation.[6]

The World Is a Service

Once you get used to the idea of having adapters mediate access between your application and external services, it's not that far a leap to have adapters internally to mediate between different parts of your application. This approach is sometimes called *hexagonal architecture*, and many resources can be found online that describe hexagonal architecture as it applies to Rails.[7] At the same time you can find many resources online saying that hexagonal architecture is an awful idea. (David Heinemeier Hansson is a particularly vocal critic.)

You've taken baby steps in this direction by creating action objects such as `CreatesProject`, which are somewhat like adapters between the controller and the model. Many web frameworks use adapters between model objects and the database. Rails does not, but the pattern is not uncommon.

What You've Done

In this chapter you looked at a pattern for testing external services while still allowing the test suite to run quickly and consistently and allowing you to set up and test for error conditions. You used an adapter in your code to

---

6. https://relishapp.com/vcr/vcr/v/2-9-2/docs
7. https://medium.com/@vsavkin/hexagonal-architecture-for-rails-developers-8b1fee64a613

convert between your application logic and the external service API. Tests internal to the codebase can use a test double to replace the adapter.

For external tests, you saw how to use the VCR gem to simulate interactions with the external server by recording and replaying the actual results of interactions. This allows you to both use real data and not be dependent on the vagaries of network connectivity for your tests to run.

Next up, you'll look at the tools you can use to diagnose failing tests.

CHAPTER 15

Troubleshooting and Debugging

Dot, dot, dot, dot, dot.

Tests are passing; looks like it's time for lunch.

Dot, dot, dot, dot, F.

F? F?

But the code works. I know it does.

I think it does.

Why is my test failing?

One of the most frustrating moments in the life of a TDD developer is when a test is failing and it's not clear why. In this chapter you'll look at tools you can use to diagnose failing tests to help improve your testing experience.

General Principles

This may be the most obvious piece of advice in the book:

> **Prescription 40** When a formerly passing test fails, something has changed.

Obvious or not, it's worth repeating, mantra-like, when confronted with a bug. When a formerly passing test fails, it means something changed.

It may be in the code, in the system, or in the test. It may be that the time of day has changed. But it's probably not sunspots, and it's probably not evil spirits possessing your MacBook (unless you're living in one of Charles Stross's Laundry Files).

The Humble Print Statement

My initial troubleshooting tool of choice is a plucky little Ruby method called p, for "print." Perhaps you've heard of it.

I realize that to many of you, debugging with the p statement sounds like trying to fix your television by kicking it. In the p method's defense, it's dirt-simple, works anywhere, and is infinitely adaptable to your current troubleshooting needs. An elegant weapon for a more civilized age, so to speak.

The p method calls inspect on its argument and then outputs it to STDOUT using Ruby's even-more-primitive puts. I prefer p to puts because the extra call to inspect generally results in more readable output. (Though in poking around, it looks like puts does a better job with mixed data these days than it did back in the Ruby 1.8.7 era.)

A couple of other methods are particularly good at displaying structured data. Ruby defines the method y, which takes its argument and outputs it to STD-OUT in YAML format. This is valuable in direct proportion to your ability to read complicated YAML formats.

I like the Awesome Print gem,[1] available with gem install awesome_print and lots of examples and docs. Including Awesome Print gives you the ap method, which awesomely prints things. Even nicer, you get the logger helper method Rails.logger.ap, which awesomely prints to the Rails log (by default, at the debug level). Awesome Print also has a number of options to customize output, but I've never used them.

One minor downside to Awesome Print is that because it's often loaded into just the development and test groups in the Gemfile, it's not available on staging or production. That sounds great until you accidentally leave an ap statement in the code and it goes to staging and causes a 500 error. With the other methods, which are core Ruby, the worst that happens is STDOUT spew.

Here's a comparison from a Rails 5 console in Ruby 2.4.1 with awesome_print in the Gemfile. This comparison uses a couple of collections, a hash with an array value, and a plain array. This output is lightly edited from a Rails console session:

```
> x = {1 => ['a', 'b'], 2 => 'c'}
> y = ["a", "b"]
```

---

1.   https://github.com/awesome-print/awesome_print

```
> puts x
{1=>["a", "b"], 2=>"c"}
> puts y
a
b

> p x
{1=>["a", "b"], 2=>"c"}
> p y
["a", "b"]

> y x
---
1:
- a
- b
2: c

> y y
---
- a
- b

> ap x
{
    1 => [
        [0] "a",
        [1] "b"
    ],
    2 => "c"
}
> ap y
[
    [0] "a",
    [1] "b"
]
```

This gives the flavor of how Awesome Print and y create somewhat easier-to-read output for structured data.

One more quick comparison using an Active Record object, again from an edited Rails console:

```
p = Project.new(name: "Project Runway", due_date: 1.month.from_now)

> puts p
#<Project:0x00000102ff3568>

> p p
#<Project id: nil, name: "Project Runway", due_date: "2014-08-16",
    created_at: nil, updated_at: nil, public: false>
```

```
> y p
--- !ruby/object:Project
concise_attributes:
- !ruby/object:ActiveRecord::Attribute::FromDatabase
  name: id
- !ruby/object:ActiveRecord::Attribute::FromUser
  name: name
  value_before_type_cast: Project Runway
  original_attribute: !ruby/object:ActiveRecord::Attribute::FromDatabase
    name: name
    type: !ruby/object:ActiveModel::Type::String
      precision:
      scale:
      limit:
<there's more here>

> ap p
#<Project:0x00000102ff3568> {
            :id => nil,
          :name => "Project Runway",
      :due_date => Sat, 16 Aug 2014,
    :created_at => nil,
    :updated_at => nil,
        :public => false
}
```

There's a nice progression here, from puts just giving the class name, to p giving a class name and key/value pairs, to y putting each key/value on a different line, to Awesome Print lining up the values for readability. The Awesome Print output is also a syntactically correct Ruby hash, should you feel the need for copy and paste.

> **Prescription 41** Using p and various related methods is a quick and easy way to get a sense of why a test is behaving badly.

Using these print statements in a successful troubleshooting section is a tug-of-war between finding interesting data and not overwhelming yourself.

One catch to keep in mind: all these kernel method calls work fine from a test console or in the server log if you run Rails via rails server. If you use a development server, such as Unicorn, that doesn't output STDOUT to the terminal, then you need to use the Rails logger to see printed output. The Rails logger is available anywhere in your application with Rails.logger, which then takes one of several methods, such as Rails.logger.error, all of which take an argument that gets printed to the log or a block whose final value gets printed to the log.

I highly recommended that when you're troubleshooting with print statements, you use one of the techniques I discuss in Chapter 16, *Running Tests Faster and Running Faster Tests*, on page 319, to run just one test at a time for clarity. Fast tests help a lot here, because the quicker you can get data on the screen, the faster you can iterate, and using print statements for test troubleshooting is definitely a rapid-iteration process.

Here are some ways to use print statements in troubleshooting.

You Are Here

Print little "You're here" messages as a cheap alternative to program traces. (Ruby does have a program tracer, called tracer, but it's going to be wild overkill for most debugging purposes.) I usually go with a simple p "here" and, if I need a second one, p "there". It's a fast way to determine if the method you're looking at is even called during the test invocation.

For the most part I use these as one-and-done quick checks to see what's going on. It's not uncommon for a check like this to save me significant time banging my head against the code looking at a method that isn't even being called.

Also helpful here is the Putsinator gem,[2] which annotates every p and puts with the line number that generated them. This is helpful in tracking down that one line of output in the test suite that you can't otherwise trace. Also, using Rubocop will by default catch stray p statements and flag them before you commit them to production.

You May Ask Yourself, "How Did I Get Here?"

At any point in Ruby, you can determine the name of the method that called the method you're in by using the cryptic incantation caller_locations(1,1)[0].label. caller_locations is a kernel method that returns the call stack as an array of objects. You can also use the caller method, which returns the call stack in a different format. The two arguments are index and length, with index 0 being the current method, and index 1 being the immediate caller. So we have an array of length 1, returning the first element via [0] and then taking that object's label attributes, which is the method name. You're encouraged to tweak the call a bit to see what other data is around: see ruby-doc.org for official docs.[3]

I recommend you keep this one on speed dial in the form of a helper method in your test_helper or rails_helper file.

---

2.   https://github.com/tobytripp/Putsinator
3.   http://www.ruby-doc.org/core-2.1.1/Kernel.html#method-i-caller_locations

Print a Value

You'll naturally want to use p and the related methods to print values from specific points in the app. Some techniques that are useful here:

- Print the arguments to a method call.
- Print an ActiveRecord object before and after an update.
- Print both sides of a compound Boolean separately.

And so on. If you're particularly industrious, use Ruby string interpolation to give a label—p "user name: #{user.name}"—but for most quick uses you don't need to bother.

Deface a Gem

You're not limited to your own application when inserting print statements. It's easy and fun to insert code into a gem (just remember to undo it).

Bundler has two commands: bundle show and bundle open. The bundle show command returns the complete path to the version of the gem that Bundler is using. If you want to go one step further, bundle open will open the gem directory in your default editor.

Add print or log statements to taste. This can be useful when first interacting with a new gem. You'll need to restart your server or Spring instance for the changes to take effect.

When you're done, use the command gem pristine <gemname> to return the gem to its original state. Or reinstall the bundle.

Show a Page

It's very important to see what's going on inside an integration test that uses Capybara or Cucumber. Capybara has the helper method save_and_open_page, which does exactly what it says. It dumps the current Capybara DOM to a temp file and opens the file in your default browser.

The resulting browser window will look a little strange. Any relative files or assets won't be displayed, meaning no CSS and only some images. But the text is usually enough to see if your integration test is even looking at the page you expect, and not, say, looking at the login page because you forgot to log in. The gem capybara-screenshot will do this automatically on any failing Capybara test.[4]

---

4. https://github.com/mattheworiordan/capybara-screenshot

There are a lot of other Ruby methods that give you insight into the internals of how code runs that you can reveal via p and puts. Most of them are a little arcane for our purposes, but Aaron Patterson has a great rundown.[5]

Git Bisect

git bisect is the kind of tool you'll use about once every six months, but when you use it, you'll be totally thrilled that it exists.

git bisect is indicated when something has gone wrong in your code, and you believe it to be the result of a code change but you cannot isolate which change resulted in the problem. git bisect's goal is to isolate the commit where the change occurred.

 **Prescription 42** Use git bisect to track down mysterious failures in your code when you have no idea how they were inserted.

You start using git bisect with two commands:

```
$ git bisect start
$ git bisect bad
```

The first command puts Git into what I'll call *bisect mode*, and the second command says that the current Git snapshot is bad, meaning it contains the behavior you're trying to fix.

You then switch the Git snapshot to the secure hash algorithm of a previous commit that you believe is good because it doesn't have the behavior. And you tell Git that branch is good. For example, I'd use this if I've determined that SHA 34ace43 is good:

```
$ git checkout 34ace43
$ git bisect good
```

You can combine those into one command, git bisect good 34ace43.

Git now does something really neat. It derives a straight line of commits between the good one and the bad one, picks the middle of that line, and checks itself into that commit. You'll see some commentary on the console explaining how many commits are in the line and roughly how many steps Git expects the bisect to take.

Your job is to do whatever you need to in the newly entered commit to determine if it is "good" or "bad" based on whether the incorrect behavior exists.

---

5.   https://tenderlovemaking.com/2016/02/05/i-am-a-puts-debuggerer.html

Based on that, you enter either git bisect good or git bisect bad. (If you really can't tell, you can do git bisect skip.)

Git now has enough information to know that the bad change was in one half of the commits. If you said the commit was bad, then the change was in the first half of the commits; if you said it was good, then the change had to come after. Git splits the narrowed-down list of commits in half and checks out the middle commit.

You repeat your checks until eventually you can isolate a change where the beginning state is good and the end state is bad. Ideally, inspecting the commit list of the commit with that change will give you a hint as to what's causing the behavior, since one of those changes is likely the cause. This process can save you hours.

Furthermore, if you can encapsulate whatever test you're running against your codebase in a script that follows the Unix convention of returning a nonzero value on failure, you can pass that script to git bisect and Git will automatically do the good/bad thing for you based on the result of the script. The syntax is of the following form:

```
$ git bisect run my_script
```

I note in passing that whichever tool you're using to run your tests has this behavior, so git bisect run rspec should work, though it'll probably be a little on the slow side.

For the full git bisect effect, a few things need to be true:

- The problem needs to have been caused by a code change, not a change in your environment.

- You need to be able to reliably trigger the problem.

- It helps if your commits are relatively small and if the system is in a loadable and executable state after each one.

That said, when this works, it can work big.

RSpec or Minitest Bisect

Minitest and RSpec both have their own version of bisect, which solves a slightly different problem. Sometimes you'll have a test failure caused by the order in which the tests are run. This usually means the tests aren't completely isolated and one test is changing global state in a way that breaks another test. This can be very difficult to reproduce, especially if the test suite is long.

The bisect option for Minitest and RSpec gives you a minimal set of specs that reproduces the error so that you can run the minimal set from the command line and reproduce the problem efficiently. Once the minimal set is identified, it's much easier to find the problem.

The two commands work almost identically, which is not surprising since RSpec explicitly cribbed the feature from Minitest. The Minitest version does require a gem, minitest-bisect, to be installed.

To make this work, you need a test suite that has an intermittent failure that you believe is due to test ordering, and you need a seed value that produces a failure. In RSpec, if you're not already running the tests in a random order, add the line --order rand to the .rspec file. Each run will then tell you what seed value RSpec used for the randomization Randomized with seed 57180. You can then reproduce the exact ordering with rspec --seed 57180. Minitest behaves similarly, except that the random ordering is the default behavior.

Once you have a seed that consistently produces an ordering with a test failure, you trigger the bisect. In RSpec that's done with the following:

```
$ rspec --seed 57180 --bisect
```

In Minitest it looks like this:

```
$ minitest_bisect --seed 57180 test/**/_*test.rb
```

In either case, replace the seed value with whatever your tests accept. In Minitest, the final argument is a file glob selecting test files. If you know that the tests are in a smaller subset already, you can specify that instead.

In both cases, the bisect tool will run tests for a while. Possibly a long while. But if a test failure is really caused by test ordering, both tools will end up with a minimal set of individual tests (not test files) that will cause it, and a command-line command suitable for cutting and pasting that will run those tests.

The test bisect is tricky. It will not help you with some kinds of intermittent failures (for example, Capybara timing issues), but like Git's bisect, when it works, it can save you hours.

Pry

Once upon a time, I was a fan of development environments that had big fancy symbolic debuggers that let you set breakpoints and watch variables and step through the code.

What can I say? I was young and programming in Java, a language that had large integrated development environments.

When I started using TDD, I largely stopped using debuggers. Having small, focused tests eliminates most of the need to walk through code in a step debugger. That said, it's sometimes nice to be able to stop a test in progress and peer inside the Ruby virtual machine to see what's going on.

Enter Pry.

Pry is technically a Ruby console—a souped-up replacement for irb, but with some add-on gems. It makes an excellent debugger. You can even coax it to reload code changes and rerun specs from inside Pry, which is as close as you can get in Ruby to programming inside a Smalltalk image.

Pry improves on irb in many ways. It offers much more powerful examination of live Ruby objects. It also has some niceties that makes it easier to enter code in the console.

Let's load Pry and a couple of extras by including them in the :development, :test group of the Gemfile:

```
gem "pry-rails"
gem "pry-byebug"
gem "pry-stack_explorer"
gem "pry-rescue"
```

The pry-rails gem allows Pry to replace irb as the console when you run rails console and adds a couple of handy commands that provide Rails info inside Pry. The other two gems both provide additional useful behavior: pry-byebug allows you to step through the code, and pry-stack_explorer allows you to go up and down the stack trace.

A quickish bundle install, and you're on your way.

Basic Pry Consoling

There's a lot of great stuff in Pry and I'm not going to cover it all. Full docs are available online.[6]

You've set Pry up as your Rails console, so you can access it with a simple rails console:

```
$ rails c
Loading development environment (Rails 5.1.3)
[1] pry(main)> 1 + 1
=> 2
[2] pry(main)> project = Project.new(name: "Project Runway")
```

---

6. https://github.com/pry/pry/wiki

```
=> #<Project:0x007fcb918be958
 id: nil,
 name: "Project Runway",
 due_date: nil,
 created_at: nil,
 updated_at: nil,
 public: false>
```

Pry allows you to closely examine the current object under scope, which you can determine with the self command. Right now the current object is main:

```
[3] pry(main)> self
=> main
[4] pry(main)> ls
ActiveSupport::ToJsonWithActiveSupportEncoder#methods: to_json
Rails::ConsoleMethods#methods: app  controller  helper  new_session  reload!
self.methods: inspect  to_s
locals: _  __  _dir_  _ex_  _file_  _in_  _out_  _pry_  project
```

Pry uses the metaphor of Unix directory navigation to work through object trees (which, honestly, I find kind of weird). So, just as typing ls in a regular Unix terminal gives you a list of files, typing ls for Pry gives you a list of all kinds of stuff about the current namespace by introspecting on the object, including the available methods on the current object and local variables. (See the Pry wiki page on GitHub for full details.[7])

You can see that the list of locals contains a bunch of preexisting special variables and then the project variable that you created at the start of the sessions.

Just as you can type ls for a listing, you can type cd to change scope. Let's go into the scope of the project object:

```
[5] pry(main)> cd project
[6] pry(#<Project>):1> self
=> #<Project:0x007fcb918be958
 id: nil,
 name: "Project Runway",
 due_date: nil,
 created_at: nil,
 updated_at: nil,
 public: false>
[7] pry(#<Project>):1> ls
==> A BUNCH OF STUFF
```

Here the cd command is used to change scope. As with Unix, cd .. will take you back up a level, and other syntax quirks move you through multiple levels in a single command.

---

7.   https://github.com/pry/pry/wiki/State-navigation

The bunch of stuff after you type ls includes all the methods project can respond to. As you might imagine, that's rather a lot. All output in Pry goes through a paginator, though, so you can just type q to get back to the command line rather than wading through the entire listing.

If you start a command with a dot (.), Pry will consider that to be a shell command, so you can keep a Pry terminal open but still interact with, say, your Git repo.

And that's not all.

You can use the show-source command to display, in the Pry console, the source code of any method. You can request methods of the object in scope:

```
[1] pry(main)> project = Project.new(name: "Project Runway")
=> #<Project:0x007fcb8ff82700
 id: nil,
 name: "Project Runway",
 due_date: nil,
 created_at: nil,
 updated_at: nil,
 public: false
[2] pry(main)> cd project
[3] pry(#<Project>):1> show-source on_schedule?

From: /Users/noel/code/github/noelrappin/gatherer/app/models/project.rb @ line 52:
Owner: Project
Visibility: public
Number of lines: 5

def on_schedule?
  return false if projected_days_remaining.infinite?
  return false if projected_days_remaining.nan?
  (Date.today + projected_days_remaining) <= due_date
end
```

You can't see it here, but the method is syntax-colored in the console. You can do this for any method in the system using the ClassName#method_name syntax. Similarly, you can use the show-doc and ri methods to see just the documentation for a method you're interested in, which is particularly useful for Rails methods.

Pry has a couple of special variables that are always available. Like irb, the _ variable always refers to the result of the most recent expression evaluated. The variable _ex_ is the most recently raised exception, even if you've moved out of the exception scope. You can use cat —ex to view the code that caused the exception, and you can see the stack trace with _ex_.backtrace.

Using Pry to Troubleshoot Test Failures

Pry is really a wonderful console, but again, this is *Rails 5 Test Prescriptions* not *Rails 5 Console Prescriptions*. Luckily, you can invoke Pry directly from inside a test.

If you add the line binding.pry to your code, then a Pry session will start when the code execution reaches that line.

Let's see how this works. I'll put a binding.pry in one of the tests in the action test file creates_project_test.rb. Can you guess which line from this session trace contains binding.pry?

```
$ rspec
..................................................
From: .../spec/workflows/creates_project_spec.rb @ line 12 :

     7:
     8:   describe "initialization" do
     9:     let(:task_string) { "" }
    10:     it "creates a project given a name" do
    11:       creator.build
 => 12:       binding.pry
    13:       expect(creator.project.name).to eq("Project Runway")
    14:     end
    15:   end
    16:

[1] pry(#<RSpec::ExampleGroups::CreatesProject::Initialization>)>
```

Pry not only opens a session; it displays the test where it stopped, and it sets the Pry scope to the test class (again, this is syntax-highlighted).

You can use the cd notation to see what's going on:

```
[1] pry(#<CreatesProjectTest>)> cd creator
[2] pry(#<CreatesProject>):1> ls
ActiveSupport::ToJsonWithActiveSupportEncoder#methods: to_json
CreatesProject#methods:
  build  create  name=   project=  success?    task_string=  users=
  convert_string_to_tasks  name    project  size_as_integer  task_string  users
self.methods: __pry__
instance variables: @name  @project  @success  @task_string  @users
locals: _  __  _dir_  _ex_  _file_  _in_  _out_  _pry_
[3] pry(#<CreatesProject>):1> cd project
[6] pry(#<Project>):2> name
=> "Project Runway"
```

And then, if you use <control>-c to exit Pry, the tests just continue on their merry way.

There's nothing special about binding as the receiver of the pry message. It's handy because it's available anywhere and gives you the entire local scope—and Pry will display the surrounding code when you drop into it. You can, however, send pry to anything. You could've used creator.pry in the same test, and you would've been dropped into Pry with the creator local variable as the top-level scope.

The pry-byebug and pry-stack_explorer gems have some commands that are useful in a debugging session.

From pry-byebug you get four commands: continue, finish, next, and step. If you've done much with interactive debuggers, these will be familiar. The step and next commands take you one command forward, with next keeping you in the same frame but step sending you into a frame. The finish command executes until the end of the current frame, and continue ends the Pry session entirely.

The pry-stack_explorer gem allows you to see the entire current stack trace with the show-stack command. You can then use the up and down methods to navigate the trace.

You can also invoke the editor directly from the Pry console using the edit command. Using just edit -c opens the editor to the file where the original binding.pry was located. Using edit ClassName#method_name opens the editor at the file where the given class and method are defined. Similarly, edit with any instance variable as an argument opens the file where that instance's class is defined.

The Pry session will wait while the edit is happening. Closing the edit window will reload that file in the Pry session and allow you to keep going.

You can be even more interactive with the pry-rescue gem. The pry-rescue gem provides a regular terminal command rescue that is prefixed to a different command. If that command raises an exception, then Pry is automatically invoked at the point of the exception. If you run rescue before your test command, Pry will also be invoked on test failure.

In RSpec, pry-rescue just works with a rescue rspec command. In Minitest you need to put the following lines in the test_helper.rb first:

```
require "minitest/autorun"
require "pry-rescue/minitest"
```

Remember how I said that editing files from Pry causes the file to be reloaded? Wouldn't it be great if you could rerun the failing test inside Pry? The command for doing just that is try-again.

Using these tools together can give you a very interactive workflow. Run the tests via rescue, drop into Pry on failure, keep editing and trying again until that test passes, and keep going. For a slightly more extreme version, check out Joel Turnbull's talk from RailsConf 2014.[8]

Common Rails Gotchas

The following patterns in Rails lead to relatively silent test failure. I stumble over them all the time.

- ActiveRecord models don't save when I expect them to. The most common cause of this problem is that the creation of the object fails a validation. Often this causes a test failure down the line because a record that was supposed to be found in the database isn't there—because it didn't save. Using a factory tool helps with this, as does using save! and create! in test setup to have the failure happen at the point of the code problem and not further down the line.

- In versions of Rails that use attr_accessible, Rails silently ignores inaccessible parameters in mass assignment. Rails 5 will still ignore parameters not specified in a strong parameter permit command, but it'll at least log them. This can lead to hours of fun as you try to figure out why that attribute, which is clearly part of the method call, is not part of the resulting object.

- In integration tests, it's common to forget to log in when required. This normally means anything you expect to be on the resulting page fails to show up. The save_and_open_page command is invaluable here since it's sometimes hard to tease out what happened from the log. But save_and_open_page will clearly show you that you're not logged in.

What You've Done

In this chapter you looked at tools you can use to diagnose a failing test. You can print values to the console using the Ruby p method or the Awesome Print gem. If you're having trouble isolating when a breaking change was introduced, you can use git bisect to isolate which change caused the problem. If you think you have a test failure caused by the interaction of multiple specs, rspec bisect or minitest bisect is your friend. If you want to walk through your code step by step, the Pry gem offers a number of tools to help you do exactly that.

Troubleshooting is only one way to improve your test experience. You can also make your test setup better in a more general way, as I'll discuss in the next chapter.

---

8. http://www.confreaks.com/videos/3365-railsconf-debugger-driven-developement-with-pry

Running Tests Faster and
Running Faster Tests

Over the course of the book, I've talked about how important rapid feedback is to getting the full benefit of the TDD process. You can make your TDD feedback happen faster in several ways. You can run a focused subset of your test suite so that you see only the tests relating to the code you're working on. You can have tests run automatically when code changes. You can make the loading of the Rails application happen in the background or you can bypass Rails altogether. And, of course, you can just avoid doing really slow things.

Let's look at the many ways to speed up tests.

Running Smaller Groups of Tests

Running just some of your tests at once is often useful. If you have a slow test suite, running a relevant subset of tests will let you get most of the value of rapid testing feedback without the cost of the entire test suite. When debugging, you often just care about one or two tests. Also, if you're being verbose about printing output to the terminal, then only running one test will spare you from potentially having to wade through a lot of spurious output. If you're running Pry, being able to only run one test will let you focus better.

> **Prescription 43** If you have a slow test suite, you can mitigate the effects in practice by being able to run a relevant subset of tests.

Each tool has its own way to allow you to run one file or one set of tests at once. Also, your editor or IDE probably has a built-in feature or common extension that allows you to run your entire test suite or just a single file of tests directly from the editor.

RSpec

I recommend using the rspec command directly rather than going through any rake tasks that RSpec defines because it's a bit faster. The rspec command can take one or more arguments—files, directories, or file globs. For file globs, all matching files are run:

```
$ rspec spec/models/project_spec.rb spec/models/task_spec.rb
```

RSpec makes it easy to run a single spec. All you need to do is add the line number to the file along with a colon:

```
$ rspec spec/models/task_spec.rb:5
```

RSpec has a less user-friendly syntax that identifies the tests by their place within each nested block. This version is more robust against adding lines to tests and is what some RSpec tools (like bisect) will output:

```
$ rspec spec/models/task_spec.rb[1:1:1]
```

When RSpec's default formatter runs, RSpec will place the file name and line number of each failing test at the end of the output, suitable for easy copy-and-paste back to the command line to run the test in isolation. You'll probably find this quite useful. There is a configuration line in RSpec's helper file to run the specs in the more verbose documentation format if only one file is being executed. It's commented out by default, but you can find it; it's the block that starts with if config.files_to_run.one?.

If you want to run a set of RSpec specs that isn't quite a single test or a set of files, you can use the RSpec metadata system to tag the tests in question:

```
it "should run when I ask for focused tests", :focus do
end

it "should not run when I ask for focused tests" do
end
```

The top spec here has been tagged with the :focus metadata tag, which can also be written more verbosely as focus: true. You can also specify a spec or example group as focused by prefixing its name with f, as in fit, fdescribe, and fcontext.

You can then run all tests tagged as focused by specifying the tag at the command line:

```
$ rspec --tag focus
```

If you want to exclude tags, you prefix the tag name with a tilde:

```
$ rspec --tag ~focus
```

RSpec's default spec_helper file contains a commented-out line that applies the :focus filter automatically if any specs in the system are marked as :focus, which is convenient if you like using focus.

There isn't much that's special about the focus tag; you can use metadata to add any tag you want in RSpec with the --tag command line option. For example, here's a fun thing you can do:

```
environment/01/spec/support/profiling.rb
class UnclaimedSlowTestException < RuntimeError
  THRESHOLD = 1

  def initialize(example)
    @example = example
  end

  def message
    "This spec at #{@example.metadata[:location]}
    is slower than #{THRESHOLD} seconds.
    Either make it faster or mark it as :slow in metadata"
  end
end

RSpec.configure do |config|
  config.append_after(:each) do |ce|
    runtime = ce.clock.now - ce.metadata[:execution_result].started_at
    if runtime > UnclaimedSlowTestException::THRESHOLD && !ce.metadata[:slow]
      raise UnclaimedSlowTestException.new(ce)
    end
  end
end
```

The exact internals of this are beside the point. What it does is this: every test that's slower than a threshold value (here it's 1 second) fails unless it's explicitly tagged as :slow in its metadata. The nice thing about this is you can then run rspec --tag ~slow and only run your fast tests when you want.

> **Prescription 44** Use RSpec metadata like :focus or :slow to be able to run arbitrary groups at once.

If the config.example_status_persistence_file_path = "spec/examples.txt" option in the spec_helper.rb is uncommented, then every time you run your specs, you get a file that includes a notation for every spec in the system, whether it passed or failed on its last run, and how long it took.

This gives you two helpful command-line tags: rspec --only-failures and rspec --next-failure. The --only-failures tag runs all the specs that failed the last time they were run (regardless of whether that run was the last time you ran any RSpec specs). The --next-failure tag does the same thing, but it stops the run once one of the specs in the list fails again.

I use these two commands all the time. In conjunction with Spring, they let me run exactly the specs I'm working on very quickly.

> **Prescription 45** Use rspec --only-failures and rspec --next-failure to only run failing specs, which allows you to focus on failures easily.

Minitest

If you're invoking Minitest through the rake tasks that Rails provides, then it's easy to run a single file's worth of output just by passing the file name at the command line:

```
$ rake test test/models/task_test.rb
```

The argument can be an individual file or a directory. You can have more than one file or directory if they're separated by spaces.

This behavior is relatively new to Rails. If you've been using Rails for a while, you may know that it provides a number of testing subtasks, such as rake test:models, that wrap the expected directories and run all the tests in that directory. Since Rails has been nice enough to add the directory behavior separately, I recommend using the actual directories rather than trying to remember the names of all the rake tasks.

It's a bit more involved if you want to run a single individual test rather than an entire file. As far as I can tell, there's no way to do that directly from the Rails rake task, so you need to drop down to the Ruby command line. The invocation looks like this:

```
$ ruby -Ilib:test test/models/task_test.rb -n test_a_completed_task_is_complete
Running tests:

.
Finished tests in 0.019890s, 50.2765 tests/s, 100.5530 assertions/s.
1 tests, 2 assertions, 0 failures, 0 errors, 0 skips
```

In this command, you're running ruby with the capitol *I* option, which specifies directories to add to the load path. Specifically, you need the lib and test directories so that you can find the test_helper file your test is going to require. (You may be able to get away with not adding lib.) Next is the name of the file, and then the -n option, which is being passed to Minitest and is the name of the individual test method you want to run. This is the test name after ActiveSupport::TestCase is done munging it, so what's in your file as test "a completed task is complete" is on the command line as test_a_completed_task_is_complete—with the word test prepended to the name and all the spaces turned into underscores.

If that seems like a lot of annoying typing, I can help a tiny bit. The minitest-line gem adds a different switch to the command line, -l,[1] which takes the line number of the test, changing your command line to this relatively brief one:

```
$ ruby -Ilib:test test/models/task_test.rb -l 5
```

The line number doesn't have to be the first line of the test. If you pick an intermediate line, it will run the test that contains that line.

 **Prescription 46** If you specify a test by line number, be sure not to add lines to the file. Added lines could make it so you aren't running the test you think you're running.

Cucumber

Cucumber's set of options is almost identical to RSpec's. Again, I recommend using the cucumber command line directly rather than going through rake. You can specify one or more files, append line numbers with a colon, and allow or deny tags with the -t or --tag option. (The main difference is that Cucumber tags start with an @, which you must include in the command line.)

Cucumber privileges one special tag, @wip, which is short for "work in progress." Cucumber scenarios tagged with @wip won't count as failures in a test run (much like RSpec's pending). Cucumber also has the separate -w or --wip, which runs Cucumber in reverse and fails if there are any passing scenarios.

Running Rails in the Background

One difference between TDD in a Rails context and TDD in SUnit's original Smalltalk environment is that testing a Rails program typically requires that Ruby be started from the command line and that the Rails environment be loaded. Starting from the command line can take quite a bit of time on even a moderate-size Rails project. If you're trying to run, say, a single file's worth of tests that you expect to take about a second, having the Rails startup take more than a minute can break your flow. In contrast, the Smalltalk tests reside inside the same live process as the code and can therefore start instantly.

---

1. https://github.com/judofyr/minitest-line

One way to simulate the Smalltalk behavior in Rails is to not restart the Rails application on every test. A way to avoid restarting the Rails application is to have it already running in a background task and use the existing background application. Rails ships with the Spring gem, which does just that. Here's how to use Spring to speed up your tests.

Installing Spring

Spring is a gem. It comes with Rails by default and you'll want it in your Gemfile. There are a couple of helper gems that you'll probably also want. All these gems go in the development group of the Gemfile:

```
gem "spring"
gem "spring-commands-rspec"
gem "spring-watcher-listen"
```

If you start a fresh Rails application with rails new, spring will already be there.

At this point you can see what all the fuss is about:

```
$ spring status
Spring is not running.
```

That was exciting. Let's try something else:

```
spring help
Version: 2.0.2

Usage: spring COMMAND [ARGS]

Commands for spring itself:

    binstub       Generate spring based binstubs.
                  Use --all to generate a binstub for all known commands.
                  Use --remove to revert.
    help          Print available commands.
    server        Explicitly start a Spring server in the foreground
    status        Show current status.
    stop          Stop all spring processes for this project.

Commands for your application:

    rails         Run a rails command.
                  The following sub commands will use spring:
                  l console, runner, generate, destroy, test.
    rake          Runs the rake command
    rspec         Runs the rspec command
```

The last command is there only because the spring-commands-rspec gem was added.

Using Spring

Spring defines a half dozen or so subcommands that can all be called with syntax like bundle exec spring <whatever>. Let's try one:

```
$ bundle exec spring rspec
Running via Spring preloader in process 60422

Randomized with seed 36292

..........................................................

Finished in 5.07 seconds (files took 0.66205 seconds to load)
72 examples, 0 failures
```

After I run the tests, I can check the status of Spring again:

```
$ spring status
Spring is running:

60412 spring server | gatherer | started 33 secs ago
60413 spring app    | gatherer | started 33 secs ago | test mode
```

After I run my tests, Spring stays running in the background, as confirmed by the spring status update. If I then enter the Rails console or Rails server, Spring will start up another instance in the development environment and hold onto both of them in the background.

If I then run my tests again with another spring rspec, the tests will start noticeably faster—but sadly, not in a way I can show you by running another set of commands. Since the part that is sped up is the part before Ruby starts timing the tests, the elapsed time shown in the terminal won't change. Trust me, though: depending on your setup you'll see a difference of 5 to 10 seconds. Given that the tests take less than 10 seconds to run, that's a significant change in how fast you can get feedback, especially if you just run a subset of fast or failing tests. It's the difference between being able to run tests without losing focus and not being able to do so.

Spring is a little bit more aggressive about reloading than Rails is in development mode; for instance, it restarts itself when a file changes in the config/initializer directory. However, you'll need to restart Spring if you add files or update gems, and I'm normally prepared to restart Spring any time things look the slightest bit strange.

You don't actually need to restart Spring; you can stop it with the command spring stop. Spring will automatically start back up the next time it's invoked.

Spring and Rails ship with commands for rails and rake. There are additional gems, including spring-commands-rspec and spring-commands-cucumber, that extend Spring to allow those tools to be aware of the Spring background applications.

Alternatively, you can connect Spring and Bundler by attaching Spring to Bundler's binstubs. Binstubs are small scripts that are placed in your application's bin directory and automatically invoke the command in the context of a bundle exec to ensure that all the correct gems are in the path and keep you from typing bundle exec before each spring command.

To integrate Spring and RSpec, with the spring-commands-rspec gem in place, run this:

```
$ bundle exec spring binstub rspec
```

To integrate Spring with all the programs that bundler lets you run from the command line, run this one command:

```
$ bundle exec spring binstub --all
```

This command will create new binstubs for executables that Bundler knows about, and it'll augment the existing binstubs to be Spring-aware. The upshot is that after this command is created, you have at least three things:

- A bin/spring script that will start Spring.

- Springified versions of bin/rake and bin/rails that use the existing Spring setup. (Spring tweaks Rails's existing rake and rails scripts.)

- A new bin/rspec that uses the Spring setup to run RSpec.

All of these scripts are Bundler-aware—that's the point of having these bin/ versions of each script. If you have other executables known to Spring, you may have grown another bin script or two.

Once Spring is installed, you can invoke the binstubs directly as, for example, bin/rspec, and the Springified version will be invoked. (I have command-line aliases called brake, brails, and bspec. You could also tweak your PATH to look at a local bin directory first, though this is a potential security issue on projects you don't know.)

It Don't Mean a Thing If It Ain't Got That Spring

How useful all this is depends on what you're trying to do.

Essentially, Spring is useful to the extent that startup time is swamping your test runtime. This normally happens in one of the following cases:

- Your test suite runtime is less than your application startup time.

- Your test suite is slow, but you're willing to run just a small subset of your tests during much of your TDD development.

- Any port in a storm—it can't hurt to have a preloader, right?

I'll pause at this point to mention that I use Spring as part of my regular test practice. Pre–4.1 Rails, I used a similar tool called Zeus. So whatever else I say in the rest of this section, I do think that Spring is valuable in a lot of cases. Especially when I'm running a very small subset of failing tests over and over, it can be a significant win.

Spring is, however, one of those tools that best helps you when you're already helping yourself. If your test suite takes 20 minutes to run, you're already sunk and the 15 extra seconds to load Rails isn't going to help much.

Spring can also hide problems in a test suite by letting you run individual pieces of the suite much faster; it can reduce the pressure you might feel to speed up each individual test file. There's a Spring "uncanny valley": if an individual file takes 30 seconds, that's both fast enough for Spring to feel like a win and slow enough for it to be a serious drain on the entire project suite as you continue to add up 30-second files. You don't want to be there. It'll feel like your suite isn't getting any worse, but trust me—it is.

That said, if you're already stuck in a bad situation because you inherited it (or for whatever reason), Spring can be great and can allow you to have fast TDD feedback on the new stuff you're building without being tied to the poor decisions of the past. Just don't keep making the same poor decisions.

Running Tests Automatically with Guard

Another way to get test feedback quickly is to allow the tests to run automatically when your code changes. In Ruby, the Guard gem allows you to trigger arbitrary events when files change.[2] It's a powerful system, and running tests is only a fraction of what it can do. You're just going to manage basic setup here; full documentation is available online. Mac users should check out the Mac-specific wiki page to make sure Guard receives file events correctly.[3]

Guard is a generic system for triggering events, and it has separate libraries that make it easy to trigger specific kinds of events, such as starting a test.

---

2. http://guardgem.org
3. https://github.com/guard/guard/wiki/Add-Readline-support-to-Ruby-on-Mac-OS-X

To set up Guard, add the Guard gem and any of the dependent libraries to the Gemfile. Note that these all go in the development group, not the test group:

```
group :development do
  gem 'guard'
  gem 'guard-minitest'
  gem 'guard-rspec'
  gem 'guard-cucumber'
  gem "guard-jasmine"
  gem "rb-readline"
end
```

Then, from the command line, run the following:

```
$ guard init
guard init
20:17:50 - INFO - Writing new Guardfile to <FILE>
20:17:51 - INFO - cucumber guard added to Guardfile, feel free to edit it
20:17:51 - INFO - jasmine guard added to Guardfile, feel free to edit it
20:17:52 - INFO - minitest guard added to Guardfile, feel free to edit it
20:17:52 - INFO - rspec guard added to Guardfile, feel free to edit it
20:17:52 - INFO - teaspoon guard added to Guardfile, feel free to edit it
```

This gives you a new file, Guardfile, which contains Guard commands for each of the tools you've added.

Here's what the Guardfile portion for RSpec might look like. This is an edited version of what the Guard plugin provides by default; among other things, I've changed the default command to be Spring-aware:

```
guard :rspec, cmd: "bin/rspec" do
  require "guard/rspec/dsl"
  dsl = Guard::RSpec::Dsl.new(self)

  # Feel free to open issues for suggestions and improvements

  # RSpec files
  rspec = dsl.rspec
  watch(rspec.spec_helper) { rspec.spec_dir }
  watch(rspec.spec_support) { rspec.spec_dir }
  watch(rspec.spec_files)

  # Ruby files
  ruby = dsl.ruby
  dsl.watch_spec_files_for(ruby.lib_files)

  # Rails files
  rails = dsl.rails(view_extensions: %w(erb haml slim))
  dsl.watch_spec_files_for(rails.app_files)
  dsl.watch_spec_files_for(rails.views)
```

```
  watch(rails.controllers) do |m|
    [
      rspec.spec.call("routing/#{m[1]}_routing"),
      rspec.spec.call("controllers/#{m[1]}_controller"),
      rspec.spec.call("acceptance/#{m[1]}")
    ]
  end

  # Rails config changes
  watch(rails.spec_helper)       { rspec.spec_dir }
  watch(rails.routes)            { "#{rspec.spec_dir}/routing" }
  watch(rails.app_controller)    { "#{rspec.spec_dir}/controllers" }

  # Capybara features specs
  watch(rails.view_dirs)         { |m| rspec.spec.call("features/#{m[1]}") }
  watch(rails.layouts)           { |m| rspec.spec.call("features/#{m[1]}") }
end
```

The guard method takes the name of one of the Guard plugins, some optional arguments (depending on the plugin), and then a block. Inside the Guard block, watched files are sent to that plugin to be processed. Right now its showing the rspec plugin, which sends changed files to RSpec to be run.

The basic idea behind Guard is this watch command, which takes a string or regular expression, or a defined method that returns one of those things, and an optional block argument. A lot of special methods are also in there, like dsl.watch_spec_files_for(rails.app_files), which effectively resolve into a series of watch commands.

The watch command is triggered when the name of a file being changed matches the string or regular-expression argument. That file name is then sent on to the plugin. If there's a block argument, you can modify the file name arbitrarily. The match data from the regular expression is the argument to the block, and the result of the block is what's sent to the plugin.

The basic idea is that if a code or spec file is changed, Guard attempts to run the related specs. So, it watches the spec helper files and reruns the entire suite if they change; but if a model file changes, it may only rerun the related spec.

The Minitest file is simpler by default. Here it is with the Spring option added and the Rails files uncommented (I slightly edited the file because the default naming conventions that Guard expects don't match what we've been doing):

```
guard :minitest, spring: true do
  watch(%r{^test/(.*)\/?test_(.*)\.rb$})
  watch(%r{^lib/(.*/)?([^/]+)\.rb$})      { |m| "test/#{m[1]}test_#{m[2]}.rb" }
  watch(%r{^test/test_helper\.rb$})       { 'test' }
```

```
  watch(%r{^app/(.+)\.rb$})  { |m| "test/#{m[1]}_test.rb" }
  watch(%r{^app/controllers/application_controller\.rb$}) { 'test/controllers' }
  watch(%r{^app/controllers/(.+)_controller\.rb$})         { |m|
        "test/integration/#{m[1]}_test.rb"
  }
  watch(%r{^app/views/(.+)_mailer/.+})                     { |m|
                "test/mailers/#{m[1]}_mailer_test.rb"
  }
  watch(%r{^lib/(.+)\.rb$})                                { |m|
        "test/lib/#{m[1]}_test.rb"
  }
  watch(%r{^test/.+_test\.rb$})
  watch(%r{^test/test_helper\.rb$}) { 'test' }
end
```

The watch commands here have the same meaning. If a test file is changed, run that file. If a file in the app directory changes, run the associated test file. If the test_helper.rb changes, run the whole suite. To run Guard, type the following:

```
$ bundle exec guard
14:26:14 - INFO - Running all features
Disabling profiles...
```

Guard will then run your tests or specs, depending on which plugin you're running. There are a bunch of plugins enabled, so Guard rather weirdly runs both of the Minitest and RSpec specs, in addition to trying to run the Jasmine tests and Cucumber files. Then it waits with a command prompt—actually a Pry console, which is useful (though it's not, by default, a Rails console). You can run a few custom commands at the prompt; the most valuable are exit, which quits Guard, and all, which runs all the plugins.

If I then make some kind of change in my program—say I change something in task.rb—Guard springs into action, running the Minitests and specs related to task. (I edited this output to remove actual test results.)

```
14:27:29 - INFO - Running: test/models/task_test.rb
Run options: --guard --seed 5338
Finished in 0.009959s, 0.0000 runs/s, 0.0000 assertions/s.
0 runs, 0 assertions, 0 failures, 0 errors, 0 skips

14:27:31 - INFO - Running: spec/models/task_spec.rb
Running via Spring preloader in process 61635

Randomized with seed 16522

.............

Finished in 0.19715 seconds (files took 0.53858 seconds to load)
14 examples, 0 failures

Randomized with seed 16522
```

My experience with Guard and related automatic test tools is that they can be useful for focused unit tests but not so useful for integration tests. It is tricky to have specific files know which integration tests they might be a part of without rerunning the entire integration-test suite on every file change. If you are willing to put a little effort into tweaking the Guardfile, though, you will not have to do anything to get the tests you are working on to continue running.

Writing Faster Tests by Bypassing Rails

Another way to run tests without loading the entire Rails framework is to write tests that don't require the entire Rails framework. That sounds crazy, I know, since you're writing a Rails application. Bear with me.

The tests you've written so far mostly fall into five groups:

- End-to-end tests. These tests require the entire Rails stack since you're testing the entire stack.

- Tests that use only ActiveRecord and need the database. Right now this group includes tests for ActiveRecord finder methods and your action object tests that save to the database.

- Request tests that require ActionPack and may or may not require ActiveRecord and may or may not touch the database, depending on how they're stubbed.

- Tests that use ActiveRecord objects but don't touch the database.

- Tests that use no Rails-specific classes at all.

The first category will, broadly speaking, be slowest, and each step down should be a faster set of tests. Right now you don't have many tests in the last category—I think the only ones there are the AvatarAdapter tests you wrote to interact with Twitter. How do you move tests to the lower and faster categories in this list? And why is removing Rails helpful?

 Rails is not your application; it is a framework on which you build your application—unless you work at Basecamp and actually develop Rails.

I'm indebted to Corey Haines and Gary Bernhardt for the ideas in this section. I particularly recommend you check out Corey's book *Understanding the Four*

Rules of Simple Design,[4] and Gary's posts "Test Isolation Is About Avoiding Mocks" and "TDD, Straw Men, and Rhetoric."[5] [6]

Why Speed Is Important

Before I explain how you'll use this information to speed up your tests, let me make a pitch for the idea of being a little obsessive about test speed.

You're going to run your tests a lot.

If you're doing the kind of rapid-feedback TDD that I've been discussing up until now, you'll be running at least a subset of your tests nearly continuously, multiple times an hour. (Any exact number that I put here is going to seem shockingly high to people who aren't used to super-fast test feedback and shockingly low to those who are.) And you're probably not the only developer on your team. And it's likely that your entire test suite runs when you commit code to your repository via some kind of continuous build system.

The speed of a test run, whether it is your entire suite or a subset you're running in development, lands in one of seven groups:

1. So fast you don't even notice.

2. Fast enough for you to watch the test run without breaking focus.

3. Slow enough that you break focus but don't have time to do anything else.

4. Slow enough for you to get a cup of coffee.

5. Slow enough for you to eat lunch.

6. Slow enough for you to sleep.

7. Effectively infinite without a big parallelized server.

A project will have thousands of runs. Tens of thousands. Hundreds of thousands if the project is big. The difference between being in group 2 and group 3 becomes a big deal when you're trying to run the tests as often as you can. There are numerous studies that say that breaking focus is a huge drain in developer productivity.

The difference between a 10-second run in group 2 and a 30-second run in group 3 is important. A group 2 run allows you get feedback without breaking focus. A group 3 run means you lose your train of thought. If you've ever been

---

4. https://leanpub.com/4rulesofsimpledesign

5. https://www.destroyallsoftware.com/blog/2014/test-isolation-is-about-avoiding-mocks

6. https://www.destroyallsoftware.com/blog/2014/tdd-straw-men-and-rhetoric

able to work in an environment with near-instantaneous test feedback, you know it's an entirely different level of dealing with tests.

Worse, there's a slow acclimation that comes with a gradually increasing test suite. You'll add only a little bit of time to the test suite every day—practically nothing. But weeks and months of practically nothing being added lead you not to notice that suddenly you have time to go get coffee during your test run. Preventing this gradual time creep takes vigilance.

I'm not saying that your entire test suite needs to run in 15 seconds. That's not feasible for most applications, and it's probably not a good idea in any case—you need some of those slow integration tests. I'm saying that the value of your testing will improve if you have a reliable way to run relevant tests in a few seconds. That way might be Guard, it might include Spring, or RSpec metadata, or the --only-failures options, but it's worth making sure you have a way of doing so. It's also true that it's much easier to isolate a subset of tests if your application is broken into relatively distinct sections.

> **Prescription 48** If you have enough time to break focus while your tests run, you aren't getting the full value of the TDD process.

Why Separation from Rails Is Useful

The primary advantage of writing your tests to avoid Rails is that doing so encourages you to structure your code to better manage increasing complexity and change over time. Super-fast tests are just a side benefit.

Here are some of the advantages, which are related to the idea that there is a minimum of coupling between any two parts of the code:

- It's easier to change one element of the code if the impact of that change is limited in how it affects other parts of the code. Limiting the access that code has to the internals of other sections makes it easier to change those internals. In Rails terms, ActiveRecord associations and attributes often qualify as internals since they're based on an implementation detail—the naming convention of the underlying database. Putting lots of logic in Rails controllers and models encourages intertwining potentially unrelated functionality.

- The framework imposes generic names on common actions, whereas it's usually valuable to name specific items in your application after domain concepts. For example, order(year: :asc) is less meaningful than chronological.

- The fewer details you need to worry about at once, the easier it is to understand code. It's easier to focus on the logic for allowing users access to a
  specific project if it's not thrown together in the same file with code for finding
  users, code to display full names, and code to list a user's undone tasks.

It's possible to overdo isolation to the point where the pieces of code are so
small that your cognitive load goes back up as you try to put the pieces
together. You probably aren't near that boundary yet.

Isolating in a Rails application like this is often mischaracterized as setting
up your application to switch away from Rails. That's not the point. If you do
need to switch from Rails, you're probably looking at significant code changes
no matter how you organize your code. The point is to make your application
best able to handle both the complexity in the current application and the
inevitable changes over time.

That said, Rails itself does change. And it's even been known to throw in changes
that are not backward-compatible. When that happens, the less intertwined
your application logic is with Rails logic, the easier your upgrade path.

However, the odds that this approach will cause the founder of Rails to call
you an architecture astronaut remain pretty high.

> **Prescription 49** This is your regular reminder that software is complex and
> there are multiple paths to success.

Rails Test Prescriptions, Hold the Rails

The basic idea is isolation: isolating your objects from each other and isolating
your code from Rails functionality that would require Rails to be loaded. Isolation means that different objects interact with each other over as small a
set of methods as possible. It means objects, ideally, know nothing about the
internal structure of other objects in the system.

This doesn't have to be all that complicated. You've been writing tests with
reasonably good habits so far. To isolate your Project tests from anything other
than ActiveRecord, all you need to do is change the header. Remove the require
rails_helper call and replace it:

```
environment/01/test/models/project_test.rb
require_relative "../active_record_test_helper"
require_relative "../../app/models/project"
require_relative "../../app/models/task"
```

Where once you had a single require, now you have three.

The first one is the most important: you've replaced your rails_helper (which loads the Rails environment) with an active_record_spec_helper (which only loads ActiveRecord). After that, since you're not loading Rails, you don't have access to Rails autoloading. As a result, you need to explicitly load the model files referenced in this test file—namely, Project and Task.

Let's take a closer look at active_record_spec_helper:

```
environment/01/spec/active_record_spec_helper.rb
Line 1  require "spec_helper"
     -  require "active_record"
     -  require "yaml"
     -  require_relative "../app/models/application_record.rb"
     5
     -  connection_info = YAML.load_file("config/database.yml")["test"]
     -  ActiveRecord::Base.establish_connection(connection_info)
     -
     -  RSpec.configure do |config|
    10    config.around do |example|
     -      ActiveRecord::Base.transaction do
     -        example.run
     -        raise ActiveRecord::Rollback
     -      end
    15    end
     -  end
```

This code is based on Corey Haines's spec helper.[7]

First, a number of things are required. The critical part of this section is what is *not* there—specifically, loading the Rails config/environment, which brings in the entire Rails system. You're loading ActiveRecord and YAML.

The next two lines, starting with line 6, load your test database information from the Rails database.yml and then dig into ActiveRecord to set up a connection to that database. This will enable your tests to save to and read from the same database setup you've been using, but again, without loading the entire Rails stack.

Finally, on line 11, you have to handle database cleanup. RSpec has a global around method that takes a block and allows you to insert code both before and after each spec. In this case, you surround the spec with an ActiveRecord transaction, then execute the test with example.run, and then roll back the database to its pretest state. If you need more-sophisticated database management, look at the DatabaseCleaner gem.[8]

---

7. http://articles.coreyhaines.com/posts/active-record-spec-helper
8. https://github.com/DatabaseCleaner/database_cleaner

With this helper and the additional requirement of your project and task files, you have all you need to run this test file directly from the command line without using the rake task provided by Rails:

```
% rspec spec/models/project_spec.rb
.................

Finished in 0.06155 seconds (files took 0.4728 seconds to load)
17 examples, 0 failures
```

rspec spec/models/project_spec.rb is run all by itself and it works, bypassing the Rails environment. The RSpec command line reports how long the file load takes preceding the test, so I can confidently tell you that on my machine the Rails version takes about 3.25 seconds and the non-Rails version takes about 0.5. That's not a bad savings, especially considering that the load time for the Rails version is only going to increase over time.

One warning: if you separate rails and non-Rails tests, you need to run your non-Rails tests separately. Otherwise Rails will load anyway, and you'll lose the speed advantage and get some extra flakiness based on Rails being loaded at an arbitrary point in the suite. Also, SQLite seems to really, really not like combining regular Rails connections with this kind of ad hoc ActiveRecord connection. As a result, you may have trouble with this technique using SQLite, but changing the database to something more production-ready like PostgreSQL or MySQL should help.

active_record_test_helper in Minitest

The same Rails-bypassing test technique works in Minitest, but there are some minor differences based on the way the RSpec executable works versus the way Minitest works.

In Minitest, the active_record_test_helper looks like this:

```
environment/01/test/active_record_test_helper.rb
require "minitest/autorun"
require "mocha/mini_test"
require "active_record"
require "active_support/test_case"
require "minitest/reporters"
require_relative "../app/models/application_record.rb"

reporter_options = {color: true}
Minitest::Reporters.use!(
  [Minitest::Reporters::DefaultReporter.new(reporter_options)])

connection_info = YAML.load_file("config/database.yml")["test"]
ActiveRecord::Base.establish_connection(connection_info)
```

```
module ActiveSupport
  class TestCase
    teardown do
      ActiveRecord::Base.subclasses.each(&:delete_all)
    end
  end
end
```

This is based on a Minitest version I got from Robert Evans on GitHub.[9]

The basic setup is similar. Load Minitest and ActiveRecord, and then load some files that will help in testing: minitest/autorun, which lets you run test files as standalone scripts; Mocha for mocks; active_support/test_case so you don't have to rewrite all your tests that use it; and minitest/reporters, which gives you color output at the terminal. You also have a couple of lines setting up the reporter.

By default, Minitest doesn't have the around behavior you used in RSpec. For the moment, you're doing a very simple and blunt thing, which is adding into your ActiveSupport::TestCase a teardown block that will be called after every test. It tells all known subclasses of ActiveRecord::Base to delete_all, cleaning up the database.

In practice this will likely be slower than the RSpec behavior, though for some reason SQLite seems to like it more. (If you want the around behavior in Minitest, you can get it with the minitest-around gem.[10]) And you can still use DatabaseCleaner if you want something fancier.

You then need to change the header of your test files as well. Here's a sample for project_test:

`environment/01/test/models/project_test.rb`
```
require_relative "../active_record_test_helper"
require_relative "../../app/models/project"
require_relative "../../app/models/task"
```

If you're trying to bypass Rails, don't use the Rails-provided rake testing tasks. All of them load the environment as a dependency, even if you don't explicitly do so in your test helper.

> **Prescription 50** The only way to know the boundaries of a new coding tool is to go past them. Try things.

---

9.   https://gist.github.com/revans/4196367

10. https://github.com/splattael/minitest-around

Workflow Tests Without Rails

Limiting model tests to use only ActiveRecord doesn't seem like that big a win overall, since almost by definition a model test doesn't explore anything beyond the model.

Ideally, you'd also be able to isolate your workflow object specs, since those workflow objects are specifically created to be plain Ruby objects. Also, if you aren't careful, testing these actions can be particularly slow because you potentially create and save a lot of model objects.

You can often isolate these objects by using test doubles as replacements for your ActiveRecord objects. However, test doubles can be difficult as replacements for Rails associations (you want to model them as lists, but they aren't exactly lists). The two techniques can also work together, in that the code you would write to make it easier to isolate ActiveRecord also often makes the remaining code easier to use with test doubles.

Your existing CreatesProject tests can be isolated without much trouble, although there are rather a lot of dependencies. The header looks like this:

environment/01/spec/workflows/creates_project_spec.rb
```
require_relative "../active_record_spec_helper"
require "devise"
require "devise/orm/active_record"
require_relative "../../app/models/project"
require_relative "../../app/models/task"
require_relative "../../app/models/role"
require_relative "../../app/models/user"
require_relative "../../app/workflows/creates_project"
```

About that list of dependencies: it seems kind of long. Especially since four of those require statements—the two devise lines, the role, and the user—are there only to support the User class. You need to import the User class in part because you have a line in the action that assigns the incoming user objects to project.users. That line causes Rails to autoload the User class, which brings in Role and indirectly brings in Devise because the User class calls the devise method to set up authentication.

That seems like a lot of dependency being brought in for a single line. When you were using Rails in this test, Rails autoload prevented you from having to care about dependencies. Now that you're specifying them explicitly, you can see how interconnected this test is.

You can remove this dependency from the action and the test by putting the dependency back in the Project method, which is already tied to users, and adding in some judicious test doubles to block the user from being called.

The new test looks like this:

```
environment/02/spec/workflows/creates_project_spec.rb
it "adds users to the project" do
  project = Project.new
  user = double
  expect(project).to receive(:add_users).with([user])
  allow(Project).to receive(:new).and_return(project)
  creator = CreatesProject.new(name: "Project Runway", users: [user])
  creator.build
end
```

The test is started with four lines setting up test doubles. There's a common pattern here, where you create a blank object of a certain type—in this case, Project—then stub Project.new to return that instance. This allows you to set further stubs on the specific project instance being used, secure in the knowledge that the code being tested will be using the same instance. Without stubbing Project.new, the new instance created in the action code would not have the stub assigned to the project instance in this test.

There are at least two other ways to handle this situation. You could use the RSpec framework's allow_any_instance_of feature:

```
allow_any_instance_of(Project).to receive(:add_users).with([user])
```

This would save a line in the setup. I try to avoid allow_any_instance_of these days on the grounds that it's too big and broad a weapon for the job. I prefer being more specific about what I want the code to do.

The RSpec team recommends against using this feature. You could instead move the Project.new call to its own method inside the workflow object and stub that method, which I would be more likely to do.

For the preceding code to work, you need to move the project.users = call inside the Project class:

```
environment/02/app/models/project.rb
def add_users(users)
  self.users << users
end
```

And then update CreatesProject to use that new method:

```
environment/02/app/workflows/creates_project.rb
def build
  self.project = Project.new(name: name)
  project.tasks = convert_string_to_tasks
  project.add_users(users)
  project
end
```

And the tests pass again. You can now remove the four user-related require statements and the tests still pass.

What have you gained by writing your test this way and what have you lost?

This is tricky because the loss is up-front and clear at the moment, while the potential gain is further down the road. You've lost a small piece of Rails convenience by bypassing the Rails users association in favor of a method specifically designed to be part of the public API.

You've gained the ability to think about creating projects without dealing with the complexity of users. (Many Rails conveniences work against separation of concerns in a complex program, which is a good summary of the community's argument over this kind of code.)

This particular case is too small for that to seem like much of a win (an occupational hazard of trying to show object-oriented techniques to manage complexity is that they all look like crazy overkill when applied to your typical book-example-sized problem). In a more complicated problem, separating one wildly complex piece from another wildly complex piece can make it easier to deal with each part separately.

> **Prescription 51** You can use test doubles to remove test dependencies.

Removing dependencies starts to get more challenging as the underlying logic becomes more complex. For example, you might need some information about the user to create projects, most likely for access-control purposes. You might want to prevent a user from having created two projects with the same name, scoped to only the projects that particular user has created.

There are a few options for managing that complexity:

- You could just give up, add User back to CreatesProject, and just deal with the dependency. I don't want to underestimate this option. Sometimes it's the correct option, or at least the minimally complex one.

- You can create a dummy User class inside the test and require that version of User rather than the ActiveRecord version. I don't recommend this, as it's really tricky to manage the namespaces and hard to keep the dummy and the real user in sync.

- You can have some other object in the system filter the necessary information to CreatesProject. In the case of access information, the controller is a logical place for that; it's arguably the controller's role to police access to other services. In other cases, whoever invokes the CreatesProject action might be responsible for sending the necessary data as simple Ruby data, like a hash or even a simple struct.

- Similarly, you can create a wrapper object—ProjectCreatingUser or something—that wraps a user and provides an API for CreatesProject. In tests, the ProjectCreatingUser can easily stub information, making the dependency a single plain Ruby object rather than a complex tree of ActiveRecord objects.

The last two options may seem like way, way too much structure to you. (Maybe you came to Rails to avoid the kind of hyper-indirect object models that characterize, say, enterprise Java projects.) And sometimes I'd agree. In most cases I wouldn't start with this level of complexity and indirection. But I would refactor to it when things start to get complex—this kind of refactoring is much easier to do if you catch it early.

The point is that writing application tests that bypass Rails requires you to be more thoughtful about your dependencies (or, looked at from the other direction, writing tests that use Rails autoloading allows you to be sloppy about dependencies). However you choose to manage the dependencies, being aware of them is the first step in keeping your program easy to change over time.

 **Prescription 52** You don't need to start with elaborate object indirection, but it's useful when logic gets complicated.

Running Rails-Free Tests

If you're going to have some tests that run without loading the Rails environment, you need to be careful to run those tests separately from the slower, Rails-loading tests. You lose the benefit of not loading Rails if some of your tests *load Rails*. Also, if you're doing any namespace munging in your fast tests, mixing and matching fast and slow tests is guaranteed to give weird errors.

The easiest way to manage running fast tests is to keep them in their own directory or directories and pass those directories as arguments to ruby. This is easy in RSpec, since the spec command will take directories or globs as arguments:

```
$ rspec spec/models spec/workflows
```

This is a little more complicated in Minitest since you're loading ruby directly, and ruby doesn't handle file globs. You could create a rake task like this:

```
require 'rake/testtask'

Rake::TestTask.new(:fast) do |t|
  t.pattern = "test/{models,actions,values}/**/*_test.rb"
end
```

Or this way:

```
task :fast_tests do
  Dir.glob("test/{models,actions,values}/**/*_test.rb").each { |file| require file }
end
```

You can also do this directly from your shell if you think the rake tasks are too slow:

```
$ for file in test/{models,actions,values}/**/*_test.rb; do ruby $file; done
```

The side effect of the last approach is that each file will run and report separately, which may not be desirable.

Whatever you do, you probably want to make it a system alias, assign it a key shortcut, or do something else that's dependent on your own workflow. You want to be able to run these tests with as little effort as possible.

Recommendations for Faster Tests

The topic of Rails code structure and the attendant ability to write tests always winds up in a mixture of things everyone should try once, things I do regularly, things I wish I could do regularly, things I don't do but generally regret not doing, and so on. In that spirit, here are a few recommendations:

- My current practice is to move complex transaction logic out of controllers into workflow objects, complex creation logic out of models and into factory or workflow objects, and (somewhat less often) view logic into presenters—all of those are plain, non-Rails Ruby objects. David Heinemeier Hansson might say all of these lead to overly complicated code. That hasn't been my experience. You should try for yourself.

- I like to use SimpleDelegator to create a new object that has functionality that applies to an ActiveRecord object only some of the time—for example, logic about whether a user has access to a resource, or logic for purchasing an item, which is needed only during the purchase process itself.

- Where I can, I like to use immutable value objects—for instance, taking a start and end date from an object and making a DateRange class or taking a name class from a first name, last name, and so on. The value objects are super-fast to test and tend to attract logic.

- In tests, I try to create as few objects as possible, touch the database as little as possible, and be aware of dependencies and places to mock that can limit the amount of setup a test needs.

- RSpec has a —profile option that shows you the slowest tests in a test run. You need to be careful with it (often the slow test will be the one that had the garbage collector run during it), but it's a good thing to run now and then to try to speed up your slowest tests. The same configuration option that allows the use of --only-failures keeps a running list of the runtimes of every spec in the system. This can be useful to look at.

- All that said, don't despair if you can't make this all work immediately. I've never quite been able to make an entire project work using the ActiveRecord-specific test helper. My main problem is not making an individual test run, and it's not keeping track of dependencies manually. Rather, my main problem has typically been integrating the separate sets of tests into the entire ecosystem of the project—that includes my ability to run the entire spec suite, other developers' ability to run the suite, extra continuous-integration setup, and the like. Being aware of dependencies (and using Spring) provides most of the benefit with a fraction of the fuss. Still, it's probably something I could be more aggressive about; most of my codebases wind up with test suites that are slower than I'd like.

What You've Done

In this chapter you explored different solutions for increasing the speed of your tests. Test speed can be important in a lot of ways. It's valuable to be able to run useful tests in development without losing your focus. It's also nice to be able to run all your tests before deploying code and not have that run take a half hour when there's a bug in production you're scrambling to fix.

You learned about strategies on the command line to run only a subset of tests at once to allow you to run them more quickly and to focus on the code that is currently being changed. You also learned about strategies to make the test suite faster in a larger sense by allowing you to isolate code from Rails or by removing dependencies so that tests don't touch the database.

A lot of this advice is particularly difficult to apply to legacy codebases that have not been built to support these ideas. The next chapter talks about strategies for dealing with the particular issues of legacy code.

CHAPTER 17

Testing Legacy Code

You won't always get to start from scratch.

There's a strong possibility that you'll need to bring your testing skills to bear on a codebase that already exists. A codebase that—gasp—may not have a complete or accurate test suite to guide you.

Not all that long ago, there were no Rails legacy projects. Now there are Rails codebases that are old enough to attend middle school and beyond. These codebases tend to be large, and almost by definition they aren't using the latest tools. All the advice in this book so far is well and good, but what if you're not starting your TDD experience with a new application? How does testing change when you're dealing with a legacy codebase?

Entire books have been written on working with legacy codebases. In this chapter you'll focus on techniques for getting legacy code under test. There are many other issues you'll need to deal with in a legacy codebase. Getting the legacy system up and running can be a chore, and there's a variety of techniques for safely adding features to or refactoring existing code. I'll discuss those topics here only as they intersect with testing. For a more detailed look at managing a legacy project, check out Michael Feathers's excellent *Working Effectively with Legacy Code [Fea04]*.

What's a Legacy?

The phrase "legacy code" is often used as a synonym for "bad code." While the two categories often overlap, assuming the legacy code is always awful isn't the most helpful way to think about a legacy.

What makes code "legacy" is not the quality, but the extent to which you have access to the context in which it was created and the reasons previous developers made the choices they made.

Prescription 53	When dealing with legacy code, respect code that works. You don't know what constraints the previous coders worked under.

Legacy code is scary—not because it's bad, but because you don't know what parts of the design are incidental and what parts are critical. When two different actions are backed by the same method but one of them has a bug, you don't know whether the other action is intended to have the current behavior.

When dealing with legacy code, testing is used for the following:

- Describing the current behavior of the code
- Making sure code changes have no unintended consequences
- Promoting isolation of new features

Set Expectations

You aren't going to convert this beast of an old project into a marvel of elegant, test-driven code overnight. And trying to do so is probably not a good idea. When you're exposed to a new codebase, you should do the following:

- If it makes you feel better, for 15 minutes shake your fists and curse the previous programmer's name (doubly effective if the previous programmer was you).

- Move on and start working with the codebase. It's yours now.

If you're like me, the temptation to immediately fix everything and/or add tests to everything is pretty strong. Lie down until the feeling passes.

There are two reasons it's a bad idea to do nothing but add test coverage to a legacy project first thing. From a purely logistical standpoint, when you take over a legacy project you're often expected to do something with it immediately. Your new client may not perceive going off in the corner and doing nothing but writing tests for weeks at a time as forward motion. Every situation is different, but it's rare to find a client that considers test coverage a "quick win."

The second problem has to do with the often-noted paradox of legacy development. Legacy code, by its nature, is often too interdependent or poorly understood to make it easy to unit-test without substantial refactoring. However, substantial refactoring without unit tests is a great way to introduce bugs into the codebase—especially when working with new code that you may not fully understand. This is also unlikely to be considered a "quick win."

Working code that does not explicitly need to be changed needs *not* to be changed. If it's working and the requirements are the same as they were, waking up the sleeping bear is far from your highest priority.

When working with legacy code, proceed incrementally, taking small steps that you can verify. Tweak the existing code as little as possible to get it to a state you can live with. Then you can ensure that the new code you write is as good—and as thoroughly tested—as possible. Making small improvements to existing code over time while writing new code as best you can will make the overall codebase better.

Getting Started with Legacy Code

When you're presented with a new codebase, your first job is to figure out exactly what the heck is going on. Toward that end, you should do three things immediately.

Get the Code in Source Control

These days it probably is already under source control, but you can't be too careful. Make sure you have all the access to any code repository that you need. While starting on a new legacy codebase is not the time to get fancy with new tools, you'll be much better served by using Git or some other source-control system that lets you easily create and manipulate branches. This will enable you to easily explore changes to the codebase using branches as scratch pads that can be kept or discarded as needed.

Get the Code Running

If the legacy project was conceived without much knowledge of Rails community practices (evidenced by the lack of tests), it won't be a surprise if the production environment is also a little sketchy. Conventional wisdom suggests that your development, staging, and production environments should be as similar as possible to prevent environment-specific errors. And although this is true in general, if your legacy project is being run by some random goofy server setup, it may be difficult or impossible to replicate that setup on your staging server, let alone your development machine.

If the exact production environment isn't available to you, the staging and development environments should be as generic as possible. If you can, push to migrate the production environment to a less fragile and more standard one as soon as possible. Container tools like Docker can be helpful here; it might be easiest to replicate the production environment in a Docker container rather than on your development computer.

Get the Test Suite Running

At first glance this may strike you as a useless piece of advice. If the legacy team has been ignoring tests, nothing is there, right? Of course everything will run.

Well, not necessarily. There are at least two things you need to look out for. Even if the previous coders totally ignored tests, Rails may still have autogenerated test code. Fixtures or factories generated early in the project have moved out of date. If columns were deleted or renamed, fixtures won't load and you'll get errors galore. If validations have changed, factories might not work. It's only slightly less likely that the generated controller tests for a scaffold have drifted out of date with the code; if authentication and roles were added later, for example, you'll need to match that authentication in the tests.

In some ways your job is harder if the previous team flirted with writing tests and then gave up because they had not yet read this book (I'm assuming). In that case, you're likely to have all kinds of tests that may or may not have passed at one point and have been broken by later code—combined with inattention. You have to assume for the moment that the code is right and the tests are wrong—the exact opposite of a standard TDD scenario. (Mike Gunderloy presents a simple rule for initial triage of legacy tests in his *Rails Rescue Handbook*: if you can't figure out what a test is doing in five minutes, delete it.)

Take this opportunity to learn how the legacy code works, but do not change the code to match the tests at this point. If you can't figure out how to make a test pass, comment it out, mark it as pending, or delete it; add a note, and come back to it when you have a more thorough test scaffold in place. As I've discussed, test coverage is not the priority at this stage. The priority is a green test run that you can use as a base for future work.

I very tentatively recommend that if the code is on an older version of RSpec, one of the first things to try is an RSpec upgrade. There's an automated tool that moves from RSpec 2 to RSpec 3 syntax.[1] Upgrading to RSpec 3 gives you a few tools, such as --only-failure, that can be useful in a legacy codebase. That said, the specs need to be running without failure for the automatic upgrade to work. And you should be prepared to back out of this upgrade quickly if there are problems. If you don't know how the tests work and the upgrade gives you a lot of failures, now is not the time to be guessing.

1.　http://rspec.info/upgrading-from-rspec-2

Test-Driven Exploration

Testing a legacy codebase starts in earnest when there is a change to make. Often the first order of business on a new project is to deal with a critical bug left by the previous team—something that must be accomplished while preserving existing behavior and that does not demand a dramatic refactoring of the application.

In this case, there are two goals to getting the code under test. You want to be able to tell when the bug has been fixed. This step involves a more or less standard TDD bug-fixing session with one or more failing tests isolating the bug. The tests should pass when the bug is fixed. Also, you must confirm that any existing correct behavior hasn't been compromised. In a project that was TDD from the beginning you'd already have this ability, but in a testless legacy project you need to build up that coverage.

Generally speaking, tests against an existing system come in two flavors: black-box and white-box testing—the phrases far predate software testing and apply to any kind of test process. A black-box test is so called because it ignores the internal structure of the application and tests only top-level input into the system and the output that is returned. Conversely, a white-box test uses knowledge about system internals to explicitly test specific paths through the code.

Black-Box Testing

A *black-box* test is a test that depends only on the external interface of code without relying on the internals. You can think of the internals as an opaque black box that you can't see inside. We already did black-box testing of Rails applications back in Chapter 8, *Integration Testing with Capybara and Cucumber*, on page 151. A black-box test of a Rails application works only at the level of user input and system output, typically HTML. That sounds a lot like a Cucumber or Capybara integration test. Since integration testing works from outside the normal Rails code, it's ideal for interaction with legacy code.

The integration tests interact with the system as a user would. Since there is no interaction with the code's internal structure, it's possible to write integration tests no matter how gunky the code is.

Integration testing can be useful in a bug situation because bugs are often specified in terms of the users' actions and responses. These actions and responses are often reasonably straightforward to translate to Cucumber or Capybara, and it's easy to recognize if you've changed the behavior. In addition, it's not unheard of for a codebase with few tests to lack written requirements; the acceptance tests act as baseline requirements as you move forward.

The general plan here is to use integration testing to quickly write high-level tests surrounding both the bug and the correct behavior it is related to—not to try to cover the entire application, but rather to cover the entire feature to discover regressions.

Acceptance-level tests are relatively easy to write for a legacy application but have limited utility. An integration test won't tell you where in the application you need to make the change that fixes the bug or adds the feature. Also, integration tests tend to run slowly, so you don't want them to be the only part of your test arsenal.

White-Box Testing

There's no way around writing real unit tests. Two distinct kinds of user tests are helpful when dealing with legacy applications. I'll talk about the standard TDD tests in a moment; first let's examine a technique that you can use to build up unit tests in hard-to-understand legacy code. You can use tests to figure out what is going on in the application—they are sometimes called *characterization tests*.

The basic process is straightforward: the difficulty of implementation depends on just how tangled the code is. First, select a method to test. Ideally the method should be related to a change you're planning to make in the app, although this process also works for "what is going on here?" exploration.

For this method, let's write a test we know will fail. You don't need to go deep into the internals for this. We're trying to behave like sonar—sending a test into the depths of the code and hoping to get a signal back:

```
it "calculates sales tax" do
  user = User.create(state: :il)
  order = user.orders.create
  order.line_items.create(:price => 250)
  order.line_items.create(:price => 300)
  expect(order.sales_tax).to eq(-300_000)
end
```

You have a simple, straightforward test, right up until the last line. (Insert cheesy DJ record-scratch sound effect.) You don't really expect the sales tax to be –300,000 dollars. But you don't want to guess what it is; you'll let the app tell you.

Run the test. At this point, one of two things will happen: the test will error because there's a missing dependency, or the test will fail because the code runs but spits out a different result. (Well, three things, if you include the remote possibility that the sales tax really is –300,000 dollars, in which case you might have bigger problems.)

Most of the time the test will raise an error because there is some object dependency you didn't know about, some value is not as expected, or you have otherwise disturbed the delicate balance of your legacy app's functionality. You'll need to figure out how to smooth things over. Often you'll have to create more objects. In this example, you might need to explicitly create product objects. The object chain can get unwieldy, which is okay at this point: the goal is to understand what's happening. If the code itself is unwieldy, let the test stand as a monument to things that need to be changed.

Eventually you'll run out of errors; the application spits out the sales tax, and the test has a normal validation failure—since, again, the answer probably isn't –300,000. At this point you insert the actual value into the test and declare victory. You now have some test coverage and a greater understanding of how the application fits together. It's time to move on to the next test, most likely trying the existing method in some other test case, such as one designed to trigger a bad response.

You don't care if the value for the sales tax is correct. Well, you care in the sense that calculating sales tax is important from a business perspective; however, from a test perspective you must assume that the code is correct so that you have a stable base when you start making changes because of all the bugs.

> **Prescription 54** When writing initial unit tests for legacy code, use the test to explore the code's behavior. Try to write a passing test without changing code.

Pry can be your friend and ally during this exploration process. The console is a great way to try some of these object interactions quickly. Once you figure things out in the console, transfer the commands to the test so they can be run repeatedly.

What Tool Should I Use? (Legacy Edition)

Taking over a legacy codebase has the side effect of clarifying tool decisions you might otherwise agonize over—if the previous coder used a tool and there's anything salvageable, use that tool. You don't want to be in the position of adding code coverage while juggling your RSpec tests with a batch of existing Minitest tests. I recommend adding a factory tool if there isn't one already in the mix. It's likely that writing tests for the legacy app will require creating complete chains of related objects. Setting up a factory tool to create the associations all at once saves a lot of time.

There are, of course, exceptions to this rule. Two spring to mind: a) the original developer has chosen a tool that's unsuitable for supporting the kind of testing weight you want to put on it or, more often, b) the existing tests are useless and it's best to delete them quickly and start over. At that point you can pick whatever tools you want.

Dependency Removal

Dependencies are the most challenging issue in legacy testing. Perhaps the greatest virtue of well-done TDD code is that the tests force individual pieces of the code to be maximally independent of each other.

Without tests, legacy code tends to be highly interdependent. This makes adding tests difficult in several ways. Multiple objects might need to be created to test a single method. It might be hard to limit a test to a true functional unit if that unit is hard to reach or encased in a massive 300-line method. There are ways to have the code you need to test be separate enough to enable the tests you must write.

Keep Things Separate

Perhaps the easiest way to keep your new code from being dependent on legacy code is to separate it yourself. Where possible, write new code in new methods or new classes, and merely call those from the existing legacy mess. In theory this leaves your new code unencumbered enough to be written via TDD.

Let's try a brief example. Consider a kind of messy method from a social-networking site called Flitter:

```ruby
class Flit
  def process_flit
    if text =~ /##/
      flit.text = "testing: remove this code after 3/10/10"
    end
    if text.ends_with?("%fb%")
      send_to_facebook
    else if user.flits_in_last_day > 423
      return
    end
```

```
    flit_server.check_for_mentions(self)
    flit_server.follower_list(user)
    user.update_attributes(:flit_count => user.flit_count + 1)
    # and so it goes …
  end
end
```

Within this tangled mess, you must add a new feature: if a flit contains text of the form $username, the user in question must be informed of the message. You could just add another if statement in the long line of if statements already in the method, but then it would be hard to test the new behavior without testing all the process_flit code, which brings in a lot of other stuff. (In real life this method could be 300 lines, and for all you know it could invoke PayPal.)

Instead, add a method check_for_dollar_sign, and then call that method in the appropriate place inside process_flit, writing the new method using regular TDD. If you're feeling adventurous and it seems plausible, a mock test to confirm that process_flit calls check_for_dollar_sign might also be appropriate.

If you're adding or extracting a lot of functionality, you might consider creating your own separate class rather than just a method. One sign that a new class is warranted is if it passes the same set of instance variables to multiple methods. I'm a big fan of classes that represent processes and replace long complex methods. For testing purposes, moving new code to a new class can make testing the new code easier because the new code is less dependent on the existing application.

Although this technique helps you make a clean break from the legacy code, it has the short-term effect of making the code more opaque. In the words of Michael Feathers, "When you break dependencies in legacy code, you often have to suspend your sense of aesthetics a bit." You know how when you're cleaning off your desk, you have an intermediate stage in which the room is covered in piles of paper and it looks like an even bigger mess? Or is that just me? In any case, you're in an intermediate state here, between the undifferentiated mass of the original and the nicely factored and organized new version. Building up the test suite one broken dependency at a time moves you steadily toward cleaner code.

Legacy Databases, Testing, and You

If your legacy application has only a nodding relationship with Rails common standards, chances are the database is also a mess. Many issues that plague a legacy database can be frustrating (such as odd naming conventions or unusual use of ActiveRecord features), but they don't affect your ability to test the features.

You do need to be careful if the database has added constraints that are not evident in the code. Typically this involves column constraints that go beyond any validations specified in the ActiveRecord model, or foreign key constraints that are not specified anywhere in the Rails code. Foreign key constraints are hardest to deal with. Older versions of Rails had no native mechanism for specifying them, but they are beloved by database admins the world over.

From a testing perspective, the problem is twofold. First there is business logic outside the Rails code and in the database. That logic is hard to find, test, and change. Even worse, foreign key constraints add dependencies that require certain objects to be created together. In a test environment, that kind of dependency leads to mysterious bugs: the database doesn't let you create test data, and objects that need to be created have nothing to do with the test but are there only to make the database happy. Keep a close eye on this in a legacy application created by a database-heavy development team that didn't trust ActiveRecord.

Using Test Doubles to Remove Dependencies

If you don't want to start off at 20,000 feet with acceptance tests, test doubles are another way to get tests started without disrupting the untested code.

In a legacy context, the advantage to using test doubles is their ability to isolate a single class and method from the rest of the application. When working with a legacy application, this allows you to temporarily put aside the issue of how shaky the rest of the application may be and focus on the single part you're trying to figure out at that very moment.

In practice this is similar to the test-double behavior-centric tests you saw in Chapter 7, *Using Test Doubles as Mocks and Stubs*, on page 129, except that the code already exists, so you don't have the element of designing the API.

Let's look at an example. Take the following legacy method (which we'll assume is part of some kind of nebulous order model):

```
def calculate_order_status
  self.total = 0
  line_items.each do |item|
    if item.quantity.blank?
      LineItem.delete(item.id)
      next
    end
    if item.cost.nil? then item.cost = 0 end
```

```
  if credit_card_is_valid? && item.ready_to_ship?
    self.total += item.cost * item.quantity
  end
end
self.to_be_paid = self.total - self.amount_paid
if self.to_be_paid == 0
  self.paid_in_full = true
end
end
```

This code is a bit of a mess. (It is a special and weird kind of fun to write deliberately awful example code.) It's doing things that should be part of the LineItem class, and it probably could stand to be split. Of course, this example barely scratches the surface of how tangled a poorly written legacy system might be. (You really want to beware the ones with 300-plus-line controller methods.)

This code uses a number of things that are probably attributes that could be set with data, such as amount_paid or item.quantity, but it also calls a few things that could be complex methods in their own rights, such as credit_card_is_valid? or item.ready_to_ship.

A possible test for this code would stub those methods and might look like this (assume we're using factory_bot):

```
it "calculates order status" do
  order = create(:order, amount_paid: 2.50)
  expect(order).to receive(:credit_card_is_valid?).at_least(:once).and_return(true)
  item1 = FactoryBot.create(:line_item, quantity: 1, cost: 3.50)
  expect(item1).to receive(:ready_to_ship?).and_return(true)
  item2 = FactoryBot.create(:line_item, quantity: 2, cost: 5)
  expect(item2).to receive(:ready_to_ship?).and_return(false)
  order.line_items << [item1, item2]
  order.calculate_order_status
  assert_equal 3.50, order.total
  assert !order.paid_in_full
end
```

Lines 2 and 3 set up the order and a mock for the credit_card_is_valid? method. (We're using factory_bot's create method even though it saves to the database, because it's the least likely to disrupt a fragile method.) This can be switched to build_stubbed after the test passes. Lines 4–8 set up individual items, with the action of the test taking place in line 9 and the last lines performing the validation.

In a full test suite you'd test a couple of other combinations of values, so some of the mock setup would probably be extracted to a repeatable method—either an explicit setup block or a method that is called by each test.

The strength of this process is that it allows you to unit-test without further tangling the existing code logic: it's possible that credit_card_is_valid? depends on another three different attributes of the order, the user, or the payment system, and that's a mess you don't want to get into at this moment. The mock test lets you isolate logic issues. This style of mock-object testing also limits test coverage to the method under test, making the coverage report more accurate.

There are some problems to watch out for. It can become time-consuming to set up the external mocks for a complex method, and you run the same risk as with any mock-object testing—namely, that your test becomes a tautology because it's just parroting the input to the mock objects. You can avoid that problem by trying not to mock the data of the exact object under test.

Find the Seam

Test doubles are a specific version of a more general technique for working with legacy code, which involves finding *seams* in the code and exploiting them to make testing the legacy functionality possible

A seam is a place where you can change your application's behavior without changing the code. A test double acts as a seam because adding the test double, which happens in the test, changes the behavior of the code by mandating a specific response to a method call without executing the method. Again, the behavior of the method under test changes in the test environment without affecting behavior in production and without changing the existing development code.

It sounds magical, but the basic idea is simple and Ruby makes it easy to execute. You redirect a method call from its intended target to some other code that you want to run during tests. A test double does this by replacing the entire method call with a return value, but the generic form lets you do anything you want instead of the method call.

You might create your own object if you wanted a side effect that a mock package wouldn't normally provide, such as diagnostic logging. (Feathers calls this a *pebble*: a fake object that logs its own path through the code.) Alternatively, you might want a more elaborate processing of arguments or state than a mock can easily provide—to re-create the output of a web service your application depends on, for example. (Even if the test-double library allows you to pass an arbitrary block as the result of the stubbed call, it's often more readable to create your own object.)

Let's take some sample Ruby code that you want to test. In this sample, flit_server is an object in your system representing an internal server, and those innocent-looking calls are genuine external service calls to a real server that exists in production but not in the test:

```ruby
def process_flit
  # a bunch of messy stuff
  flit_server.check_for_mentions(self)
  # more messy stuff
  flit_server.follower_list(user)
  # more messy stuff
end
```

Now you need to get the process_flit method under test. The test might look like:

```ruby
it "processes a flit correctly if it has followers" do
  user = User.create(screen_name: "zot")
  follower = user.followers.create(screen_name: "jennyw")
  flit = Flit.new(user, "Hello to $jennyw, How are things on earth?")
  flit.process_flit
  expect(follower.timeline.size).to eq(1)
end
```

For this test to work, you need to prevent the flit_server object in the original code from calling the production server that will not exist in the test environment. For the sake of argument, let's assume there's a compelling reason a normal test-double package can't be used here—possibly because the flit_server object is too tightly intertwined with the rest of the code. You have two problems to solve: you need to create a flit_server object that will perform test-safe activities when called, and you need to inject that object into the test so it's used when the method is run under test.

Luckily, Ruby is extremely flexible when it comes to redirecting code execution. (Of course, this is exactly the kind of flexibility that drives security-minded programmers from other languages crazy. But here you're using for it good, not evil.) In a compiled object-oriented language, you might have to create a new subclass of the expected object and override the methods in question. You can do that in Ruby, too:

```ruby
class TestFlitServer < FlitServer
  def check_for_mentions(flit)
    # test code
  end

  def follower_list(user)
    # test code
  end
end
```

Depending on the details of the FlitServer class, you may have to override other methods, such as the constructor.

There are a couple of other Ruby ways to do something similar. Rather than create a subclass, you can create an instance for testing and add overriding methods to that instance's singleton class.

That class might be defined like this:

```ruby
test_server = FlitServer.new
class << test_server
  def check_for_mentions(flit)
    # test code
  end
  def follower_list(user)
    # test code
  end
end
```

Alternatively, you could create a complete dummy class that covers the calls made by your method under test. Since Ruby doesn't do any type-checking beyond seeing whether the object responds to methods, that's perfectly fine:

```ruby
class FakeServer
  def check_for_mentions(flit)
    # test code
  end
  def follower_list(user)
    # test code
  end
end
```

Now you need to inject the new object into the test code. In some sense you're reimplementing what a mock-object package would be doing. You can try to inject the object in the test itself by doing the same thing to the flit object that you did to the flit_server object. Here's an example:

```ruby
Class TestFlit < Flit
  def flit_server
    TestFlitServer.new
  end
end

it "processes a flit correctly if it has followers" do
  user = User.create(screen_name: "zot")
  follower = user.followers.create(screen_name: "jennyw")
  flit = TestFlit.new(user, "Hello to $jennyw, How are things on earth?")
  flit.process_flit
  expect(follower.timeline.size).to eq(1)
end
```

In this case you're mimicking the first way we dealt with FlitServer by by subclassing Flit. The two options shown earlier, singletons and dummy classes, also have analogous usages inside the test.

If you're willing to allow a little bit of manipulation of the original code, you can use Ruby's default arguments to get an almost-seam:

```ruby
def process_flit(flit_server = nil)
  flit_server ||= self.flit_server
  # a bunch of messy stuff
  flit_server.check_for_mentions(self)
  # more messy stuff
  flit_server.follower_list(user)
  # more messy stuff
end
```

In the new method, flit_server is a local that, if not passed as an argument, is given the value of the object's instance method. Thanks to the magic of Ruby's ||= operator, if the argument is passed a value, the passed value is used for the rest of the method. The existing legacy code, which does not use this argument, behaves as is. But it gives you a lever to insert your own server in the test by calling process_flit with the test server as an argument:

```ruby
it "processes a flit correctly if it has followers" do
  user = User.create(screen_name: "zot")
  follower = user.followers.create(screen_name: "jennyw")
  flit = Flit.new(user, "Hello to $jennyw, How are things on earth?")
  flit.process_flit(TestFlitServer.new)
  expect(follower.timeline.size).to eq(1)
end
```

Although this mechanism is slightly intrusive to the original code, you'll probably find you use this pattern often, not just for testing code but also as you add new features to existing code. The default argument lets new code have new behavior while leaving old code behavior untouched.

Each legacy program you work on is going to have its own quirks and require its own kind of creativity, using these methods or others to bring the code the kind of test coverage needed to confidently move forward with bug fixes and new features. As you tackle new problems, remember that reducing dependencies makes it easier to test your code, makes the code cleaner, and makes future work that much easier.

Don't Look Back

It's almost certainly not worth your time and effort to cover an entire complex legacy application before writing any code. I love tests, but the risks involved in doing that much coverage work at once are high, especially if the customer is expecting you to start working on new functionality.

You draw a line in the sand and start working in a test-driven mode moving forward. One critical element is to ensure that every bug fix starts by writing a failing test somewhere—whether unit, functional, or integration. This is a good way to ramp up tests on your project and it allows you to organically build test coverage over time with relatively small risk to your deadlines and fairly little chance of breaking existing functionality.

Similarly, new features must be added using a TDD process. In the beginning this often requires the heightened use of mock objects, but over time the codebase and the test coverage both improve.

If you're like me, the temptation to clean up the entire codebase at once can be almost overwhelming. In this situation, lie down until the feeling passes or you're so close to your deadline that fixing everything is no longer a viable option.

Finally, *do one thing at a time, to the extent possible.* Don't extend test coverage while you're adding new functionality. And don't try to clean up the code while you're extending test coverage (occasionally this will be unavoidable, but keep it to a minimum). The fewer things you have moving at any one time, the easier it will be to identify the culprit when things go wrong.

What You've Done

In this chapter you explored a couple of techniques to help you when you're trying to test a legacy Rails project. You saw how integration tests can be used to create test coverage without being concerned with the structure of the legacy code. You then saw how to use unit tests to build an understanding of how the code works. You also explored techniques to inject code into the system to change its behavior during test so as to focus the test on a particular piece of code.

Over the entire book, you've seen how to use automated developer testing to improve your Rails application, making it easier to validate behavior, and how to use tests to create good code that is easy to change. I've always found writing tests to be fun, and making tests pass is a great way to give myself small challenges along the way to understanding and writing code. I hope that you can use these techniques to save yourself time, make your coding less stressful, and write code that has value.

Bibliography

[FBBO99]   Martin Fowler, Kent Beck, John Brant, William Opdyke, and Don Roberts. *Refactoring: Improving the Design of Existing Code*. Addison-Wesley, Boston, MA, 1999.

[Fea04]   Michael Feathers. *Working Effectively with Legacy Code*. Prentice Hall, Englewood Cliffs, NJ, 2004.

[Hen13]   Elisabeth Hendrickson. *Explore It!*. The Pragmatic Bookshelf, Raleigh, NC, 2013.

[KP78]   Brian W. Kernighan and P.J. Plauger. *The Elements of Programming Style, Second Edition*. McGraw-Hill, Emeryville, CA, 1978.

[Mes07]   Gerard Meszaros. *xUnit Test Patterns*. Addison-Wesley, Boston, MA, 2007.

[Rub13]   Sam Ruby. *Agile Web Development with Rails 4*. The Pragmatic Bookshelf, Raleigh, NC, 2013.

[Wie03]   Karl Wiegers. *Software Requirements, 2nd Edition*. Microsoft Press, Redmond, WA, 2003.

Index

Thank you!

How did you enjoy this book? Please let us know. Take a moment and email us at support@pragprog.com with your feedback. Tell us your story and you could win free ebooks. Please use the subject line "Book Feedback."

Ready for your next great Pragmatic Bookshelf book? Come on over to https://pragprog.com and use the coupon code BUYANOTHER2017 to save 30% on your next ebook.

Void where prohibited, restricted, or otherwise unwelcome. Do not use ebooks near water. If rash persists, see a doctor. Doesn't apply to *The Pragmatic Programmer* ebook because it's older than the Pragmatic Bookshelf itself. Side effects may include increased knowledge and skill, increased marketability, and deep satisfaction. Increase dosage regularly.

And thank you for your continued support,

Andy Hunt, Publisher

SAVE 30%!
Use coupon code
BUYANOTHER2017

Explore Testing and Cucumber

Explore the uncharted waters of exploratory testing and beef up your automated testing with more Cucumber—now for Java, too.

Explore It!

Uncover surprises, risks, and potentially serious bugs with exploratory testing. Rather than designing all tests in advance, explorers design and execute small, rapid experiments, using what they learned from the last little experiment to inform the next. Learn essential skills of a master explorer, including how to analyze software to discover key points of vulnerability, how to design experiments on the fly, how to hone your observation skills, and how to focus your efforts.

Elisabeth Hendrickson
(186 pages) ISBN: 9781937785024. $29
https://pragprog.com/book/ehxta

The Cucumber for Java Book

Teams working on the JVM can now say goodbye forever to misunderstood requirements, tedious manual acceptance tests, and out-of-date documentation. Cucumber—the popular, open-source tool that helps teams communicate more effectively with their customers—now has a Java version, and our bestselling *Cucumber Book* has been updated to match. *The Cucumber for Java Book* has the same great advice about how to deliver rock-solid applications collaboratively, but with all code completely rewritten in Java. New chapters cover features unique to the Java version of Cucumber, and reflect insights from the Cucumber team since the original book was published.

Seb Rose, Matt Wynne & Aslak Hellesøy
(338 pages) ISBN: 9781941222294. $36
https://pragprog.com/book/srjcuc

Advanced Ruby and Rails

What used to be the realm of experts is fast becoming the stuff of day-to-day development—jump to the head of the class today.

Crafting Rails 4 Applications

Get ready to see Rails as you've never seen it before. Learn how to extend the framework, change its behavior, and replace whole components to bend it to your will. Eight different test-driven tutorials will help you understand Rails' inner workings and prepare you to tackle complicated projects with solutions that are well-tested, modular, and easy to maintain.

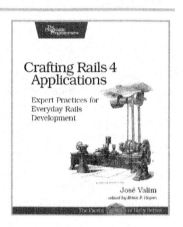

This second edition of the bestselling *Crafting Rails Applications* has been updated to Rails 4 and discusses new topics such as streaming, mountable engines, and thread safety.

José Valim
(208 pages) ISBN: 9781937785550. $36
https://pragprog.com/book/jvrails2

Metaprogramming Ruby 2

Write powerful Ruby code that is easy to maintain and change. With metaprogramming, you can produce elegant, clean, and beautiful programs. Once the domain of expert Rubyists, metaprogramming is now accessible to programmers of all levels. This thoroughly revised and updated second edition of the bestselling *Metaprogramming Ruby* explains metaprogramming in a down-to-earth style and arms you with a practical toolbox that will help you write your best Ruby code ever.

Paolo Perrotta
(278 pages) ISBN: 9781941222126. $38
https://pragprog.com/book/ppmetr2

Fix Your Hidden Problems

From technical debt to deployment in the very real, very messy world, we've got the tools you need to fix the hidden problems before they become disasters.

Software Design X-Rays

Are you working on a codebase where cost overruns, death marches, and heroic fights with legacy code monsters are the norm? Battle these adversaries with novel ways to identify and prioritize technical debt, based on behavioral data from how developers work with code. And that's just for starters. Because good code involves social design, as well as technical design, you can find surprising dependencies between people and code to resolve coordination bottlenecks among teams. Best of all, the techniques build on behavioral data that you already have: your version-control system. Join the fight for better code!

Adam Tornhill
(270 pages) ISBN: 9781680502725. $45.95
https://pragprog.com/book/atevol

Release It! Second Edition

A single dramatic software failure can cost a company millions of dollars—but can be avoided with simple changes to design and architecture. This new edition of the best-selling industry standard shows you how to create systems that run longer, with fewer failures, and recover better when bad things happen. New coverage includes DevOps, microservices, and cloud-native architecture. Stability antipatterns have grown to include systemic problems in large-scale systems. This is a must-have pragmatic guide to engineering for production systems.

Michael Nygard
(376 pages) ISBN: 9781680502398. $47.95
https://pragprog.com/book/mnee2

The Pragmatic Bookshelf

The Pragmatic Bookshelf features books written by developers for developers. The titles continue the well-known Pragmatic Programmer style and continue to garner awards and rave reviews. As development gets more and more difficult, the Pragmatic Programmers will be there with more titles and products to help you stay on top of your game.

Visit Us Online

This Book's Home Page
https://pragprog.com/book/nrtest3
Source code from this book, errata, and other resources. Come give us feedback, too!

Register for Updates
https://pragprog.com/updates
Be notified when updates and new books become available.

Join the Community
https://pragprog.com/community
Read our weblogs, join our online discussions, participate in our mailing list, interact with our wiki, and benefit from the experience of other Pragmatic Programmers.

New and Noteworthy
https://pragprog.com/news
Check out the latest pragmatic developments, new titles and other offerings.

Save on the eBook

Save on the eBook versions of this title. Owning the paper version of this book entitles you to purchase the electronic versions at a terrific discount.

PDFs are great for carrying around on your laptop—they are hyperlinked, have color, and are fully searchable. Most titles are also available for the iPhone and iPod touch, Amazon Kindle, and other popular e-book readers.

Buy now at *https://pragprog.com/coupon*

Contact Us

Online Orders:	*https://pragprog.com/catalog*
Customer Service:	*support@pragprog.com*
International Rights:	*translations@pragprog.com*
Academic Use:	*academic@pragprog.com*
Write for Us:	*http://write-for-us.pragprog.com*
Or Call:	+1 800-699-7764

CPSIA information can be obtained
at www.ICGtesting.com
Printed in the USA
BVOW08s1928270218
509249BV00001B/2/P